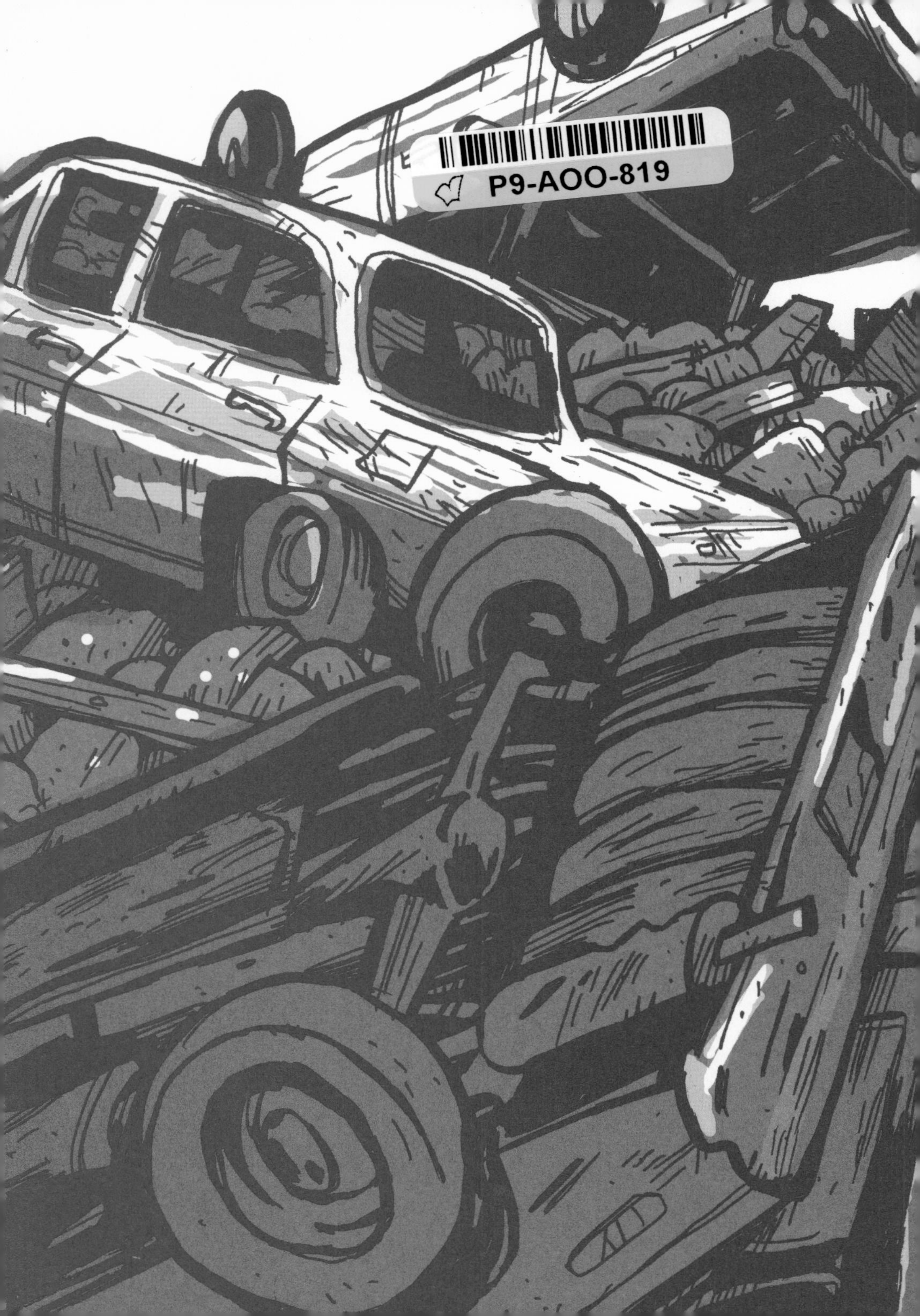

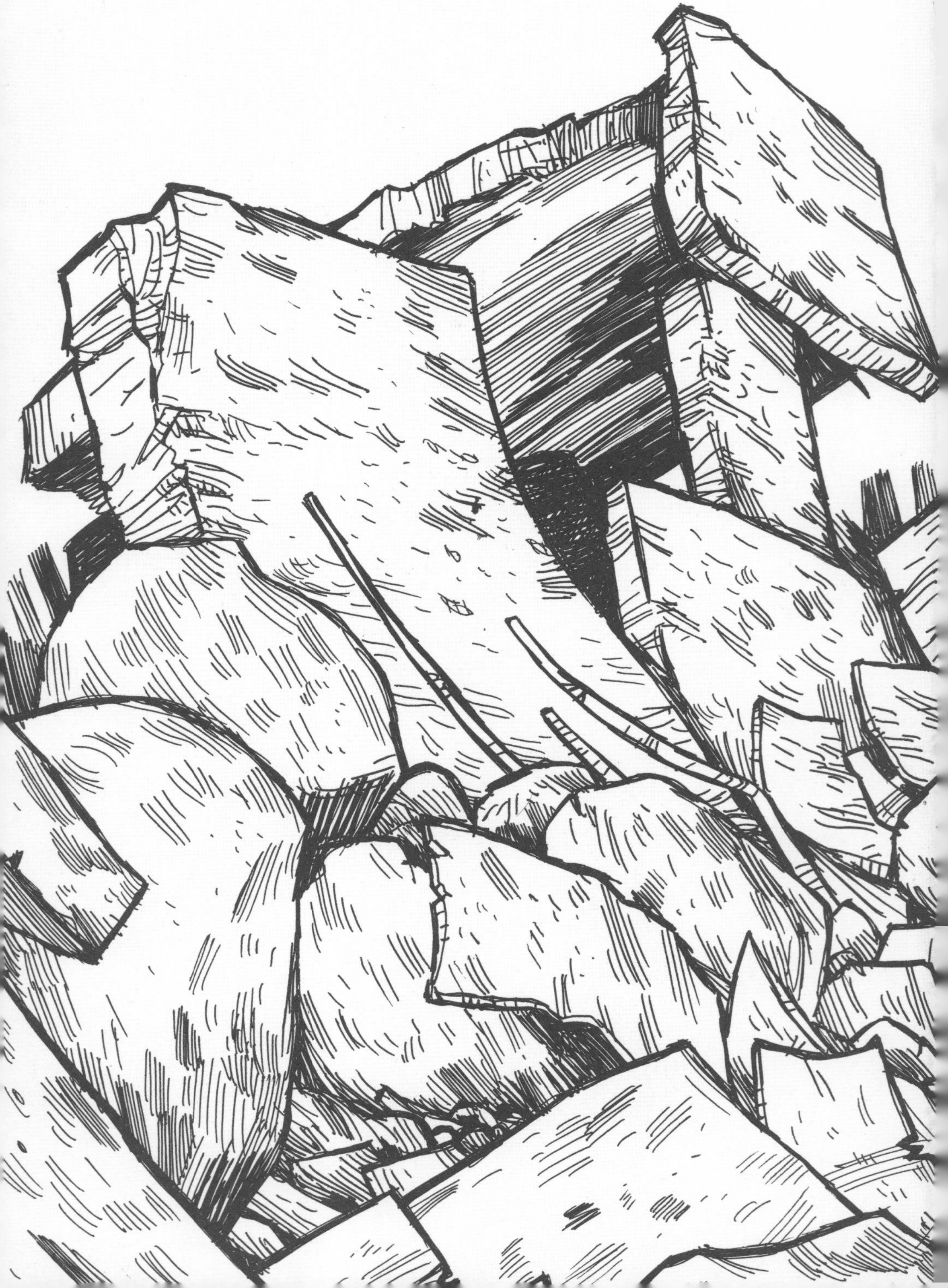

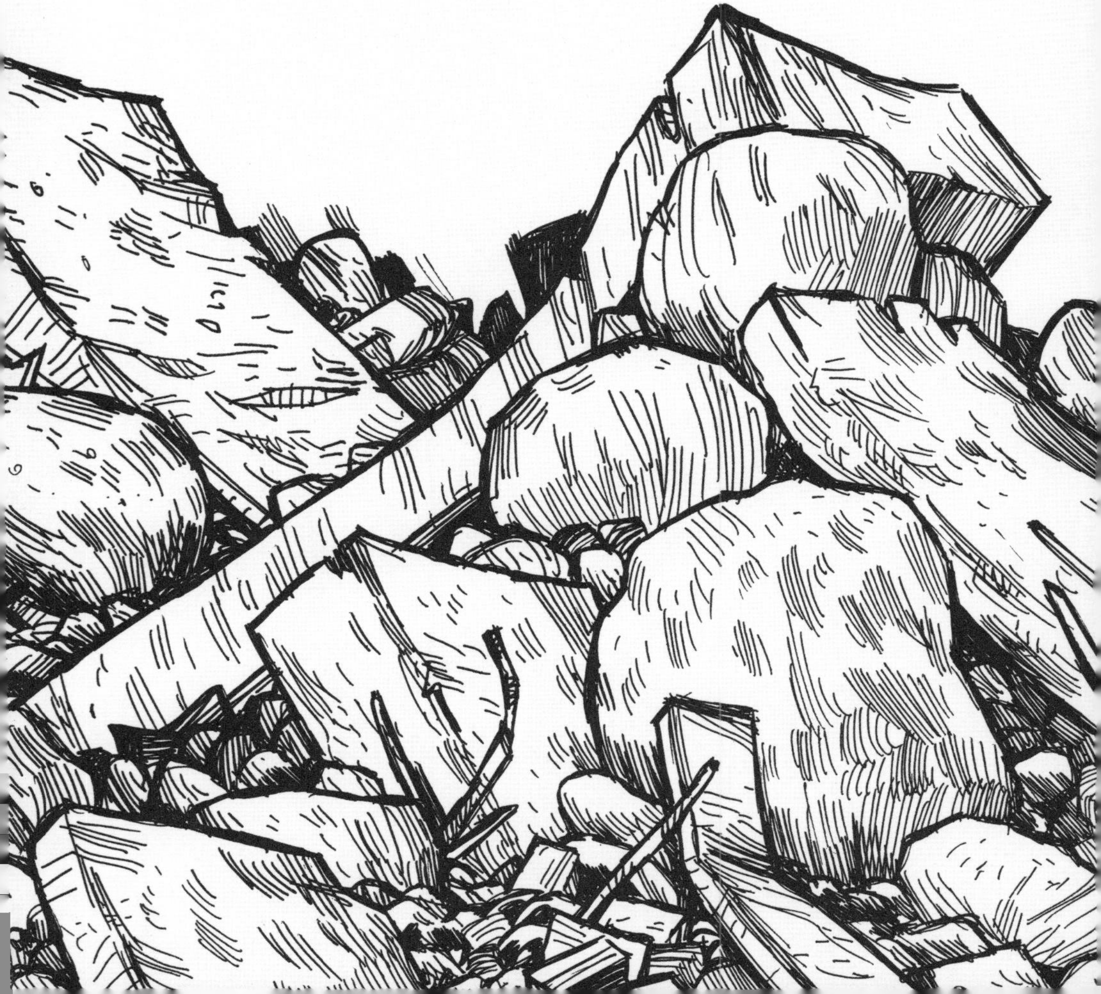

DAYBREAK

BRIAN RALPH

DRAWN & QUARTERLY MONTREAL

MOST OF THIS BOOK WAS PRINTED IN PAMPHLET FORM (DAYBREAK 1, 2, AND 3) BY BODEGA
PRODUCTION BY RANDY CHANG WITH ASSISTANCE BY RAY SOHN, ANDREW ARNOLD, AND SHANNON TIEN.

DRAWN & QUARTERLY
POST OFFICE BOX 48056
MONTREAL, QUEBEC
CANADA, H2V 4S8
WWW.DRAWNANDQUARTERLY.COM

FIRST EDITION: AUGUST 2011
PRINTED IN SINGAPORE.

10 9 8 7 6 5 4 3 2 1

LIBRARY AND ARCHIVES CANADA CATALOGUING IN PUBLICATION

RALPH, BRIAN, 1973-
DAYBREAK / BRIAN RALPH.

ISBN 978-1-77046-055-3
I. TITLE.

PN6727.R35D38 2011 741.5'973
C2011-901771-7

DISTRIBUTED IN THE USA BY:
FARRAR, STRAUS AND GIROUX
18 WEST 18TH STREET
NEW YORK, NY 10011
ORDERS: 888.330.8477

DISTRIBUTED IN CANADA BY:
RAINCOAST BOOKS
2440 VIKING WAY
RICHMOND, BC V6V 1N2
ORDERS: 800-663-5714

DISTRIBUTED IN THE UK BY:
PUBLISHERS GROUP UK
8 THE ARENA
MOLLISON AVENUE
ENFIELD
EN3 7NL
ORDERS: 020 8216 6070

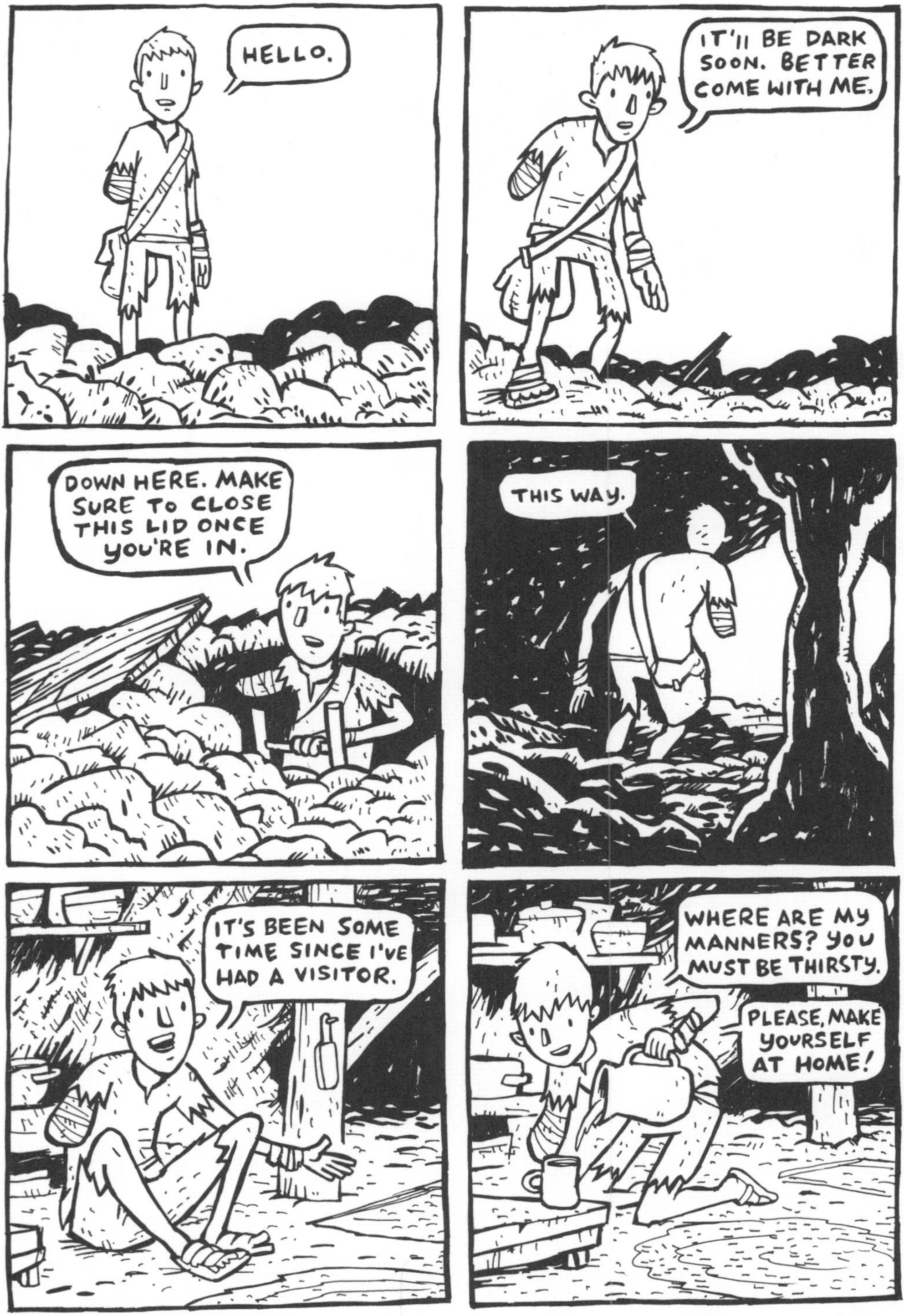
HELLO.
IT'll BE DARK SOON. BETTER COME WITH ME.
DOWN HERE. MAKE SURE TO CLOSE THIS LID ONCE YOU'RE IN.
THIS WAY.
IT'S BEEN SOME TIME SINCE I'VE HAD A VISITOR.
WHERE ARE MY MANNERS? YOU MUST BE THIRSTY.
PLEASE, MAKE YOURSELF AT HOME!

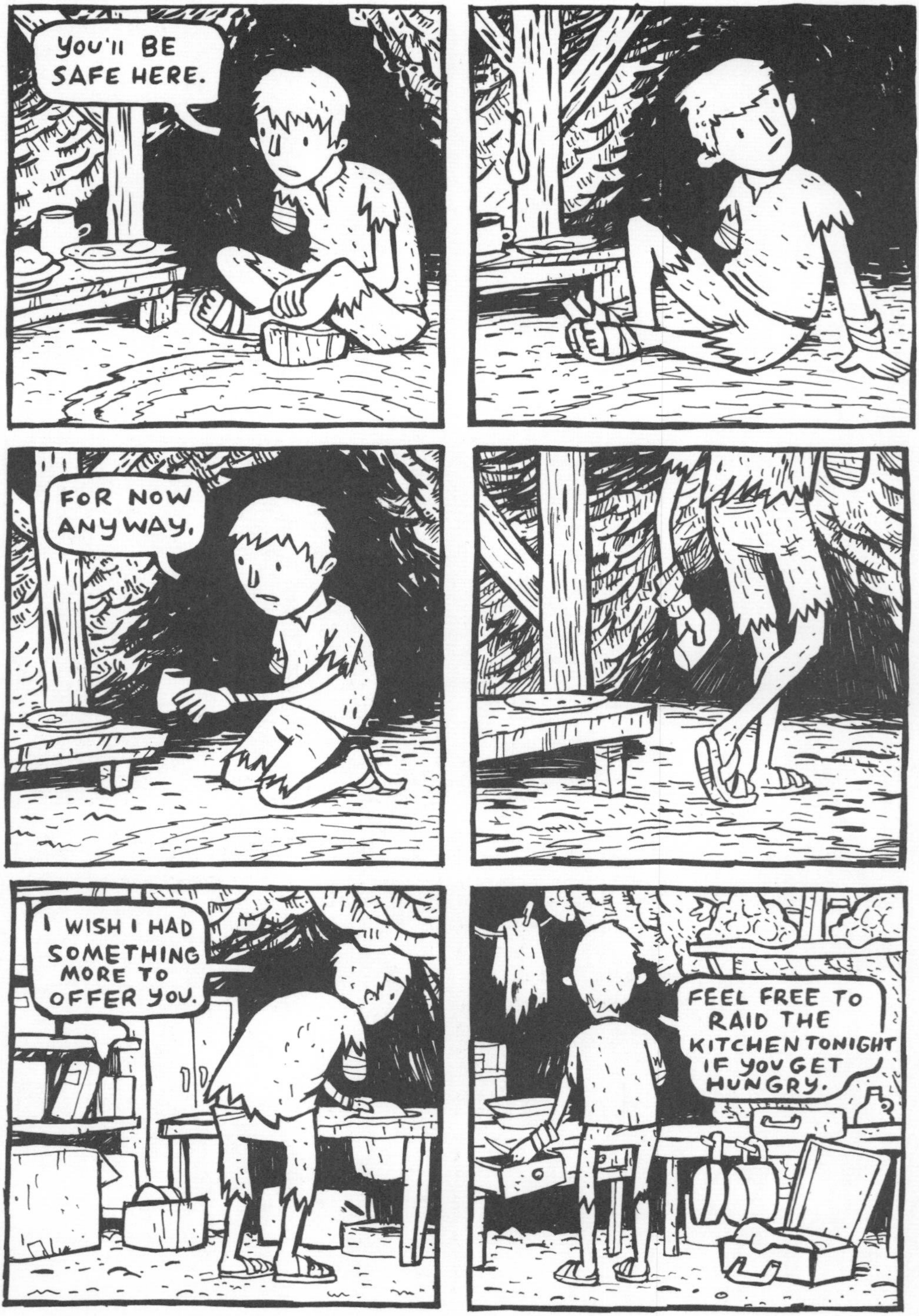
YOU'll BE SAFE HERE.
FOR NOW ANYWAY.
I WISH I HAD SOMETHING MORE TO OFFER YOU.
FEEL FREE TO RAID THE KITCHEN TONIGHT IF YOU GET HUNGRY.

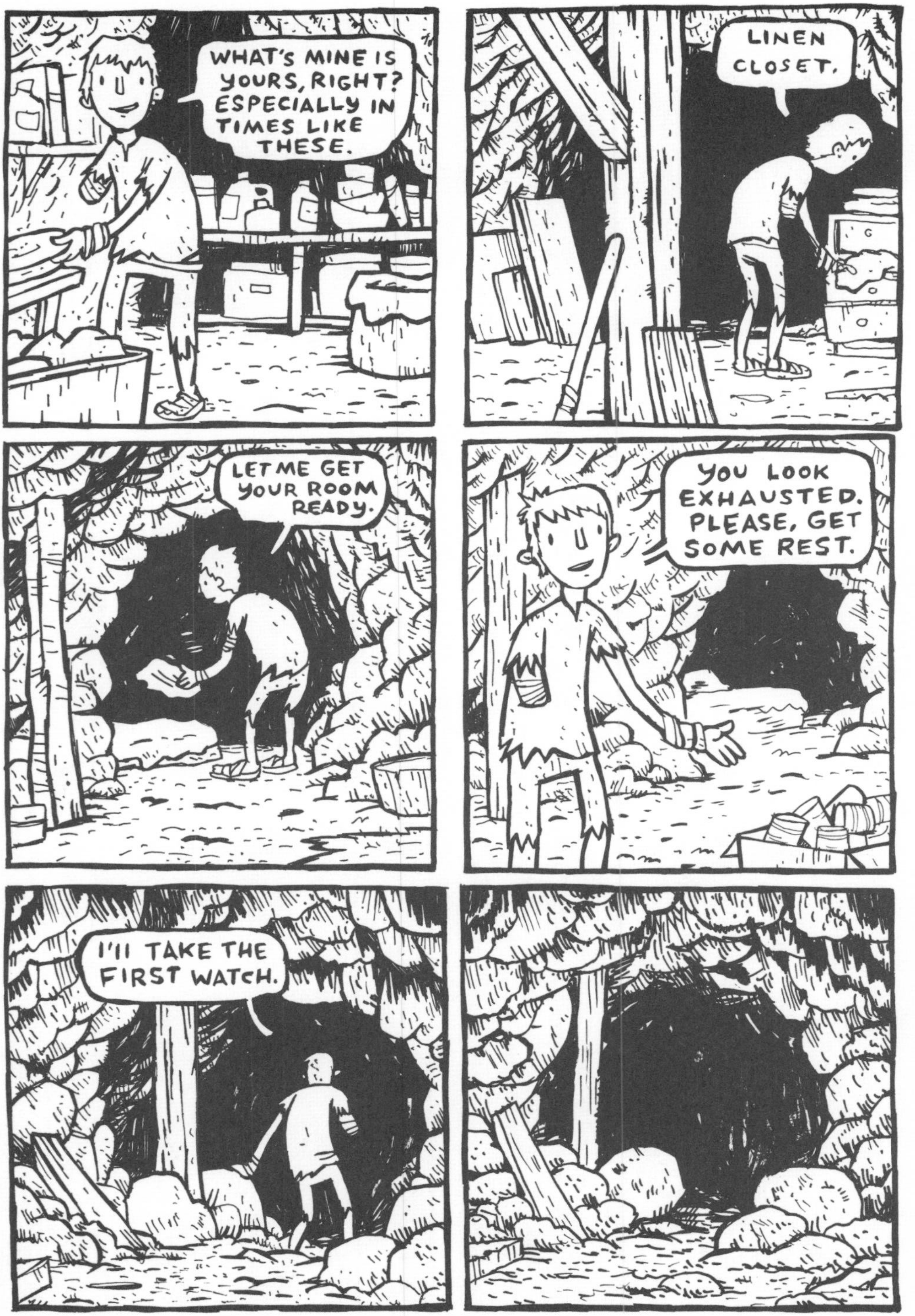
WHAT'S MINE IS YOURS, RIGHT? ESPECIALLY IN TIMES LIKE THESE.
LINEN CLOSET.
LET ME GET YOUR ROOM READY.
YOU LOOK EXHAUSTED. PLEASE, GET SOME REST.
I'll TAKE THE FIRST WATCH.

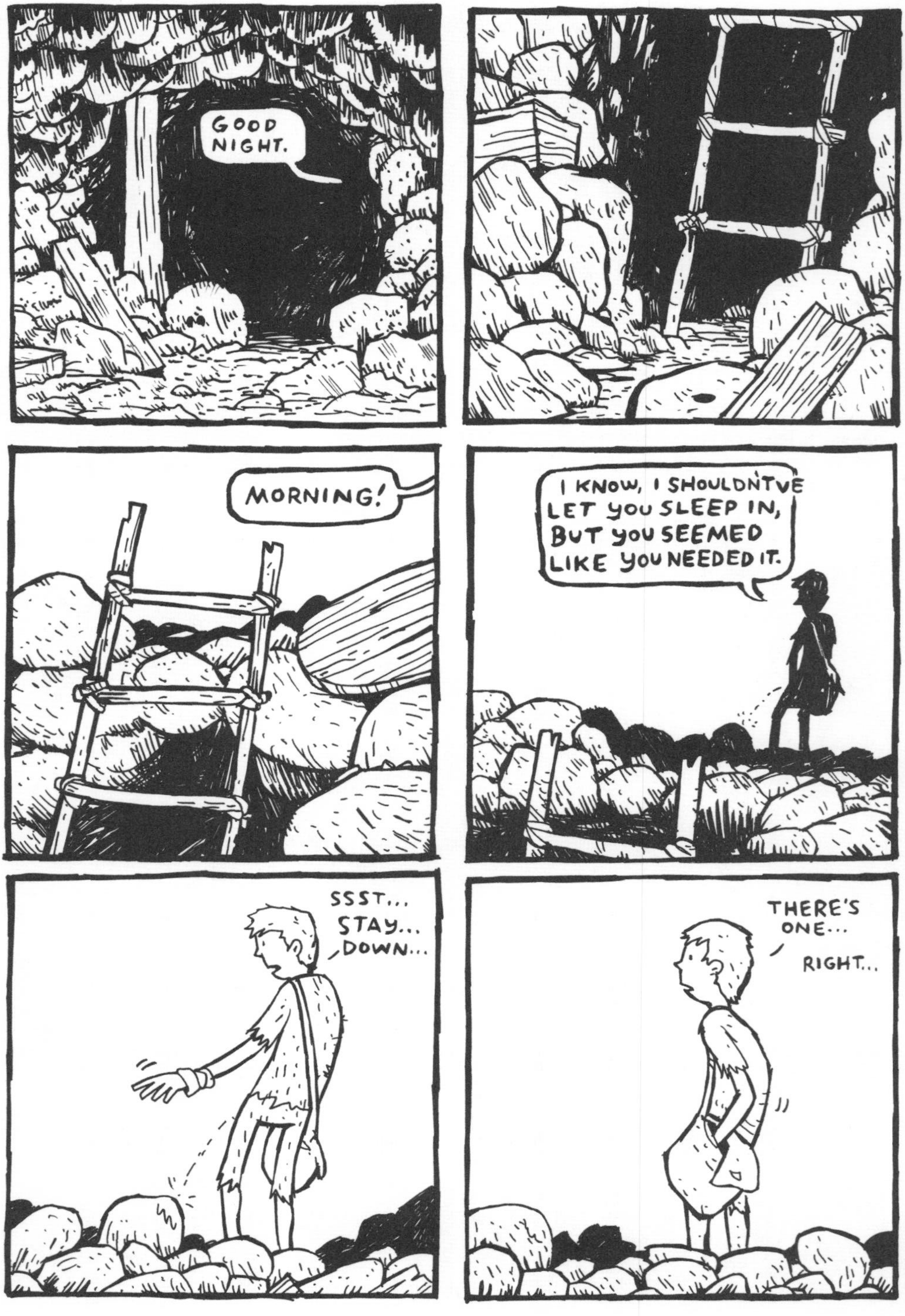
GOOD NIGHT.
MORNING!
I KNOW, I SHOULDN'T'VE LET YOU SLEEP IN, BUT YOU SEEMED LIKE YOU NEEDED IT.
SSST... STAY... DOWN...
THERE'S ONE...
RIGHT...

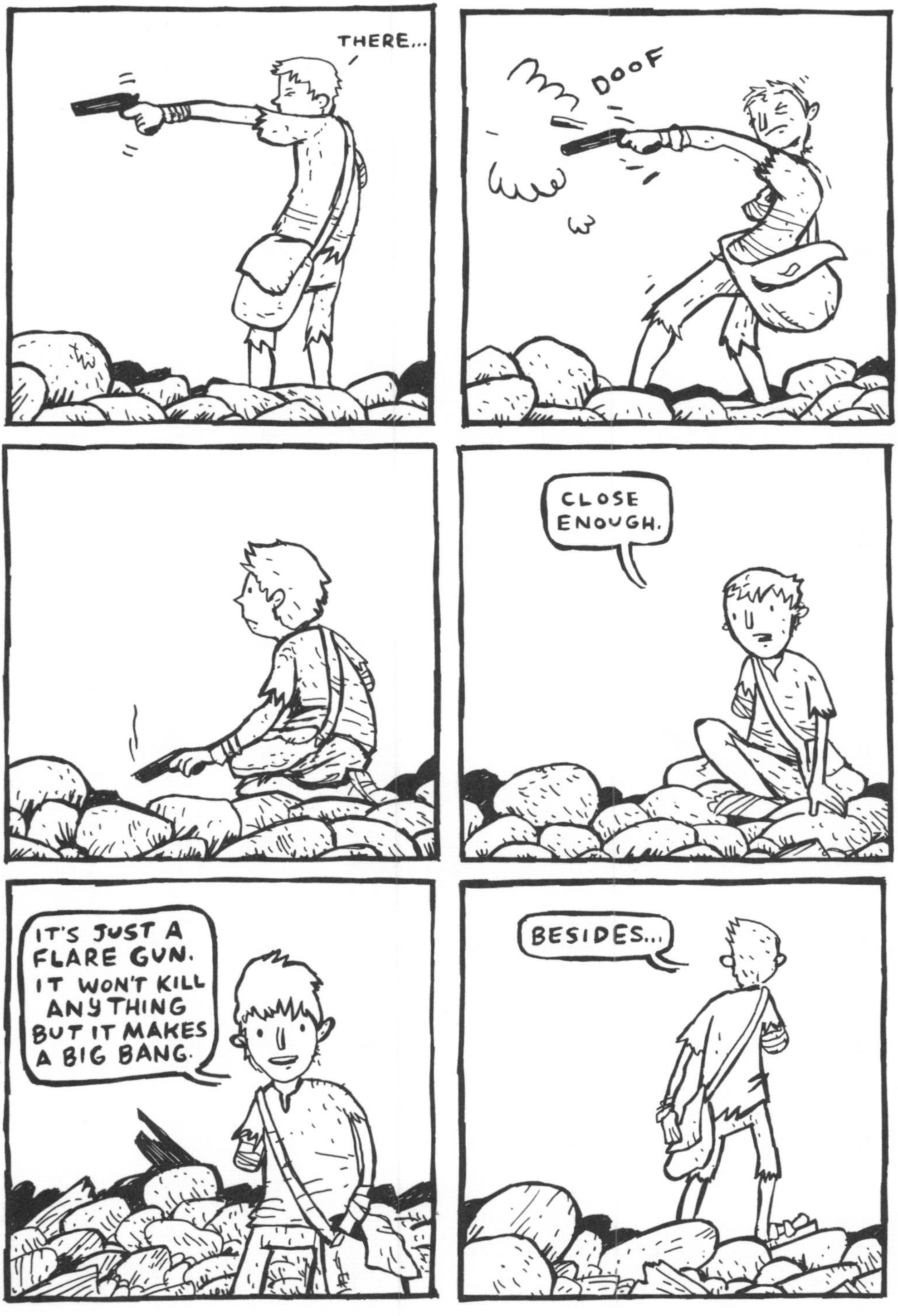
THERE...
DOOF
CLOSE ENOUGH.
IT'S JUST A FLARE GUN. IT WON'T KILL ANYTHING BUT IT MAKES A BIG BANG.
BESIDES...

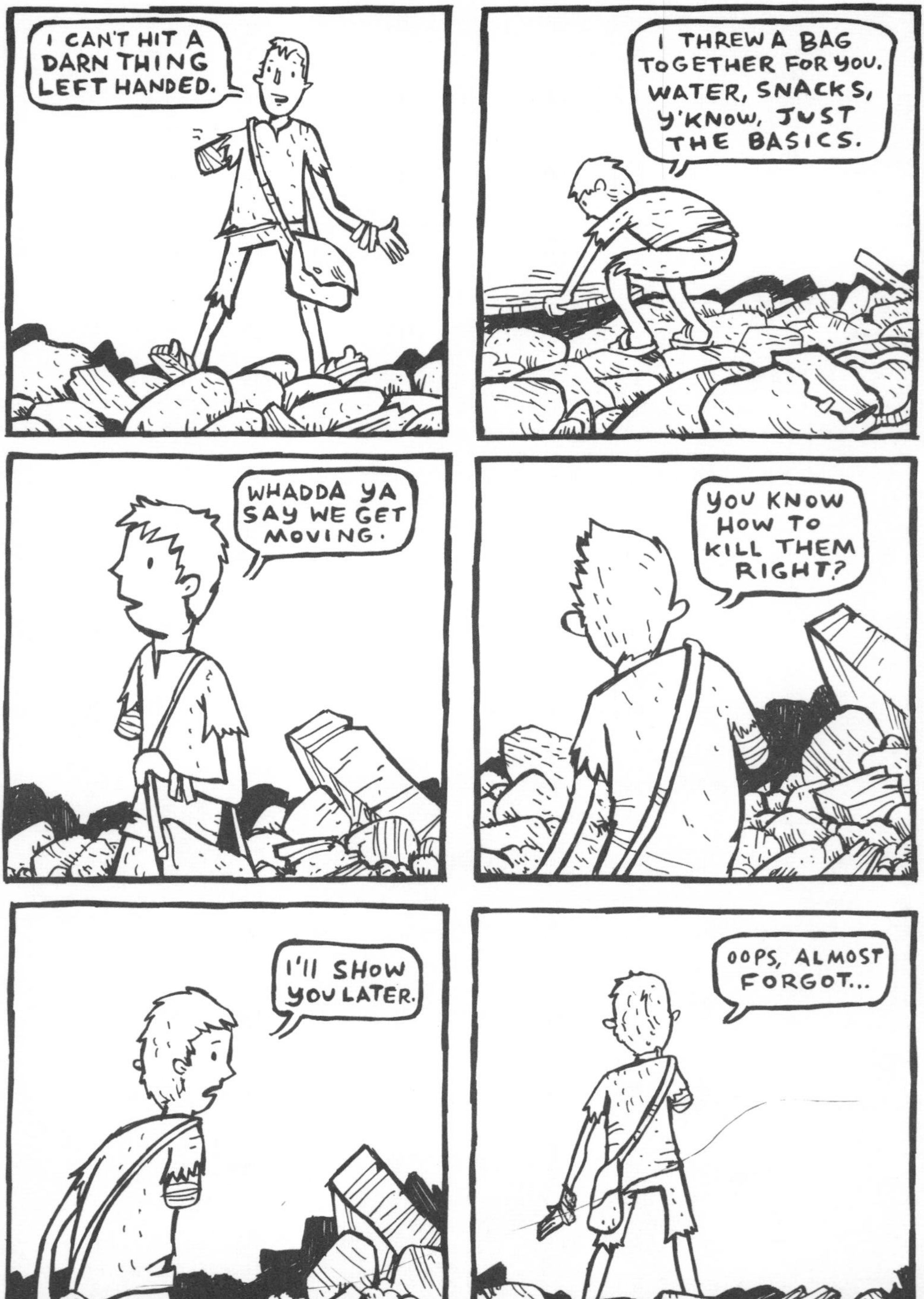
I CAN'T HIT A DARN THING LEFT HANDED.
I THREW A BAG TOGETHER FOR YOU. WATER, SNACKS, Y'KNOW, JUST THE BASICS.
WHADDA YA SAY WE GET MOVING.
YOU KNOW HOW TO KILL THEM RIGHT?
I'LL SHOW YOU LATER.
OOPS, ALMOST FORGOT...

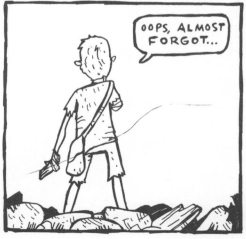

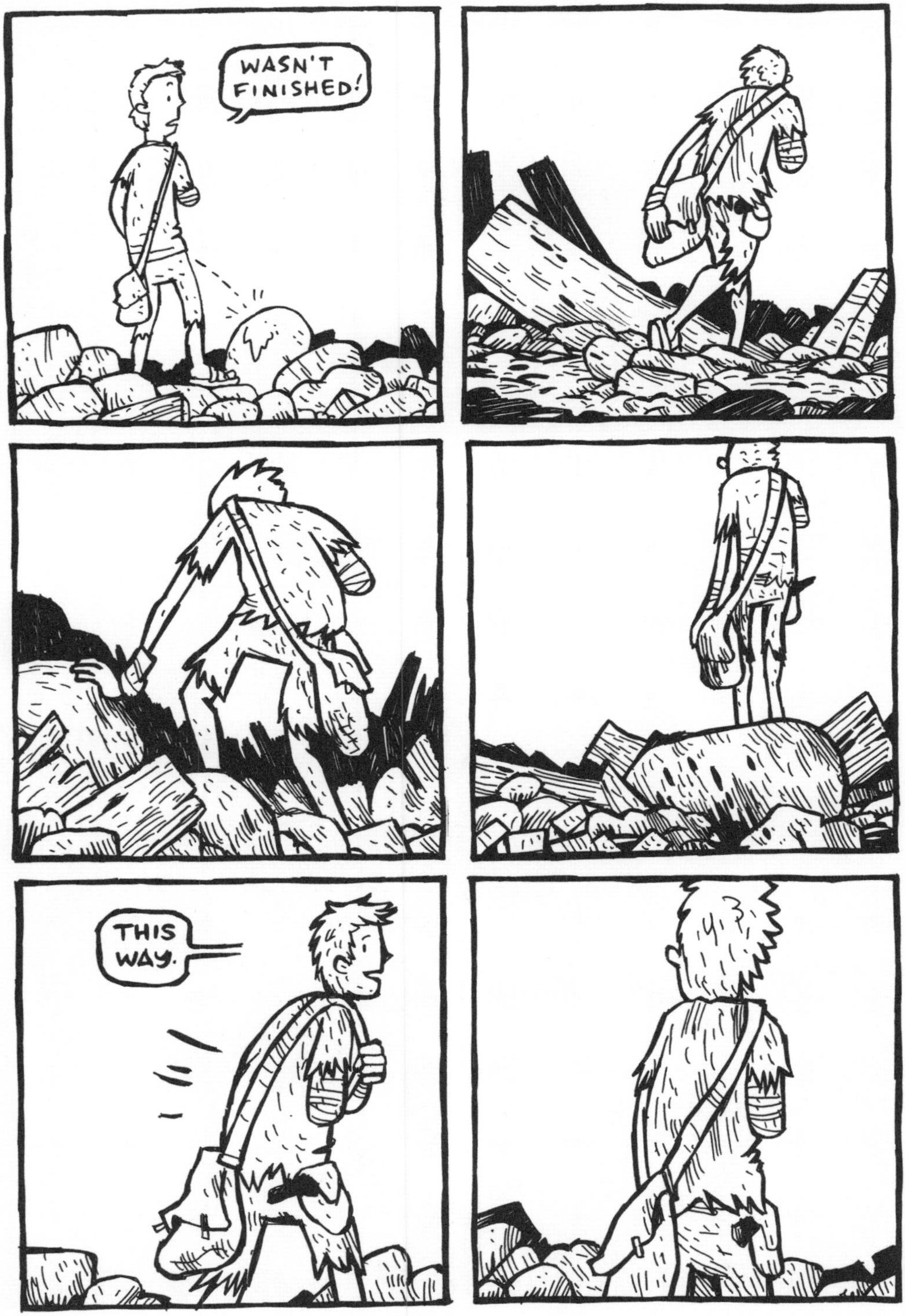
WASN'T FINISHED!
THIS WAY.

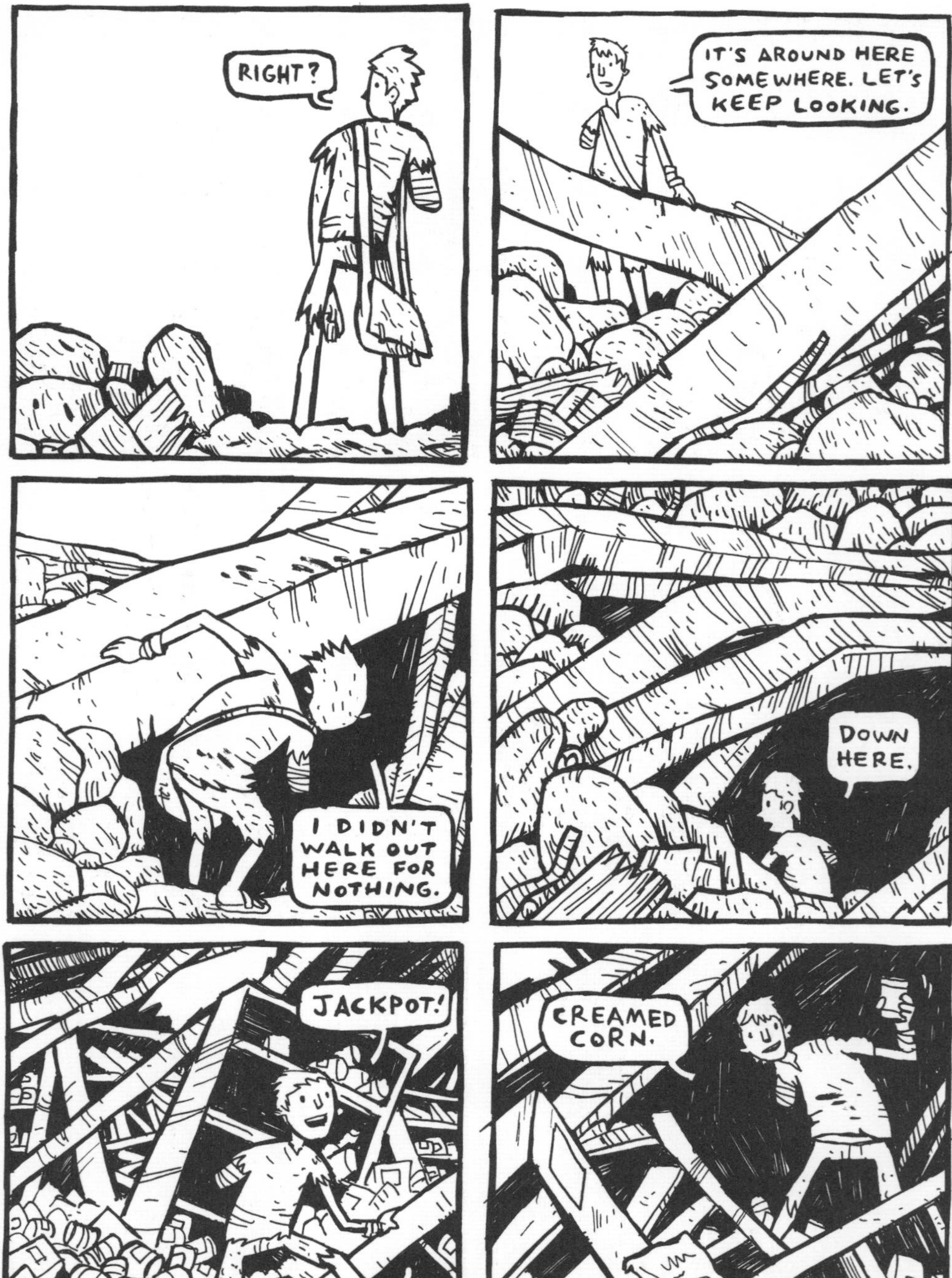
RIGHT?
IT'S AROUND HERE SOMEWHERE. LET'S KEEP LOOKING.
I DIDN'T WALK OUT HERE FOR NOTHING.
DOWN HERE.
JACKPOT!
CREAMED CORN.

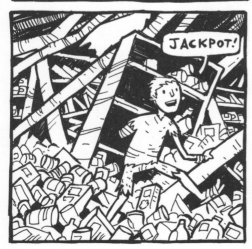

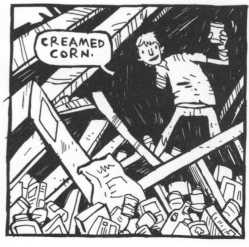

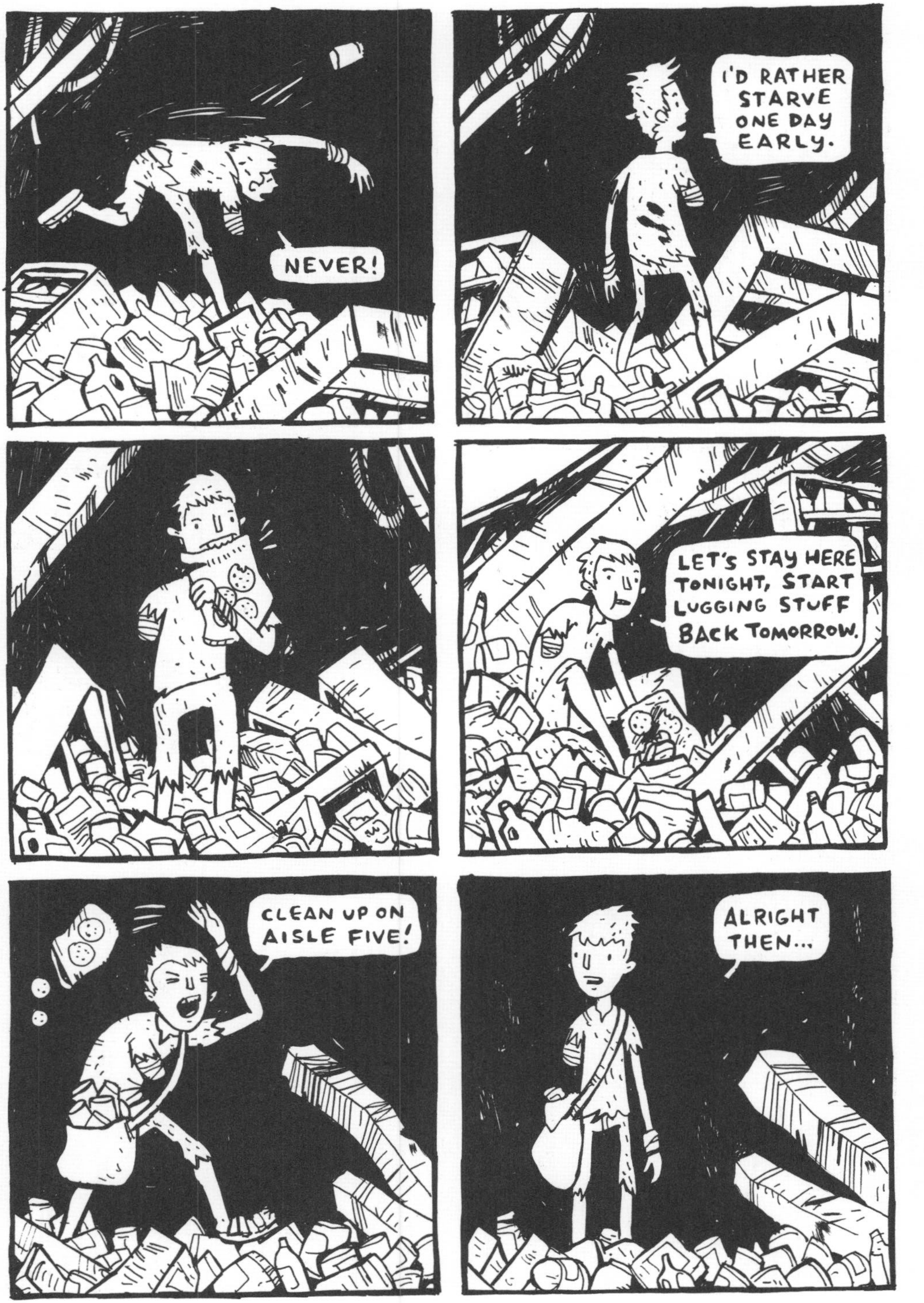
NEVER!
I'D RATHER STARVE ONE DAY EARLY.
LET'S STAY HERE TONIGHT, START LUGGING STUFF BACK TOMORROW.
CLEAN UP ON AISLE FIVE!
ALRIGHT THEN...

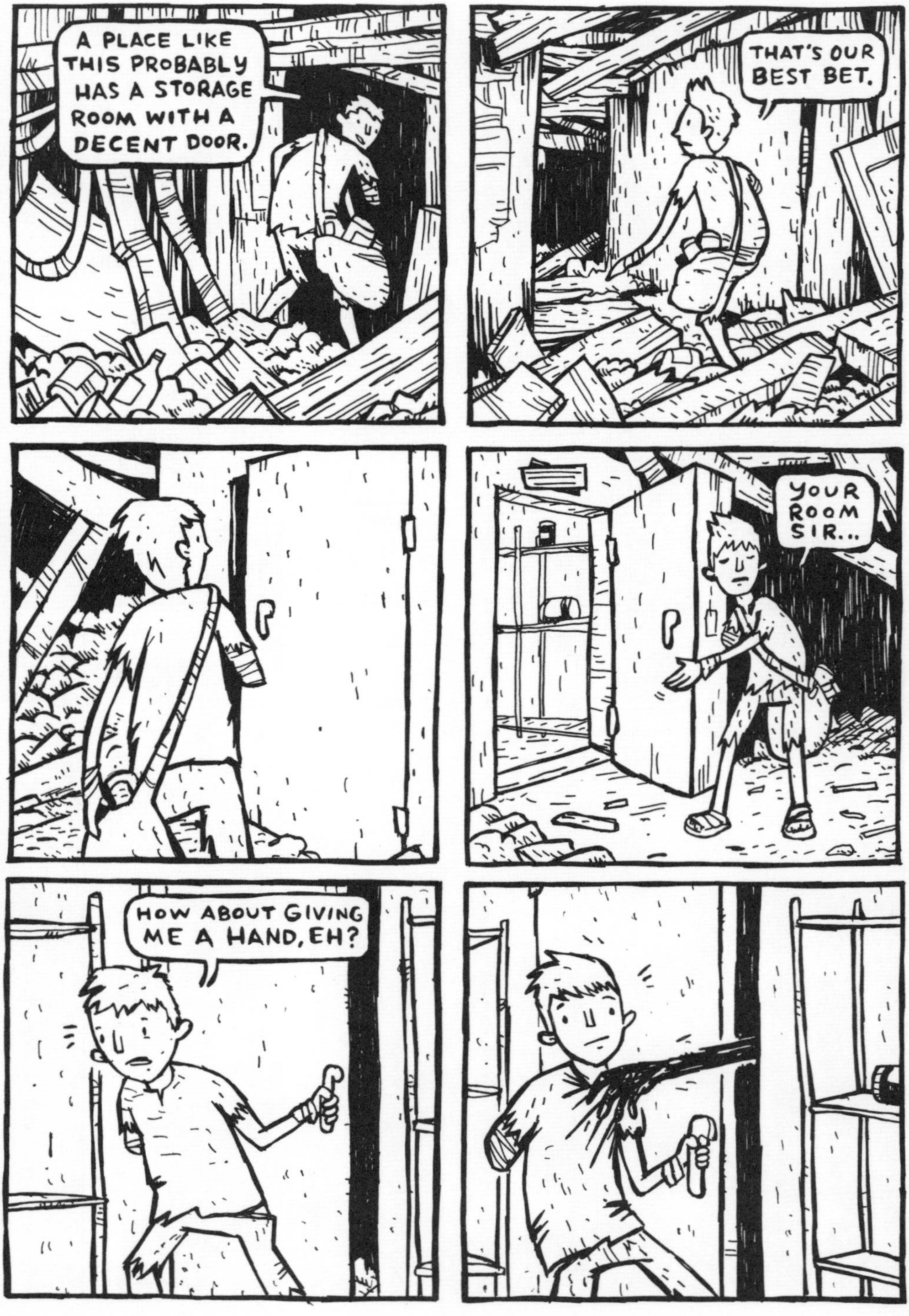
A PLACE LIKE THIS PROBABLY HAS A STORAGE ROOM WITH A DECENT DOOR.
THAT'S OUR BEST BET.
YOUR ROOM SIR...
HOW ABOUT GIVING ME A HAND, EH?

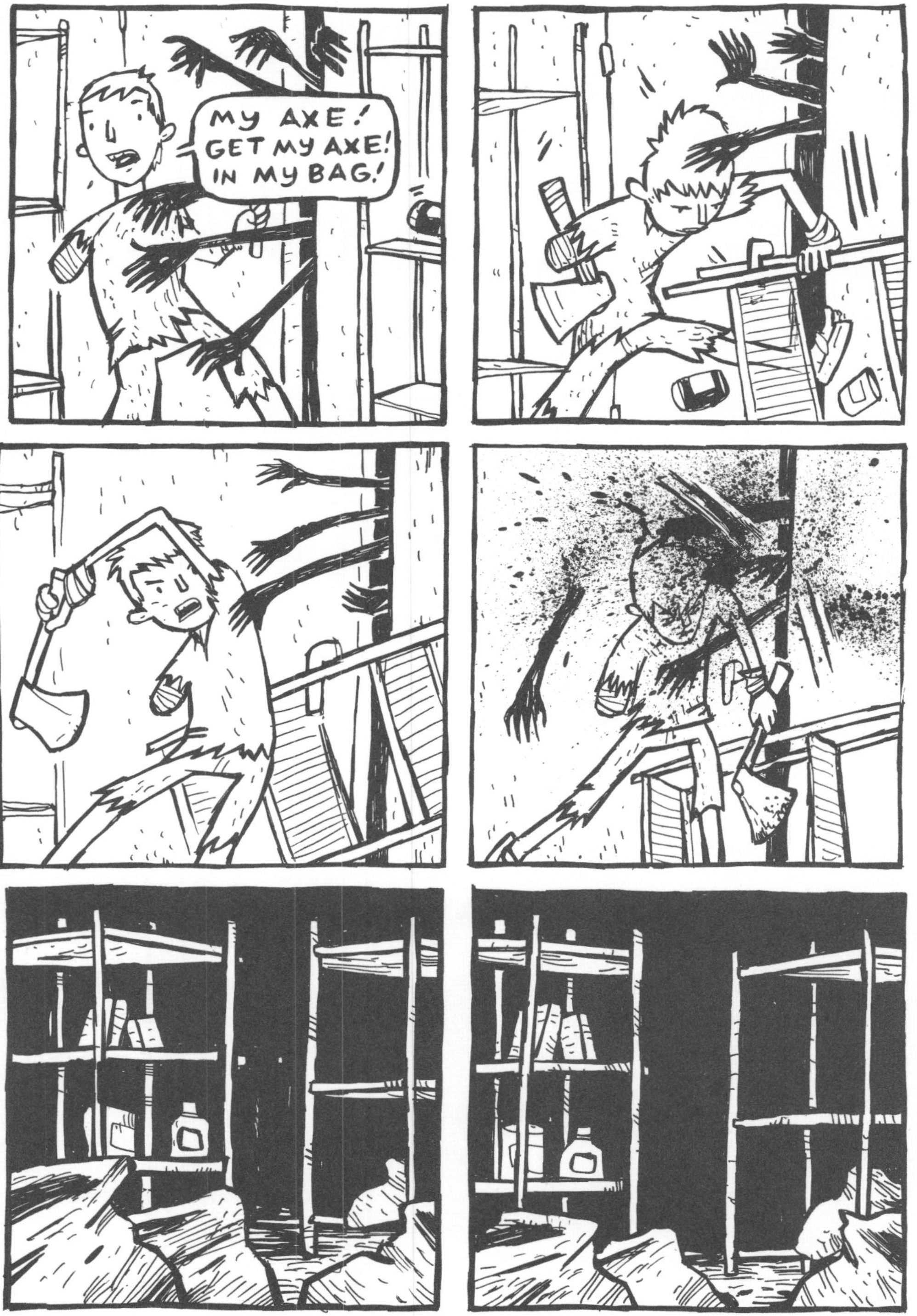
MY AXE! GET MY AXE! IN MY BAG!

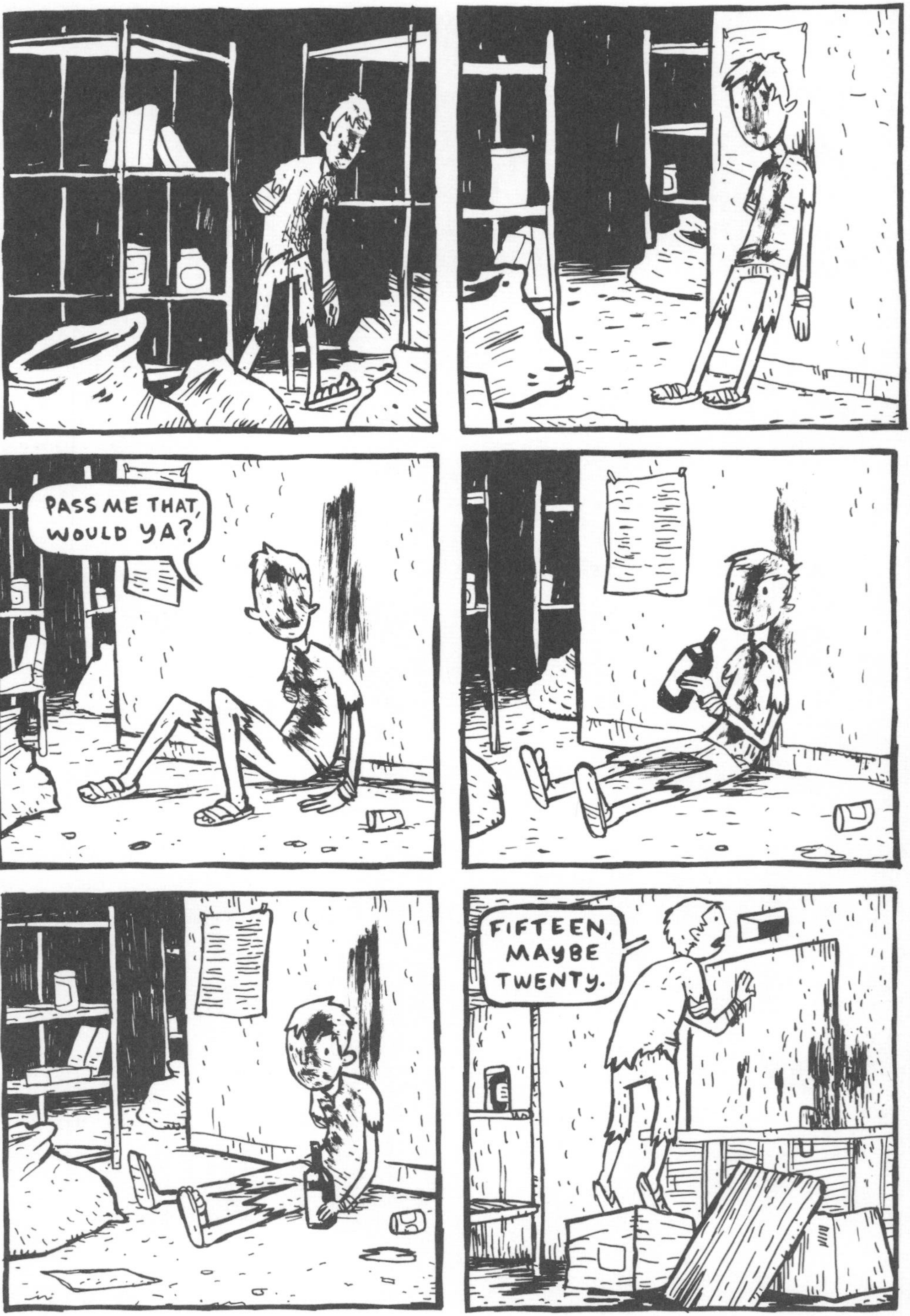
PASS ME THAT, WOULD YA?
FIFTEEN, MAYBE TWENTY.

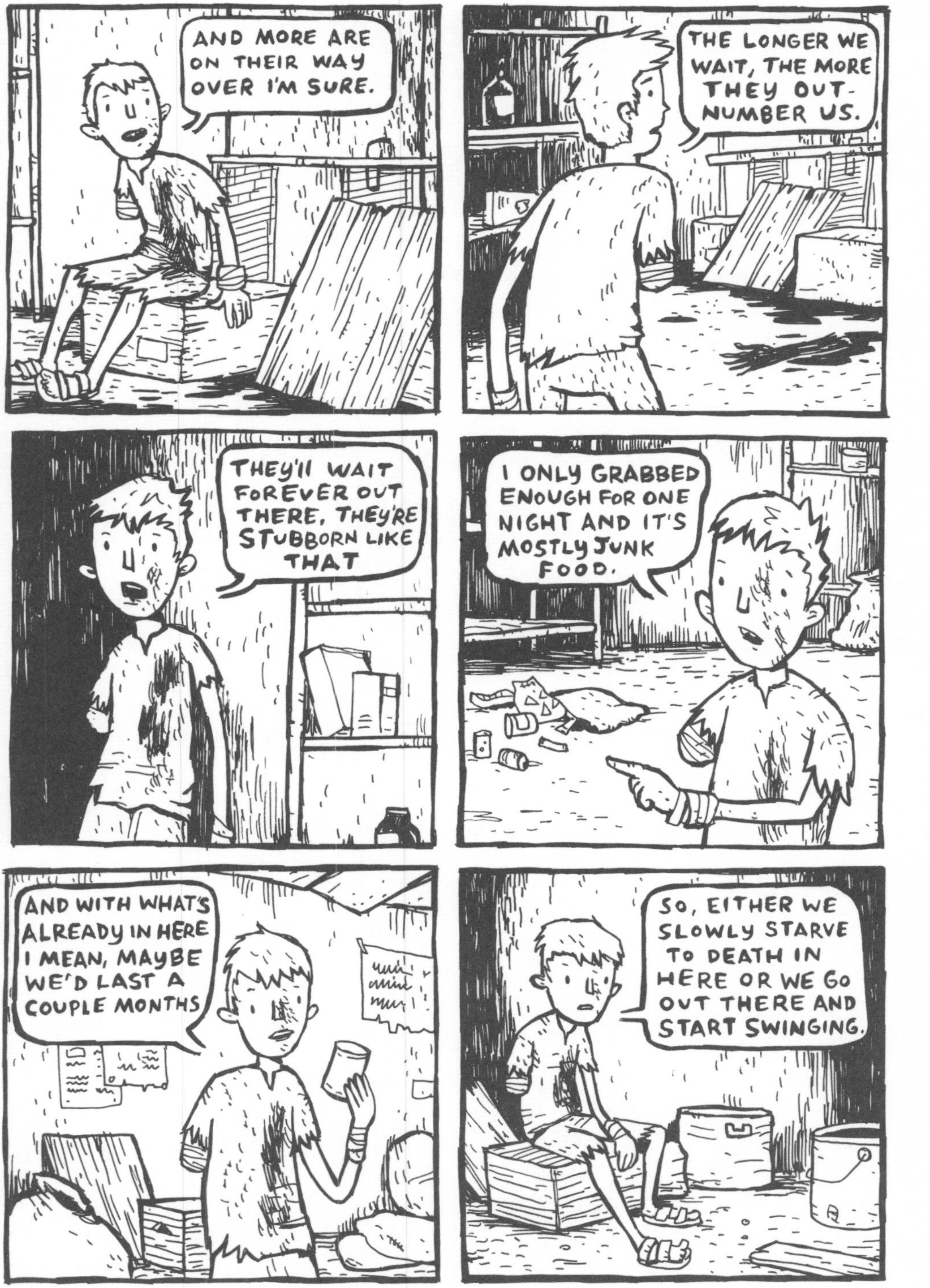
AND MORE ARE ON THEIR WAY OVER I'M SURE.
THE LONGER WE WAIT, THE MORE THEY OUT-NUMBER US.
THEY'll WAIT FOREVER OUT THERE, THEY'RE STUBBORN LIKE THAT
I ONLY GRABBED ENOUGH FOR ONE NIGHT AND IT'S MOSTLY JUNK FOOD.
AND WITH WHAT'S ALREADY IN HERE I MEAN, MAYBE WE'D LAST A COUPLE MONTHS
SO, EITHER WE SLOWLY STARVE TO DEATH IN HERE OR WE GO OUT THERE AND START SWINGING.

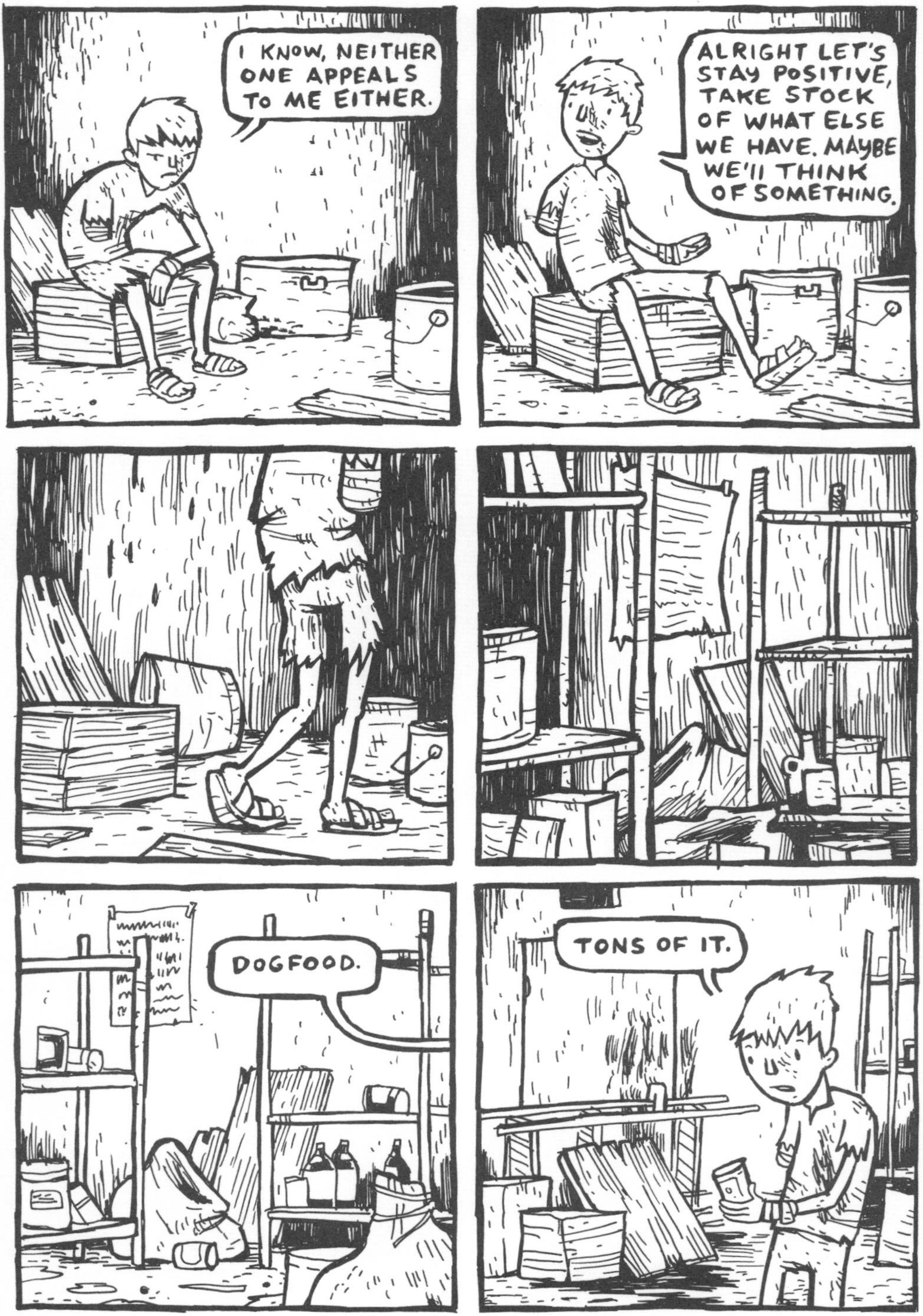
I KNOW, NEITHER ONE APPEALS TO ME EITHER.
ALRIGHT LET'S STAY POSITIVE, TAKE STOCK OF WHAT ELSE WE HAVE. MAYBE WE'll THINK OF SOMETHING.
DOGFOOD.
TONS OF IT.

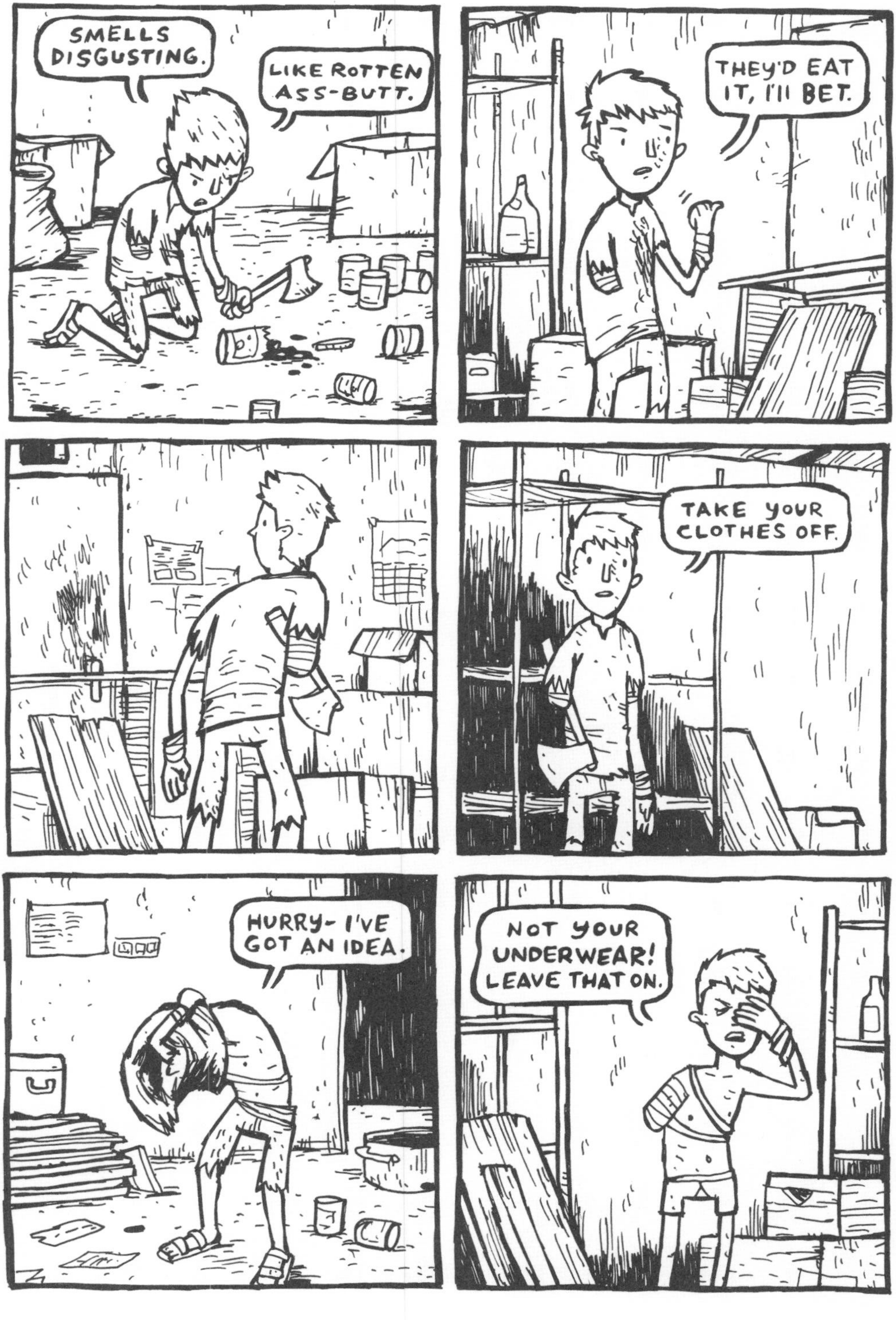
SMELLS DISGUSTING.
LIKE ROTTEN ASS-BUTT.
THEY'D EAT IT, I'll BET.
TAKE YOUR CLOTHES OFF.
HURRY- I'VE GOT AN IDEA.
NOT YOUR UNDERWEAR! LEAVE THAT ON.

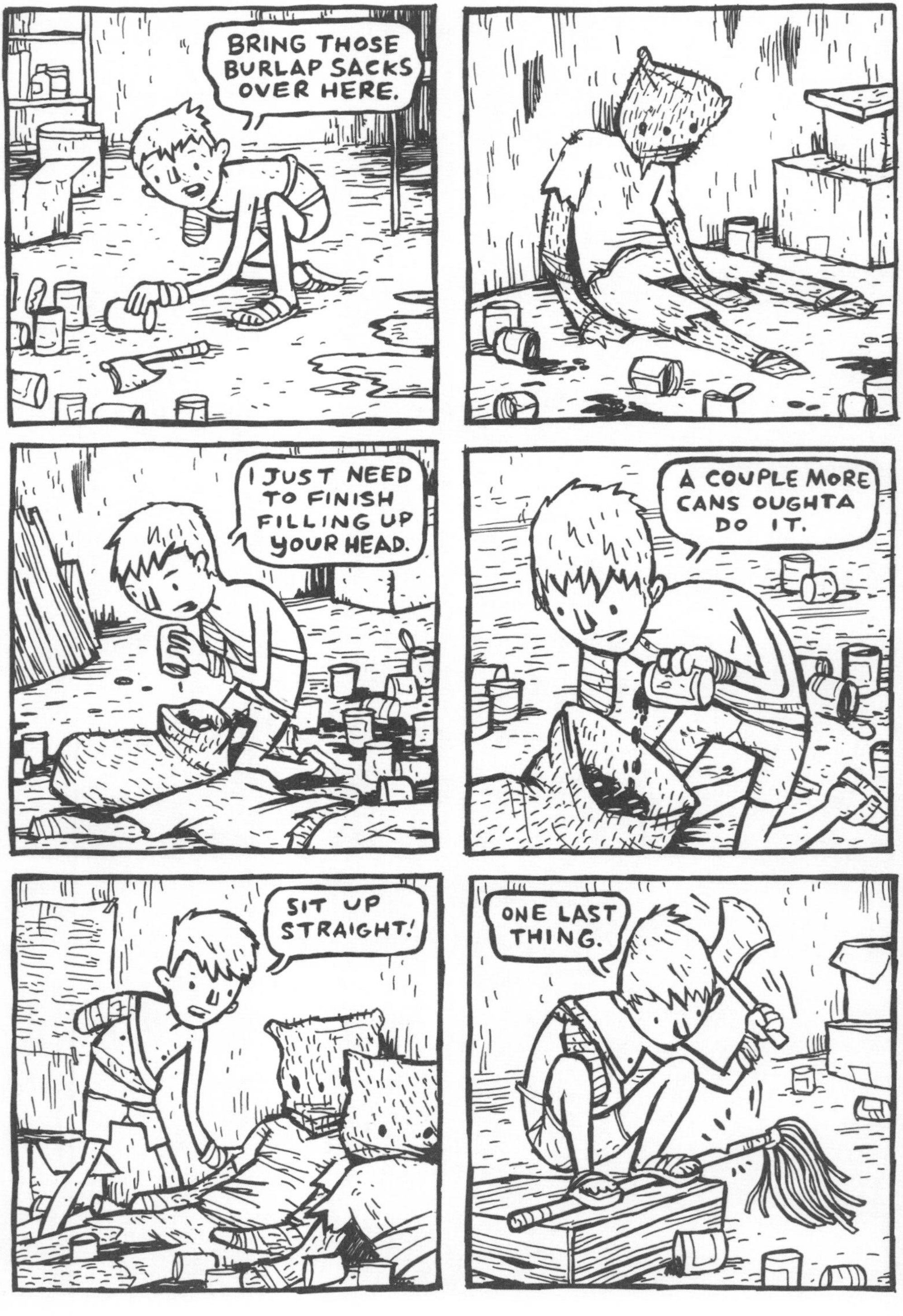
BRING THOSE BURLAP SACKS OVER HERE.
I JUST NEED TO FINISH FILLING UP YOUR HEAD.
A COUPLE MORE CANS OUGHTA DO IT.
SIT UP STRAIGHT!
ONE LAST THING.

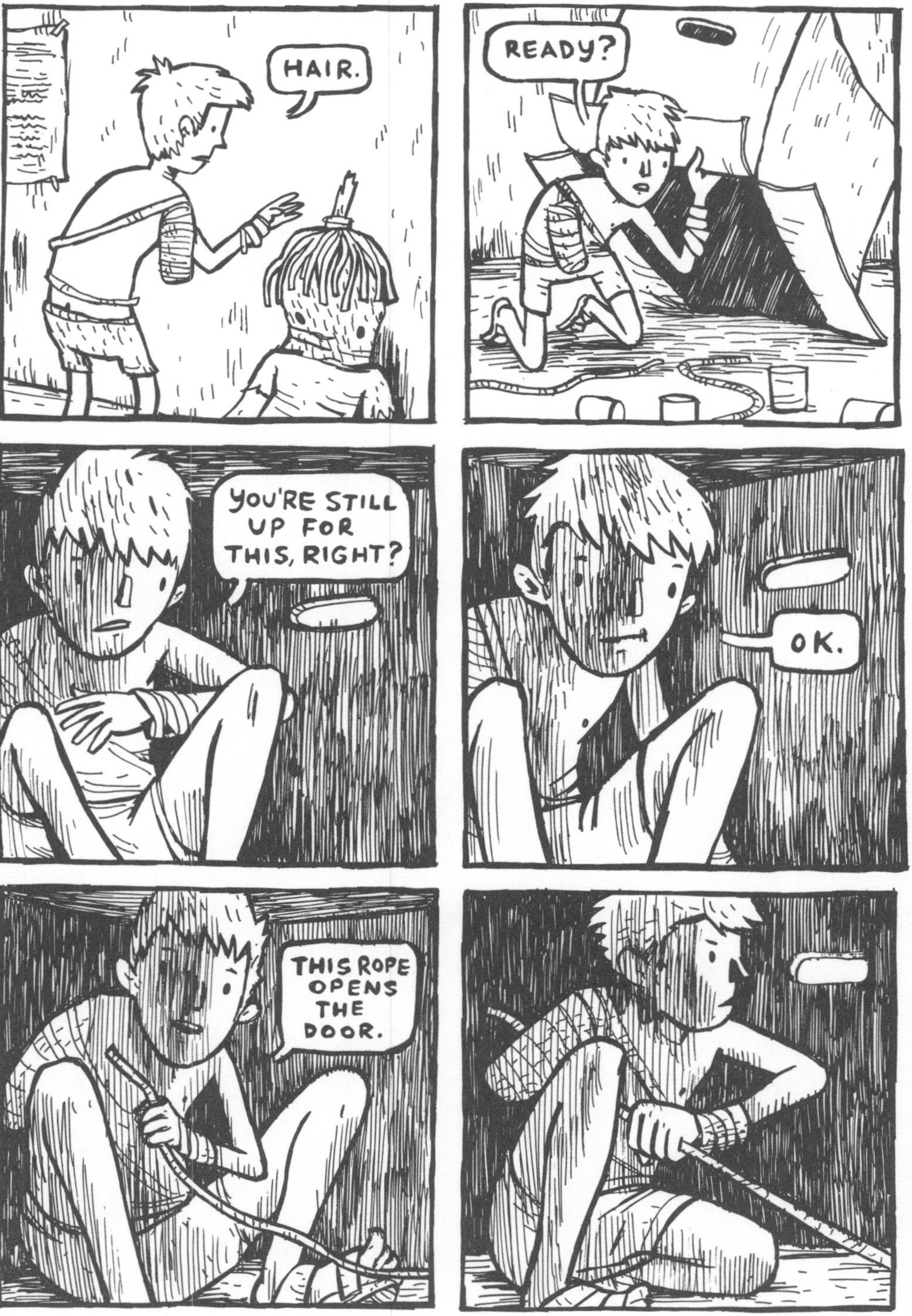
HAIR.
READY?
YOU'RE STILL UP FOR THIS, RIGHT?
OK.
THIS ROPE OPENS THE DOOR.

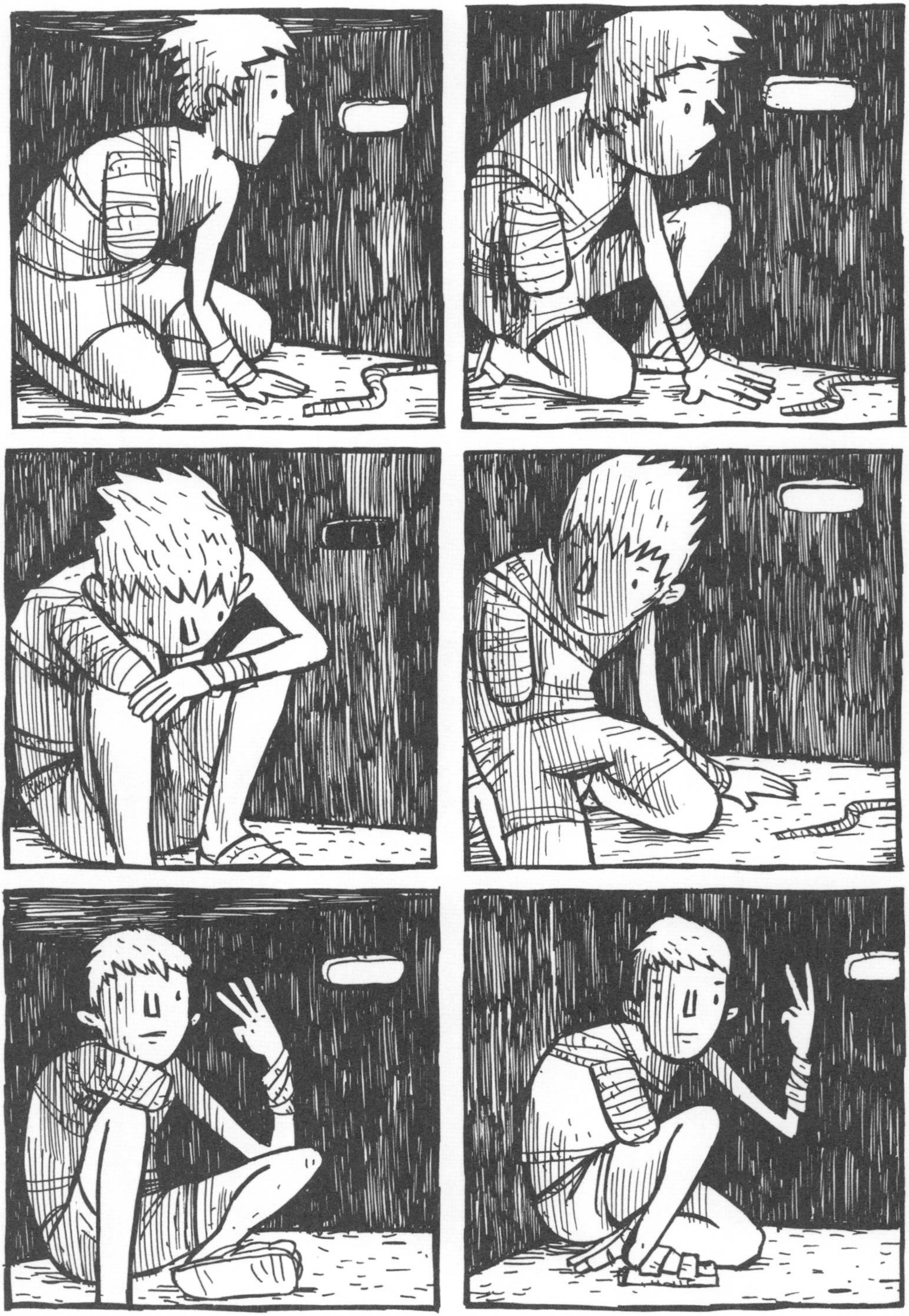

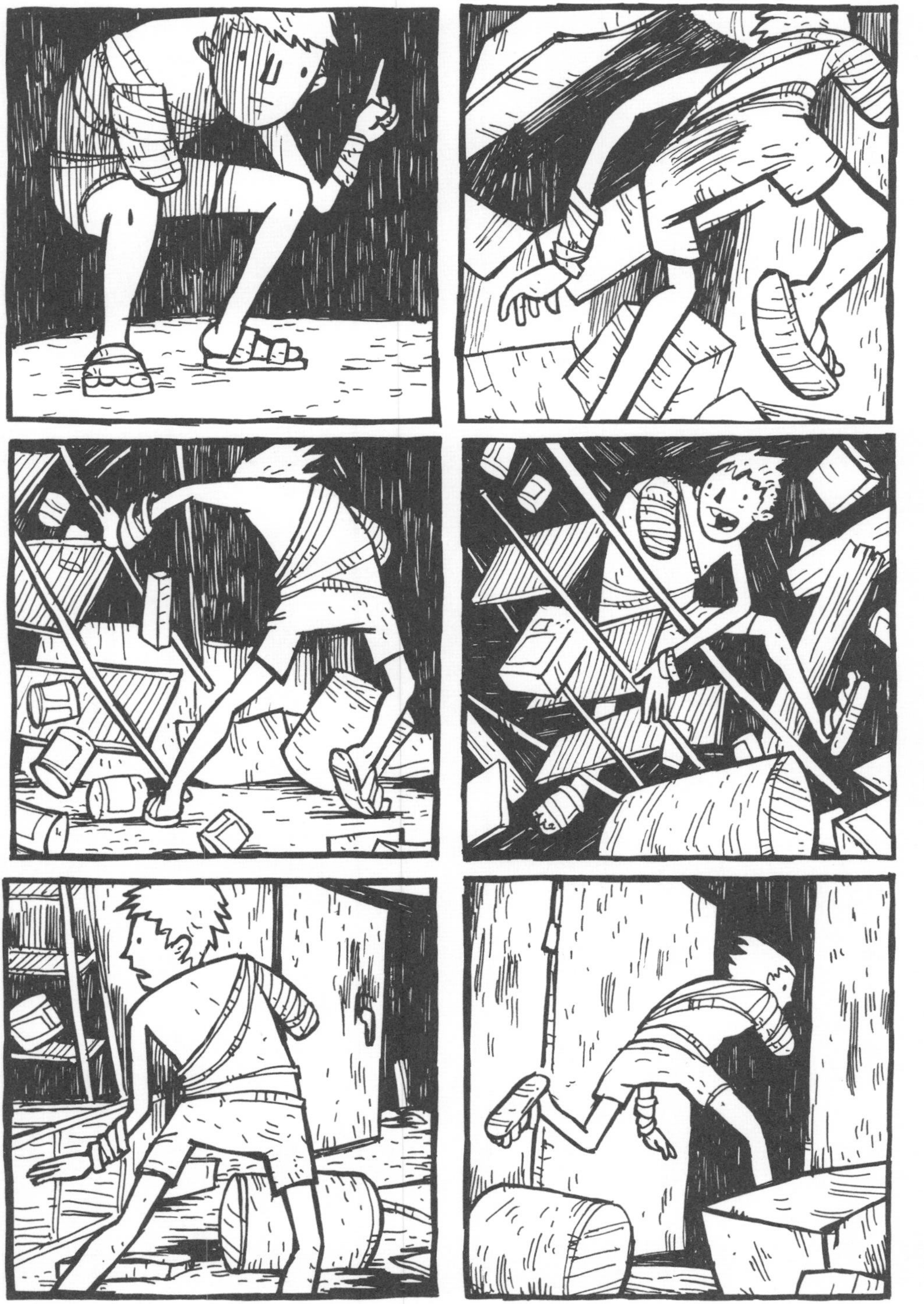

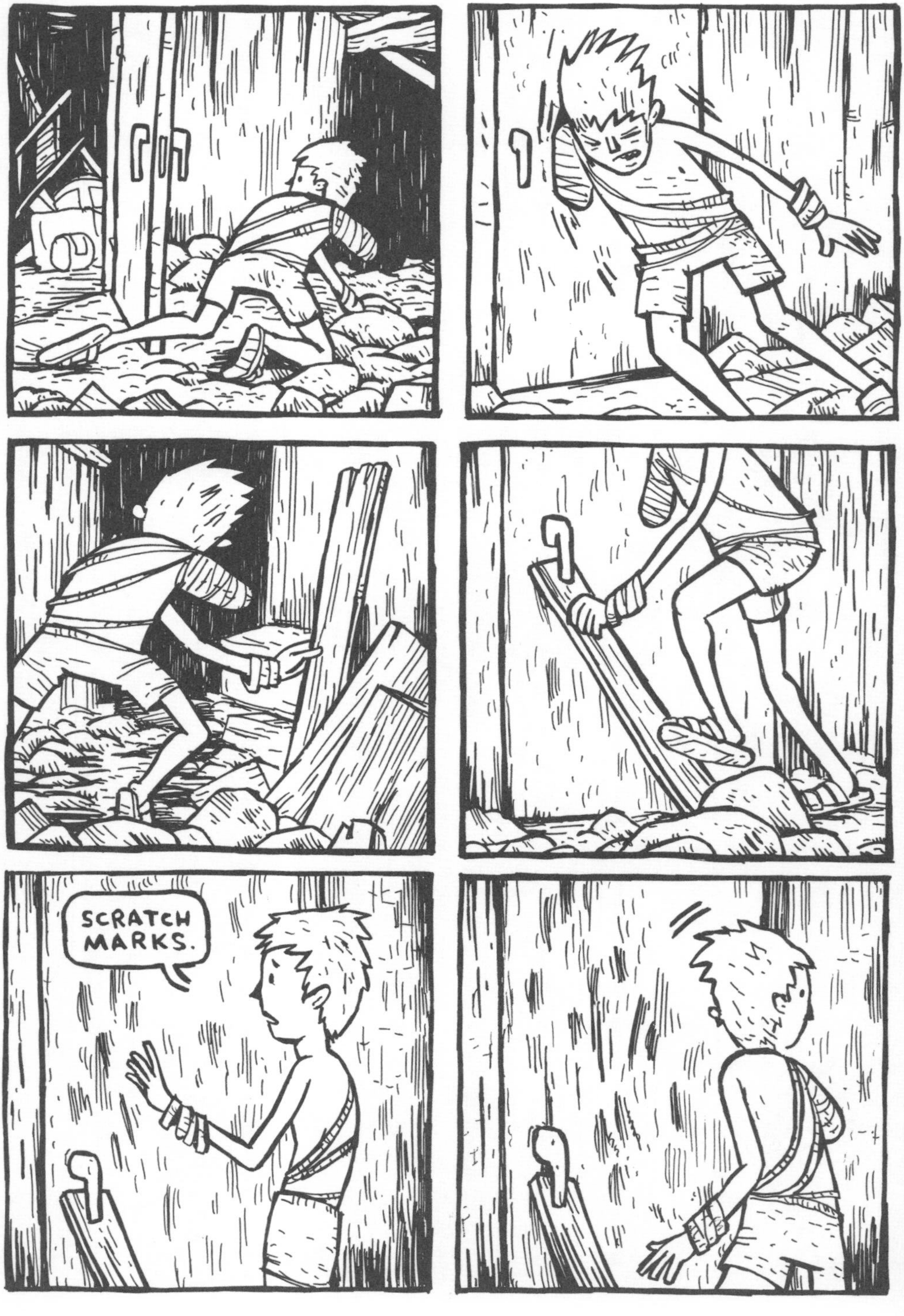
SCRATCH MARKS.

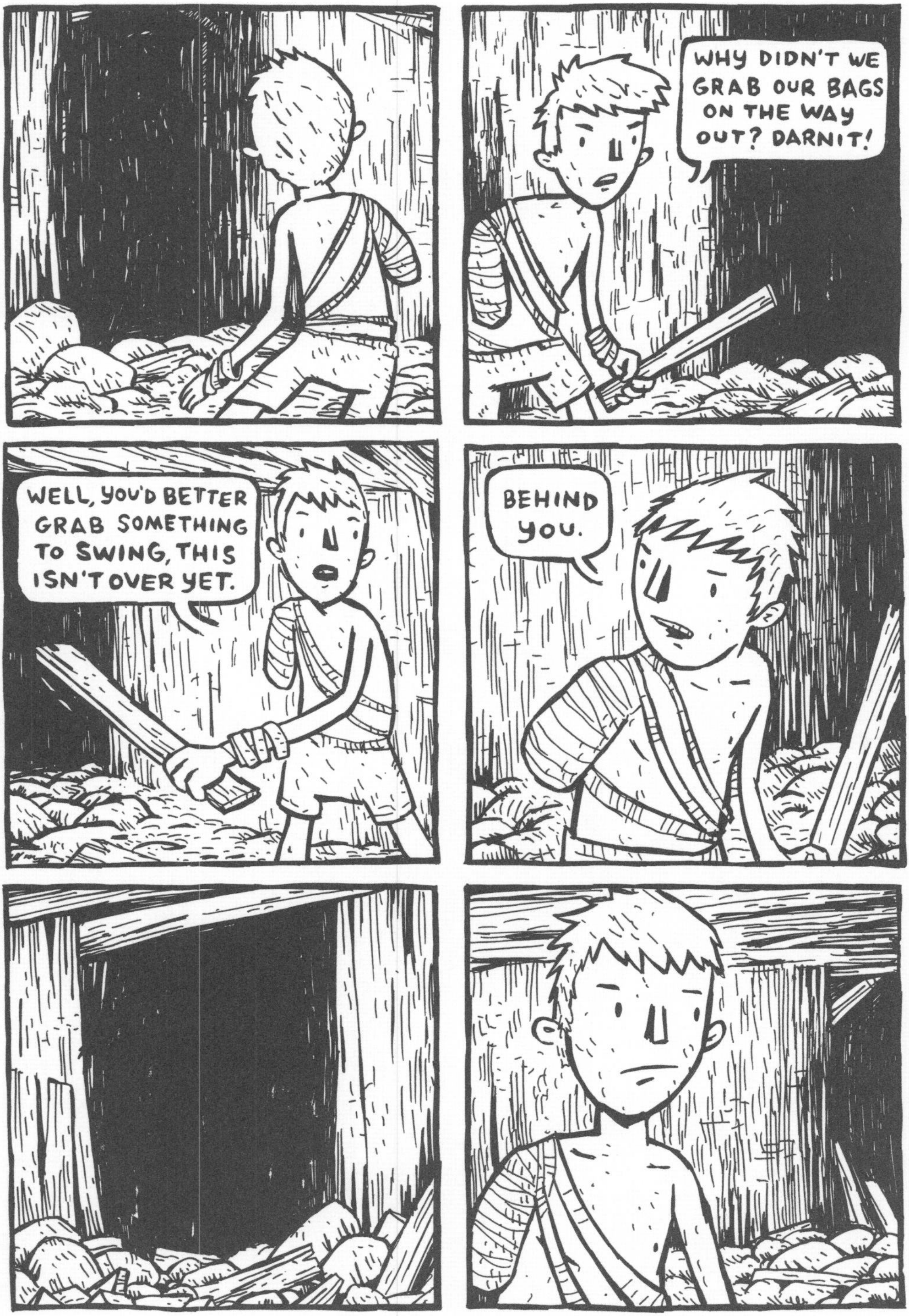
WHY DIDN'T WE GRAB OUR BAGS ON THE WAY OUT? DARNIT!
WELL, YOU'D BETTER GRAB SOMETHING TO SWING, THIS ISN'T OVER YET.
BEHIND YOU.

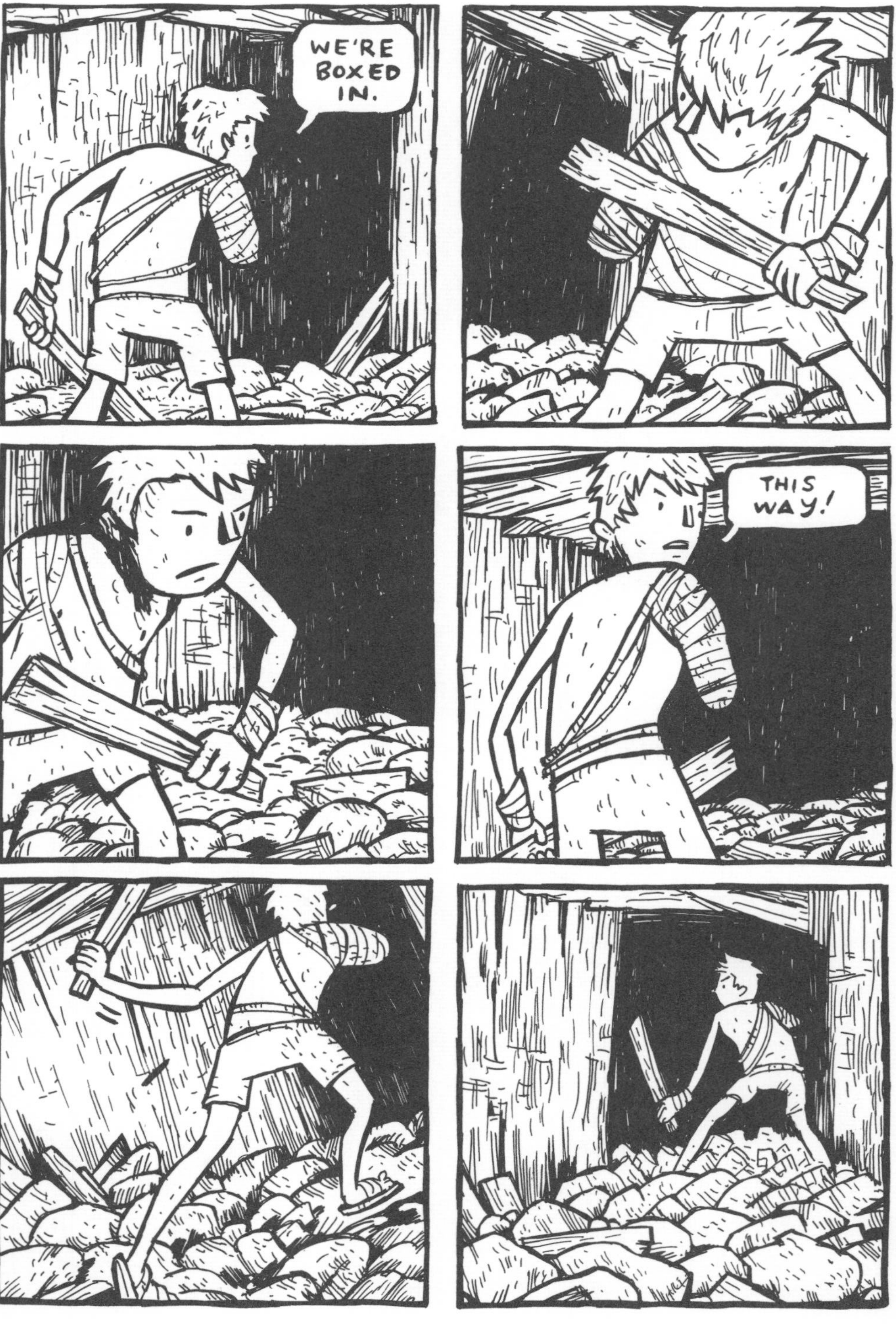
WE'RE BOXED IN.
THIS WAY!

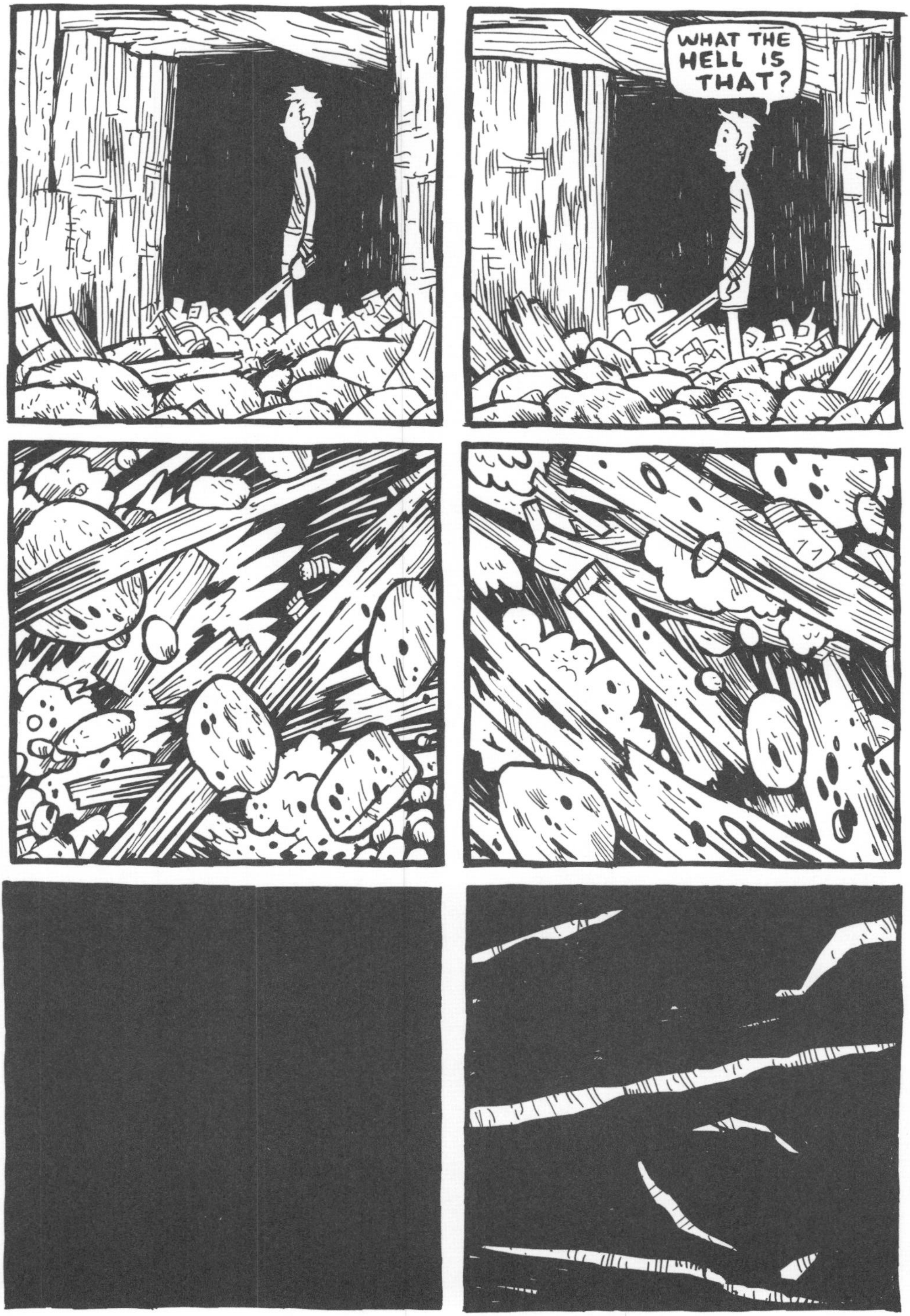
WHAT THE HELL IS THAT?

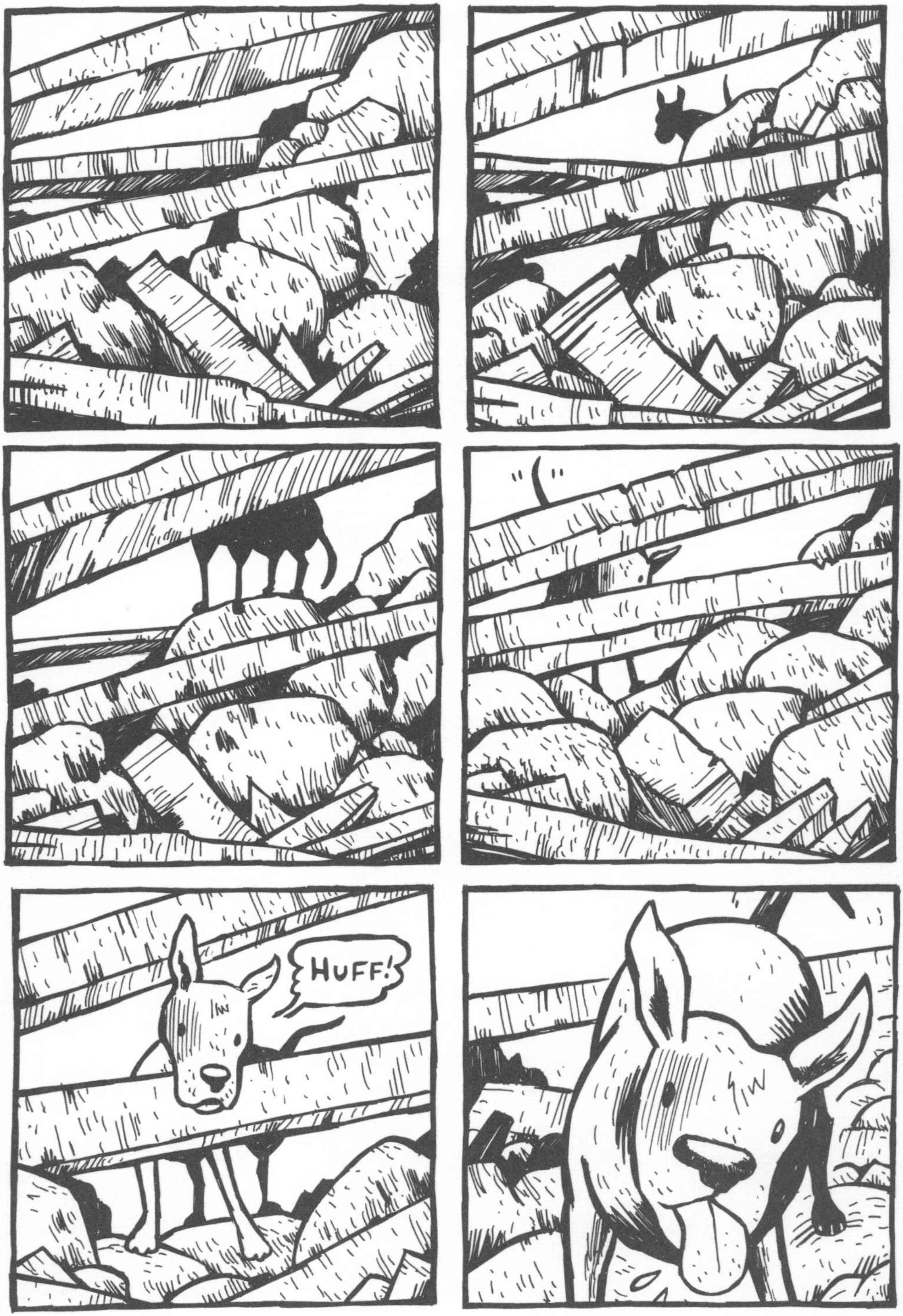
HUFF!

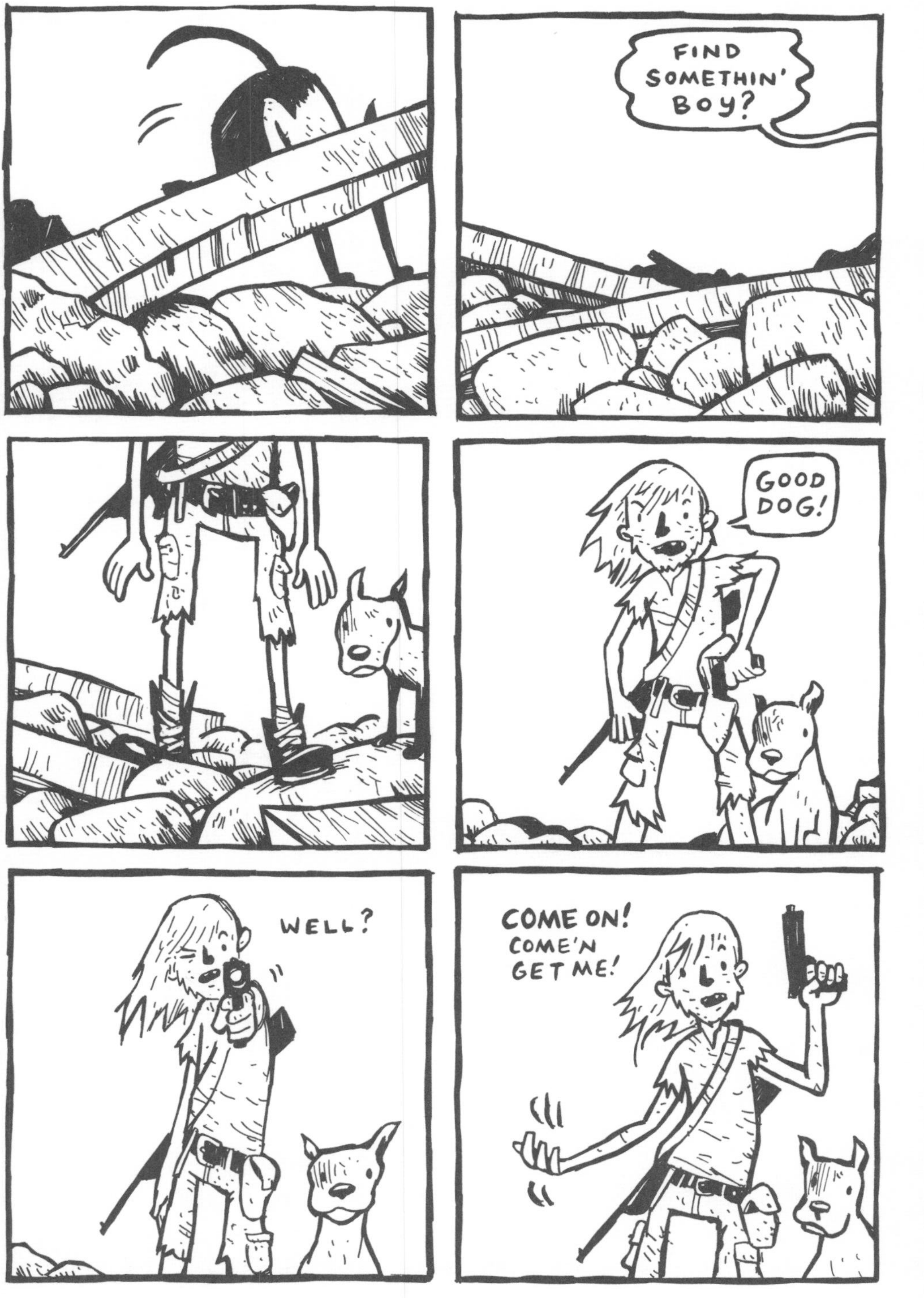
FIND SOMETHIN' BOY?
GOOD DOG!
WELL?
COME ON!
COME'N GET ME!

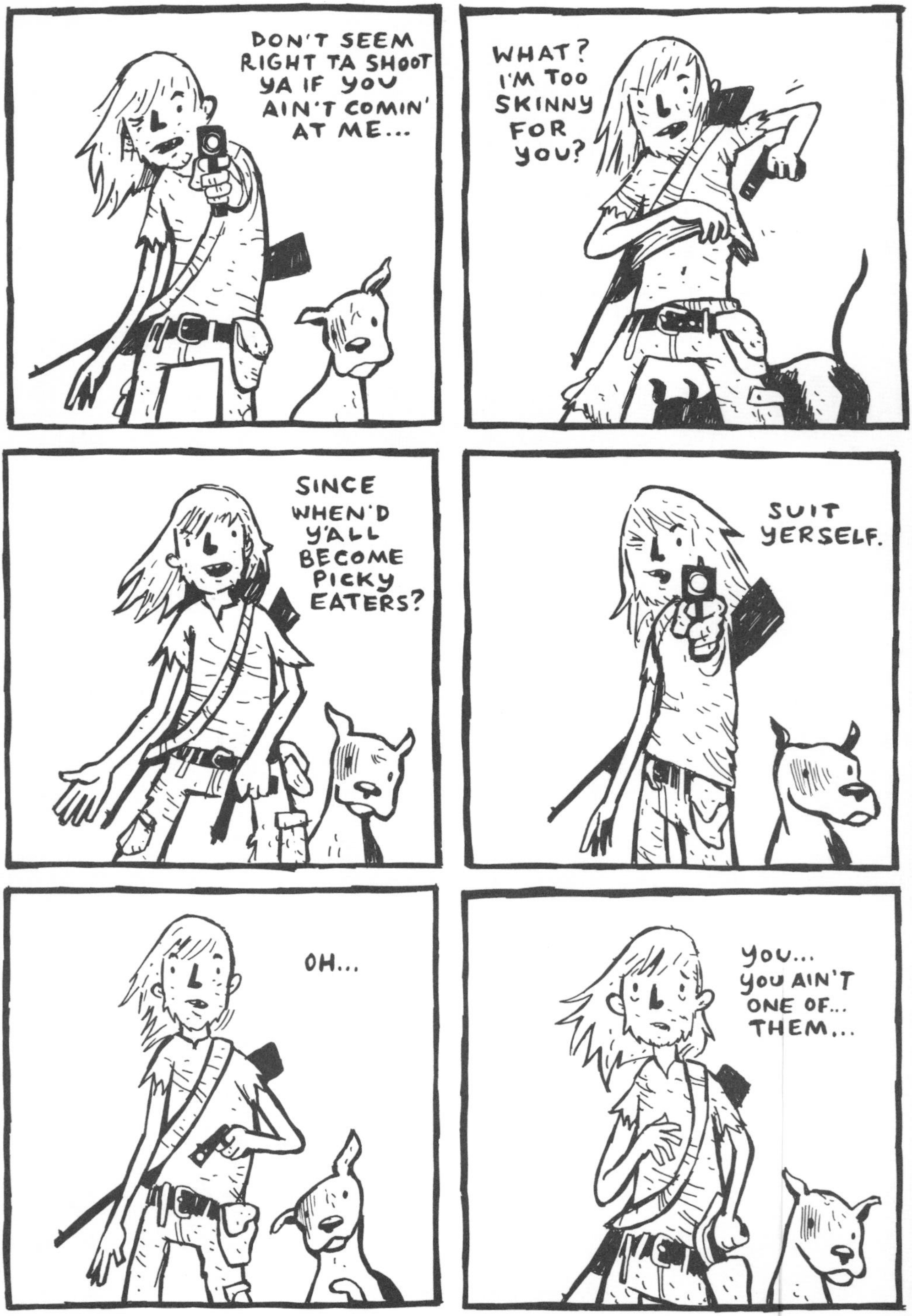
DON'T SEEM RIGHT TA SHOOT YA IF YOU AIN'T COMIN' AT ME...
WHAT? I'M TOO SKINNY FOR YOU?
SINCE WHEN'D Y'ALL BECOME PICKY EATERS?
SUIT YERSELF.
OH...
YOU... YOU AIN'T ONE OF... THEM...

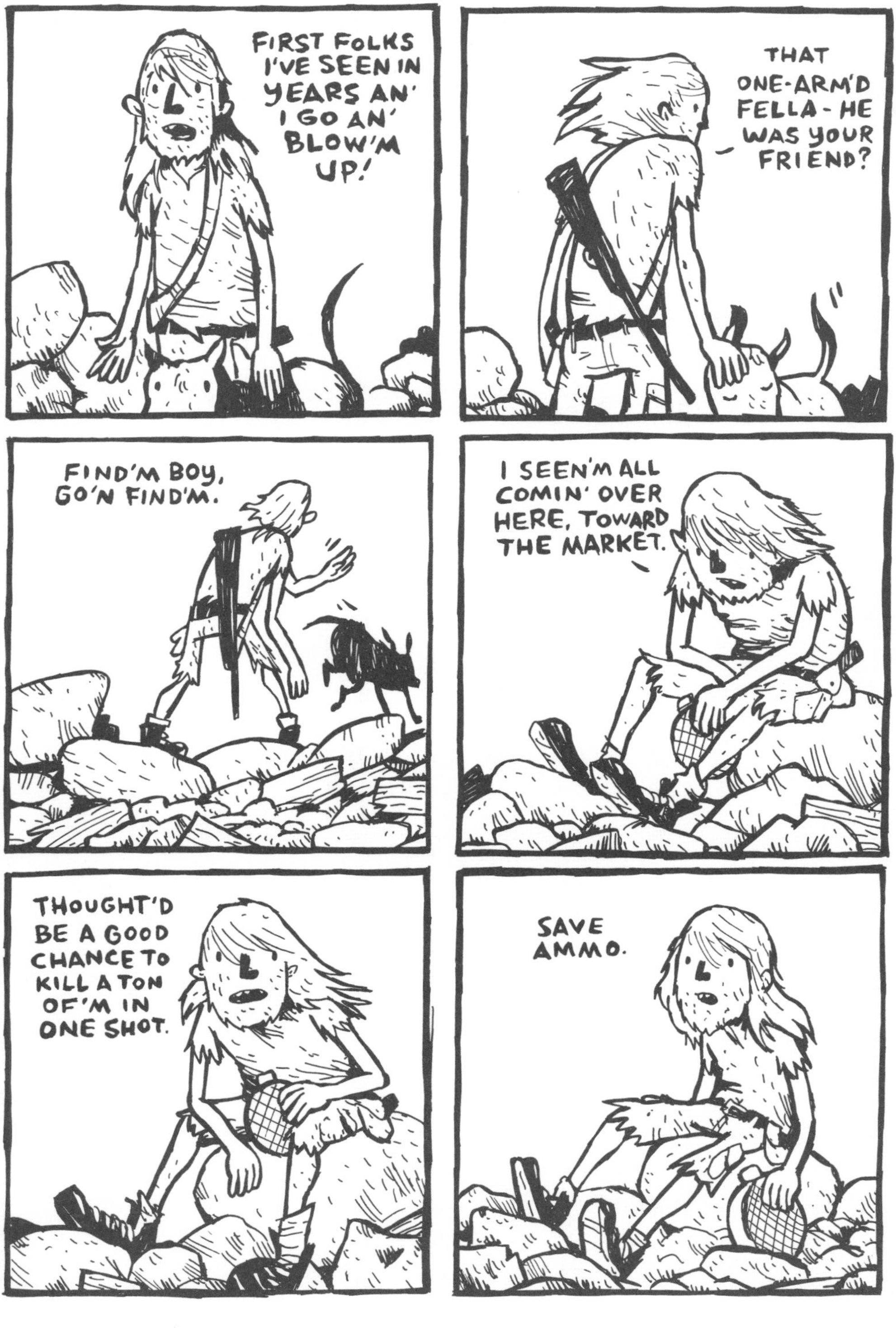
FIRST FOLKS I'VE SEEN IN YEARS AN' I GO AN' BLOW'M UP!
THAT ONE-ARM'D FELLA - HE WAS YOUR FRIEND?
FIND'M BOY, GO'N FIND'M.
I SEEN'M ALL COMIN' OVER HERE, TOWARD THE MARKET.
THOUGHT'D BE A GOOD CHANCE TO KILL A TON OF'M IN ONE SHOT.
SAVE AMMO.

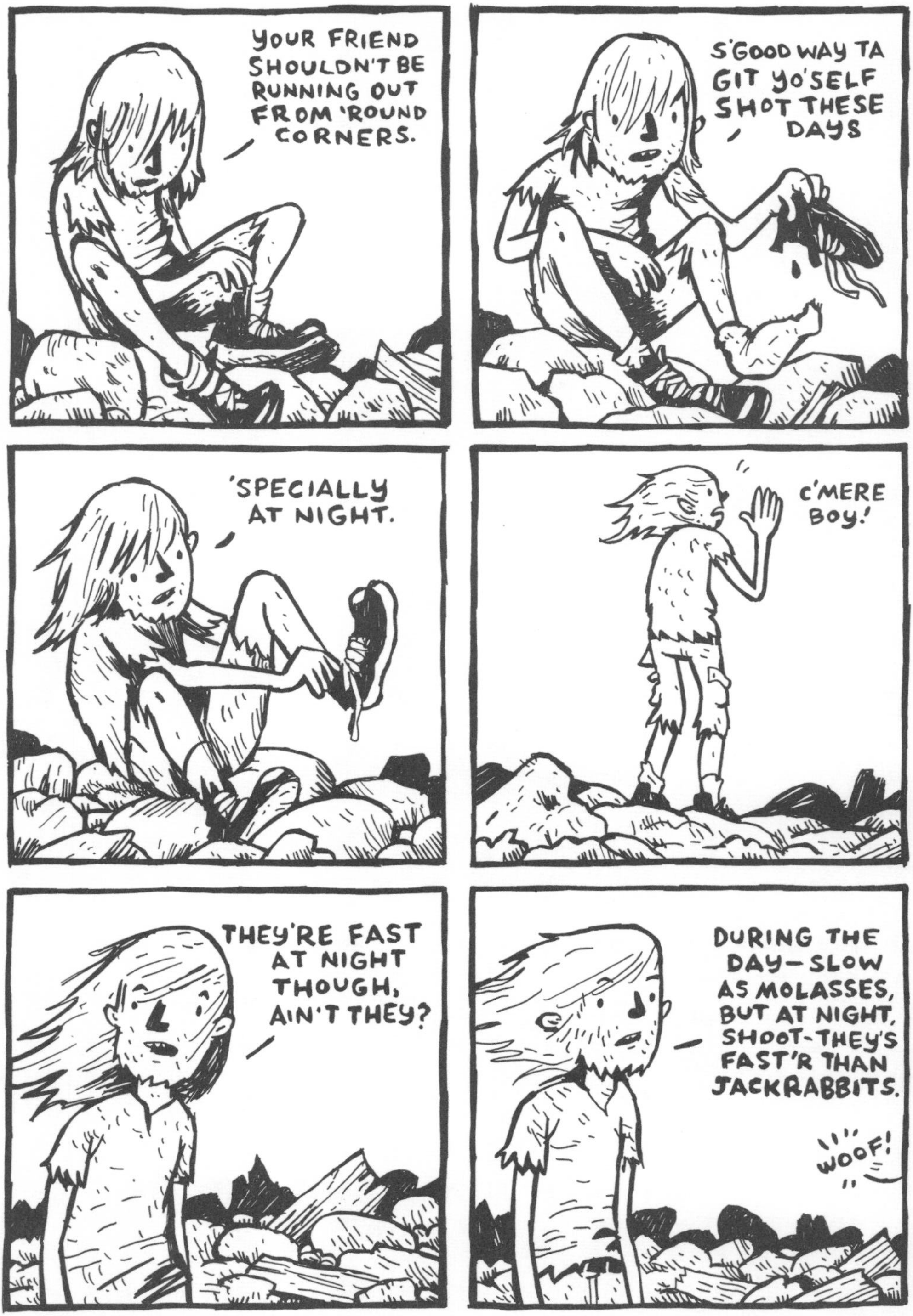
YOUR FRIEND SHOULDN'T BE RUNNING OUT FROM 'ROUND CORNERS.
S'GOOD WAY TA GIT YO'SELF SHOT THESE DAYS
'SPECIALLY AT NIGHT.
C'MERE BOY!
THEY'RE FAST AT NIGHT THOUGH, AIN'T THEY?
DURING THE DAY—SLOW AS MOLASSES, BUT AT NIGHT, SHOOT-THEY'S FAST'R THAN JACKRABBITS.
WOOF!

WAHT'CHA GOT? DROP IT!

THAT'S NOT GOOD...

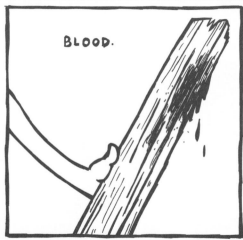

BLOOD.

WELL...

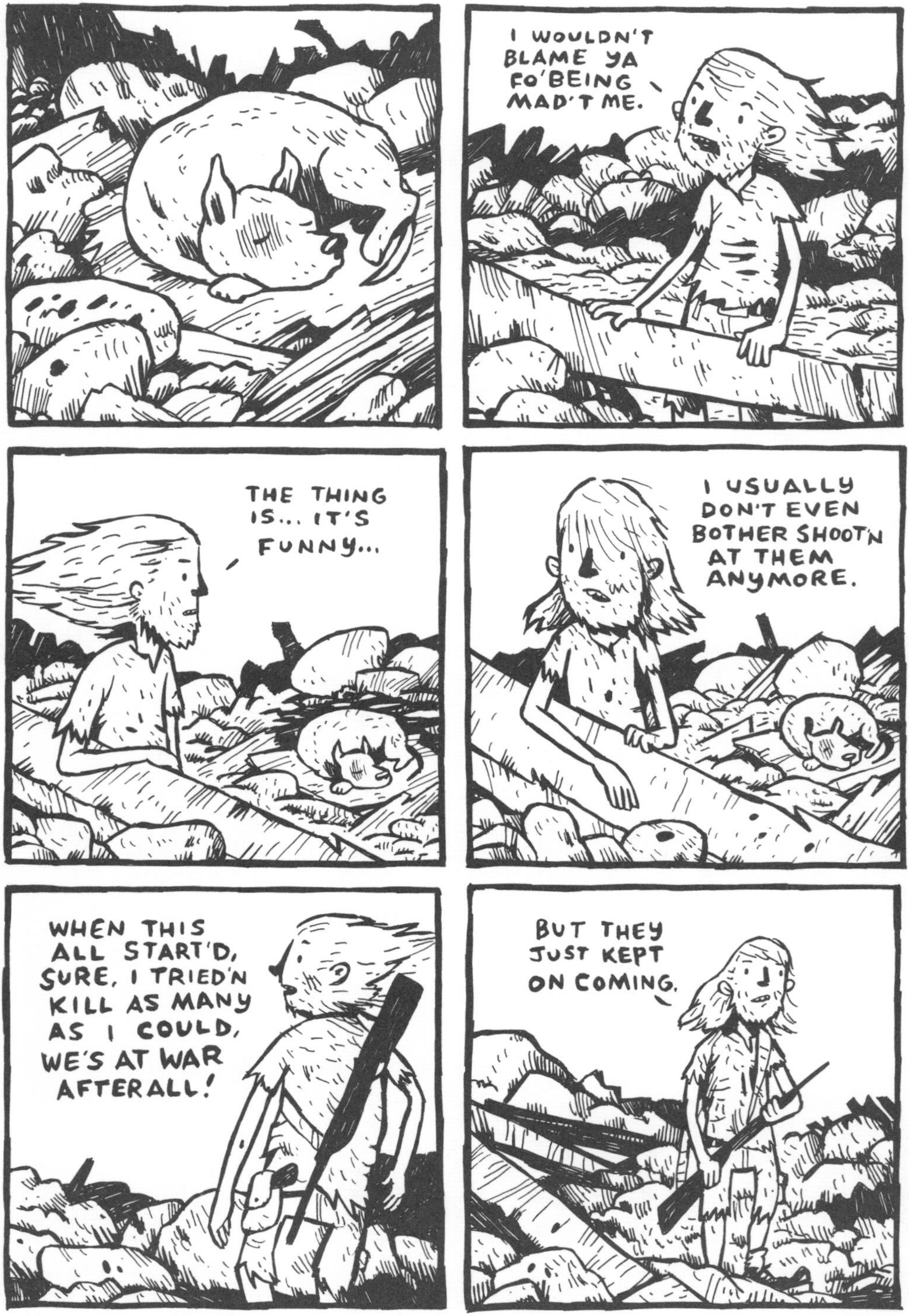
I WOULDN'T BLAME YA FO'BEING MAD'T ME.
THE THING IS... IT'S FUNNY...
I USUALLY DON'T EVEN BOTHER SHOOT'N AT THEM ANYMORE.
WHEN THIS ALL START'D, SURE, I TRIED'N KILL AS MANY AS I COULD, WE'S AT WAR AFTERALL!
BUT THEY JUST KEPT ON COMING.

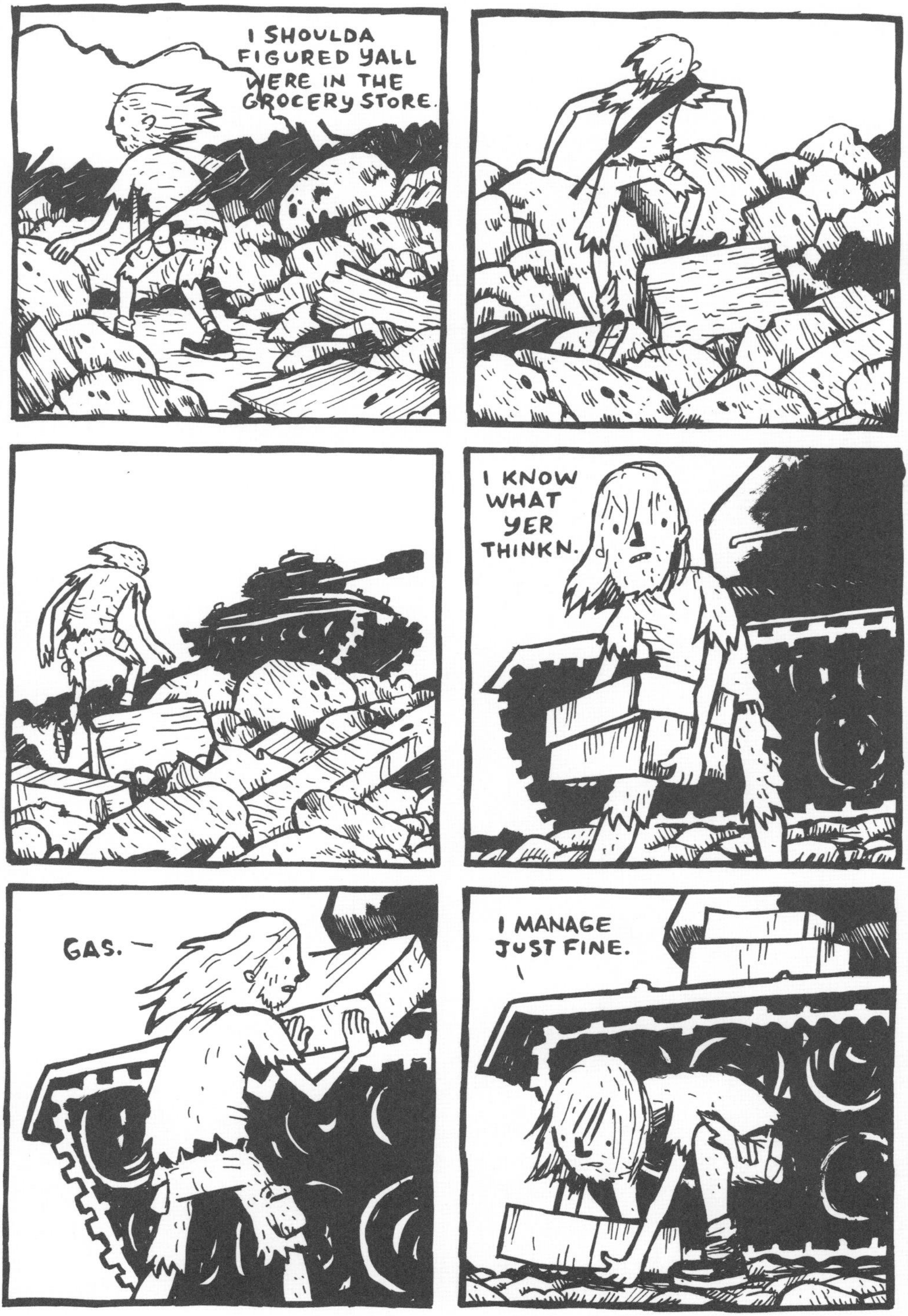
I SHOULDA FIGURED YALL WERE IN THE GROCERY STORE.
I KNOW WHAT YER THINKN.
GAS.
I MANAGE JUST FINE.

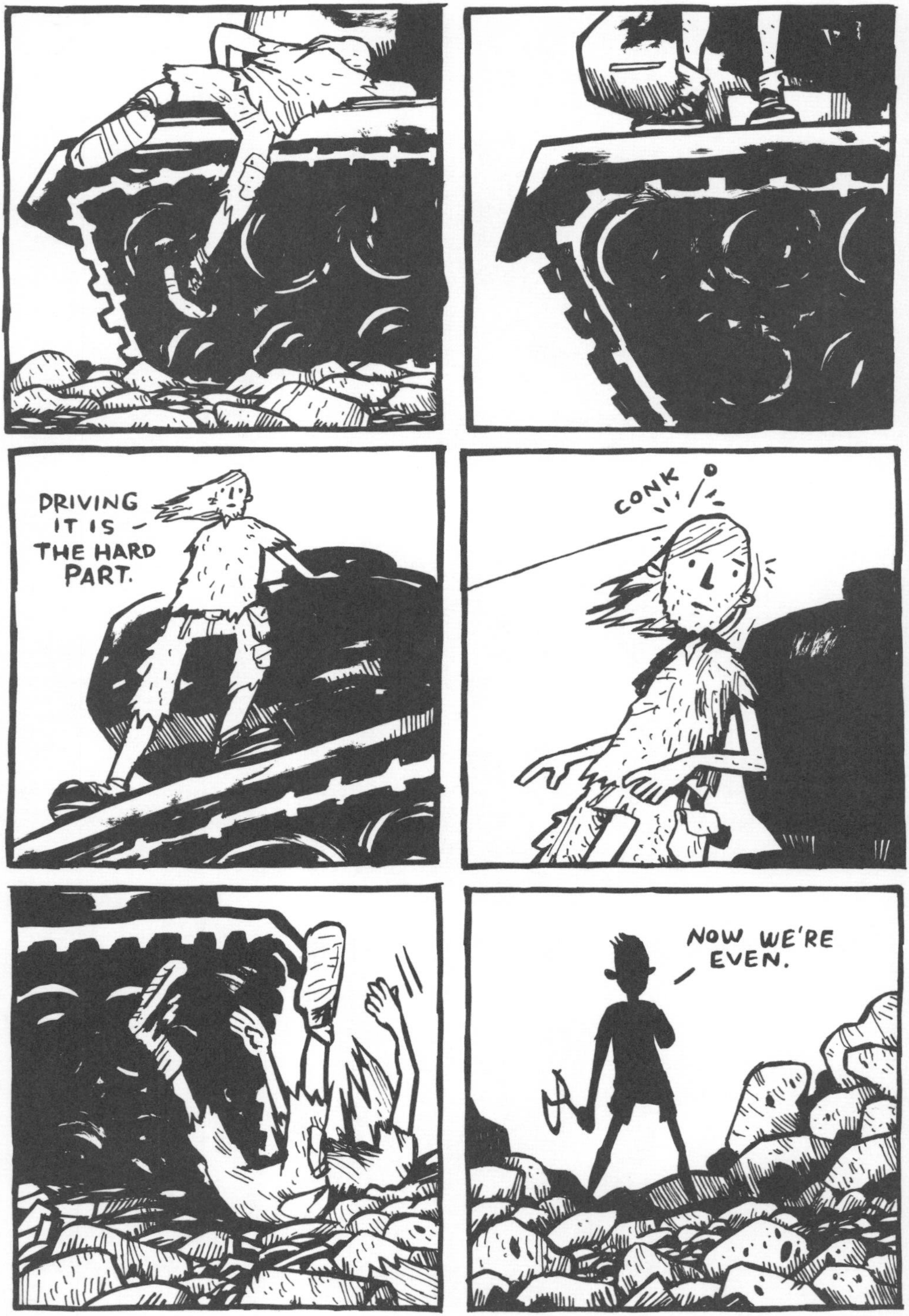
DRIVING IT IS THE HARD PART.
CONK
NOW WE'RE EVEN.

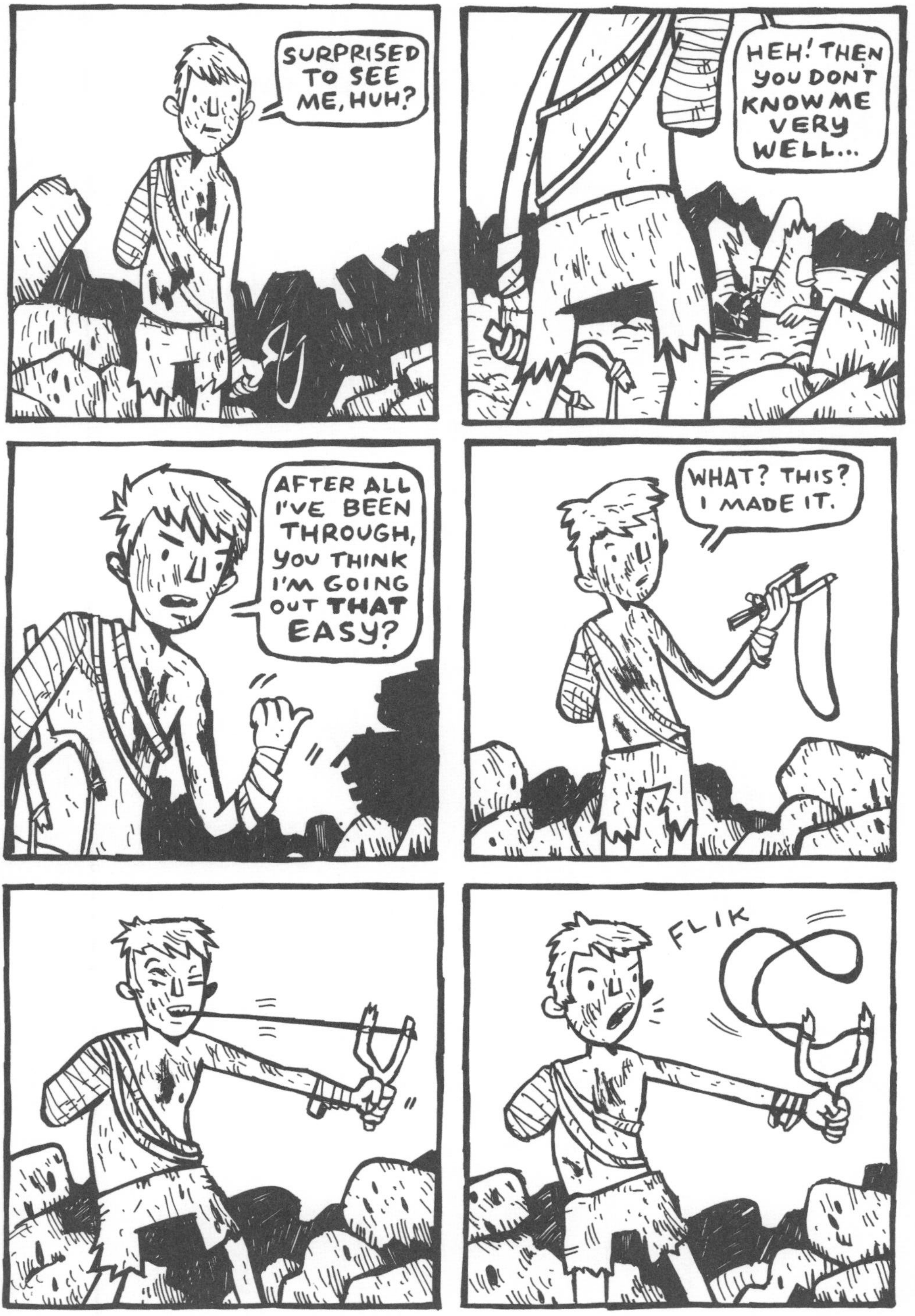
SURPRISED TO SEE ME, HUH?
HEH! THEN YOU DON'T KNOW ME VERY WELL...
AFTER ALL I'VE BEEN THROUGH, YOU THINK I'M GOING OUT **THAT** EASY?
WHAT? THIS? I MADE IT.
FLIK

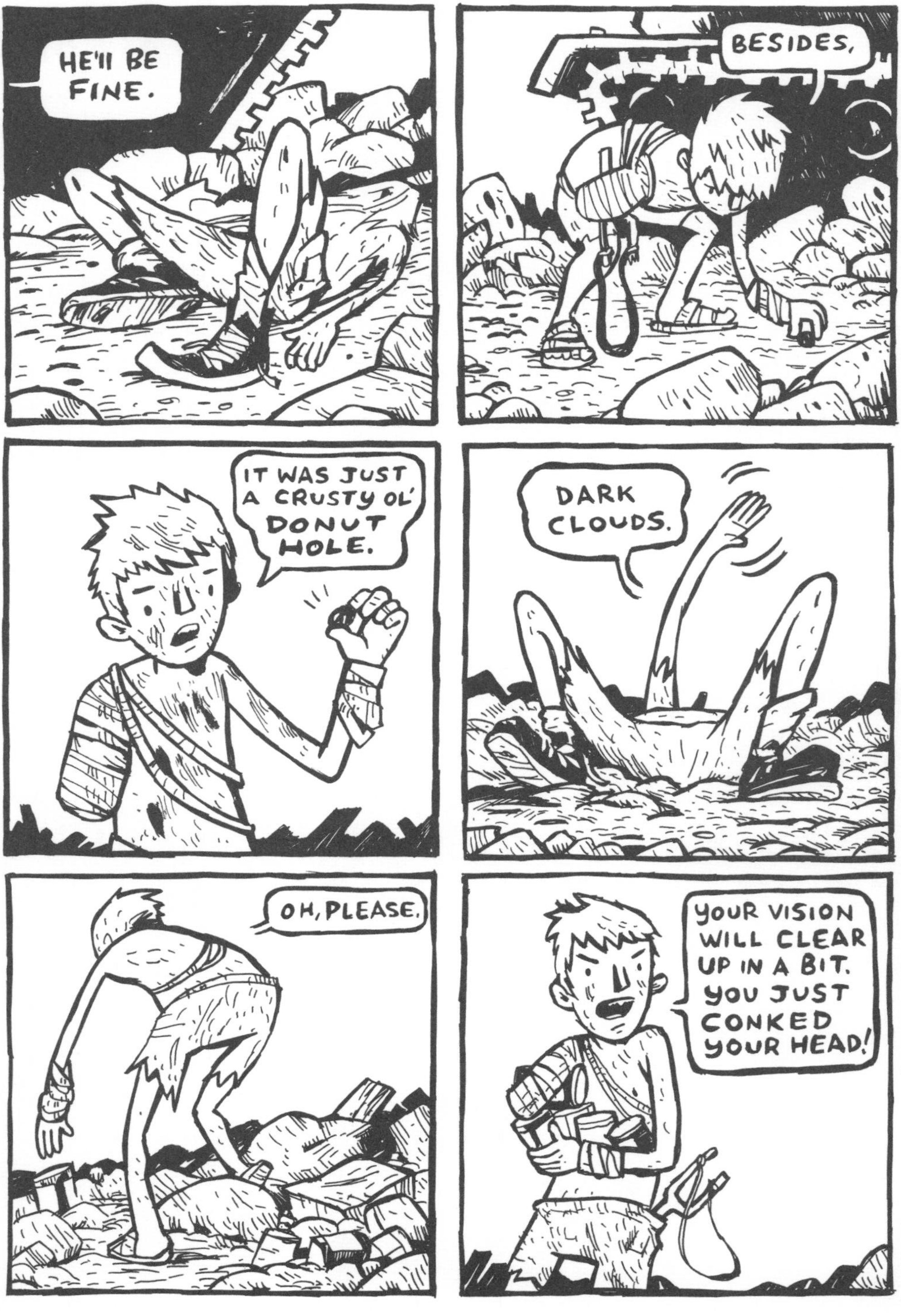
HE'll BE FINE.
BESIDES,
IT WAS JUST A CRUSTY OL' DONUT HOLE.
DARK CLOUDS.
OH, PLEASE.
YOUR VISION WILL CLEAR UP IN A BIT. YOU JUST CONKED YOUR HEAD!

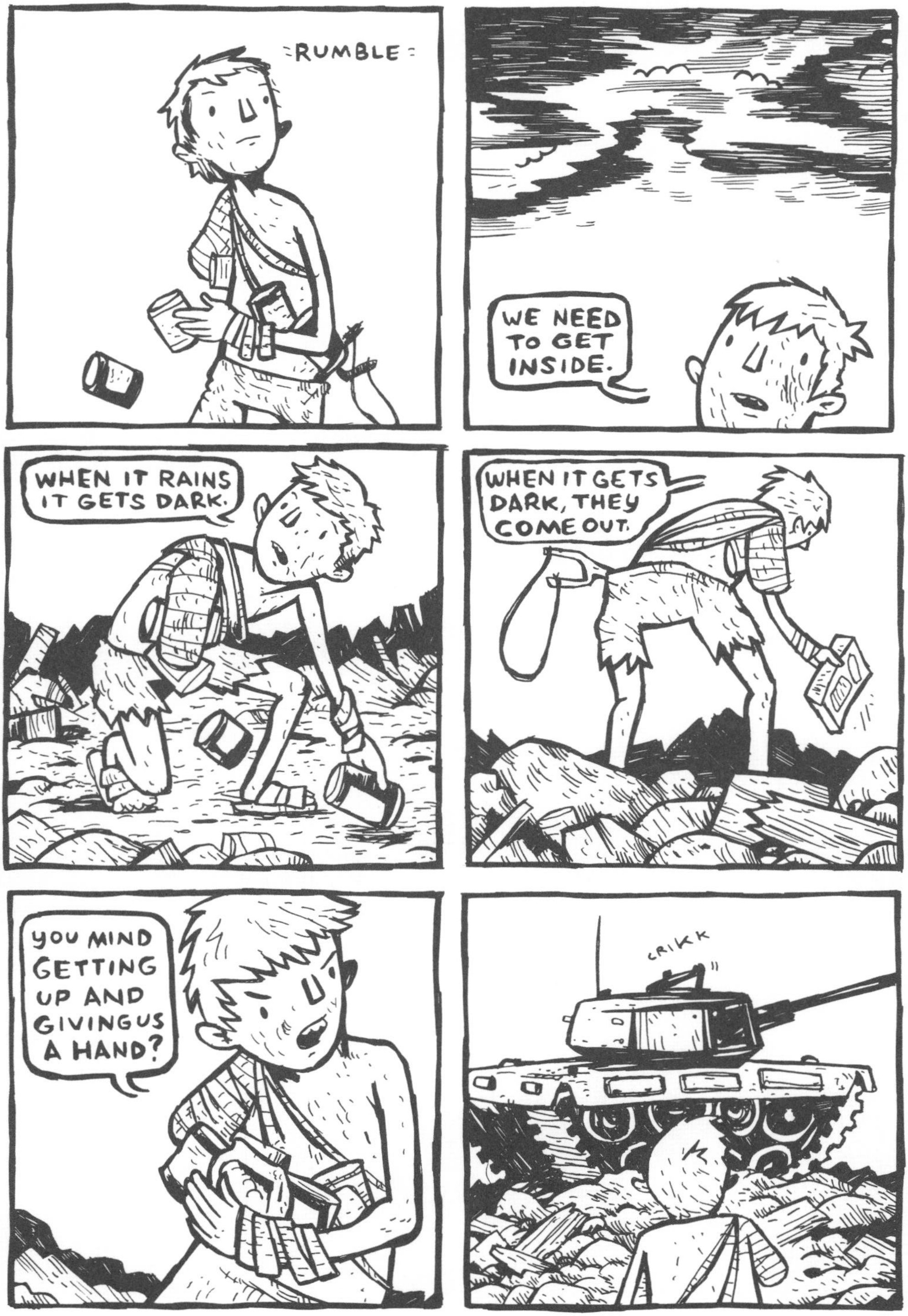
RUMBLE
WE NEED TO GET INSIDE.
WHEN IT RAINS IT GETS DARK.
WHEN IT GETS DARK, THEY COME OUT.
YOU MIND GETTING UP AND GIVINGUS A HAND?
CRIKK

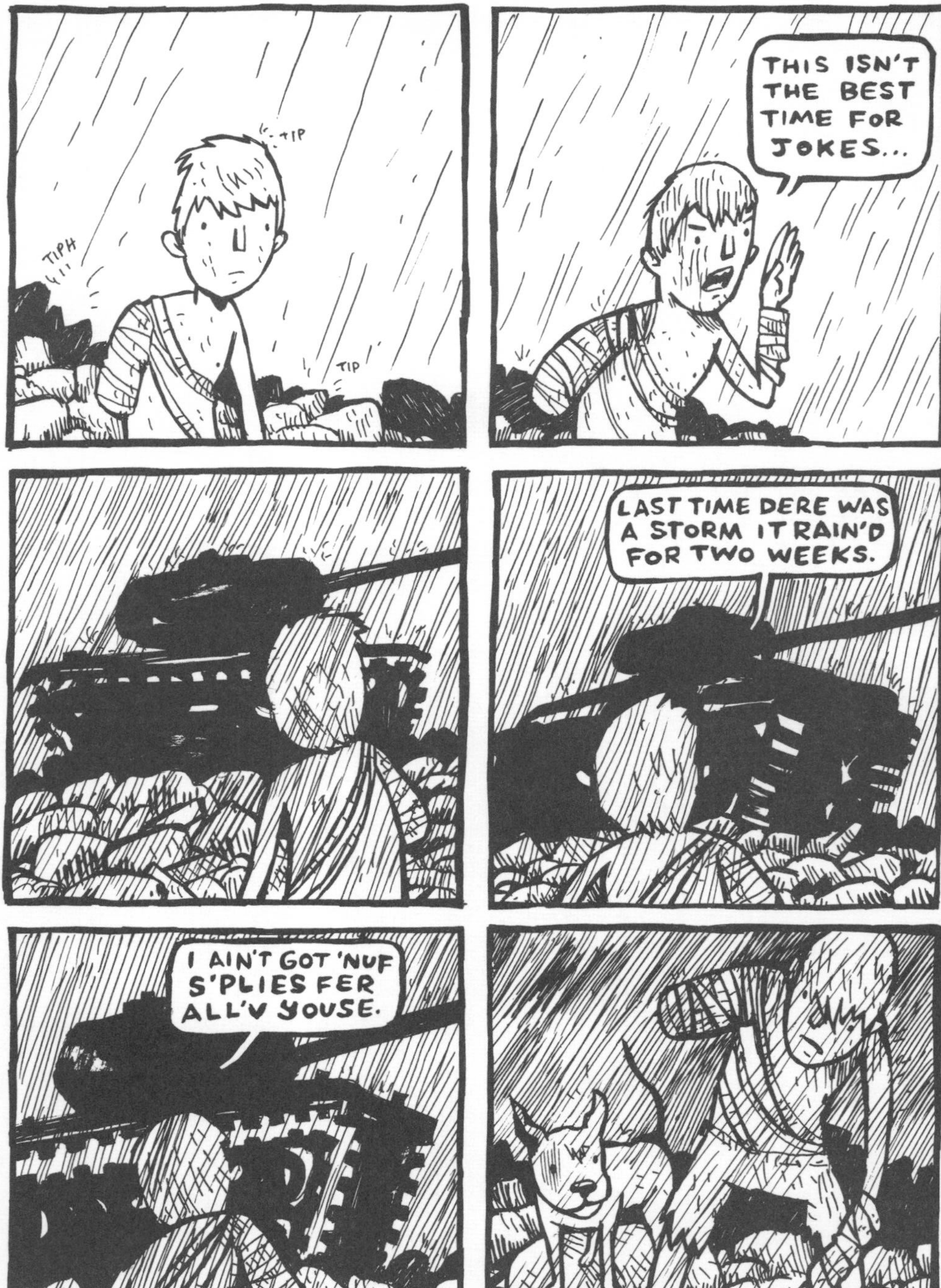
TIP
TIPH
TIP
THIS ISN'T THE BEST TIME FOR JOKES...
LAST TIME DERE WAS A STORM IT RAIN'D FOR TWO WEEKS.
I AIN'T GOT 'NUF S'PLIES FER ALL'V YOUSE.

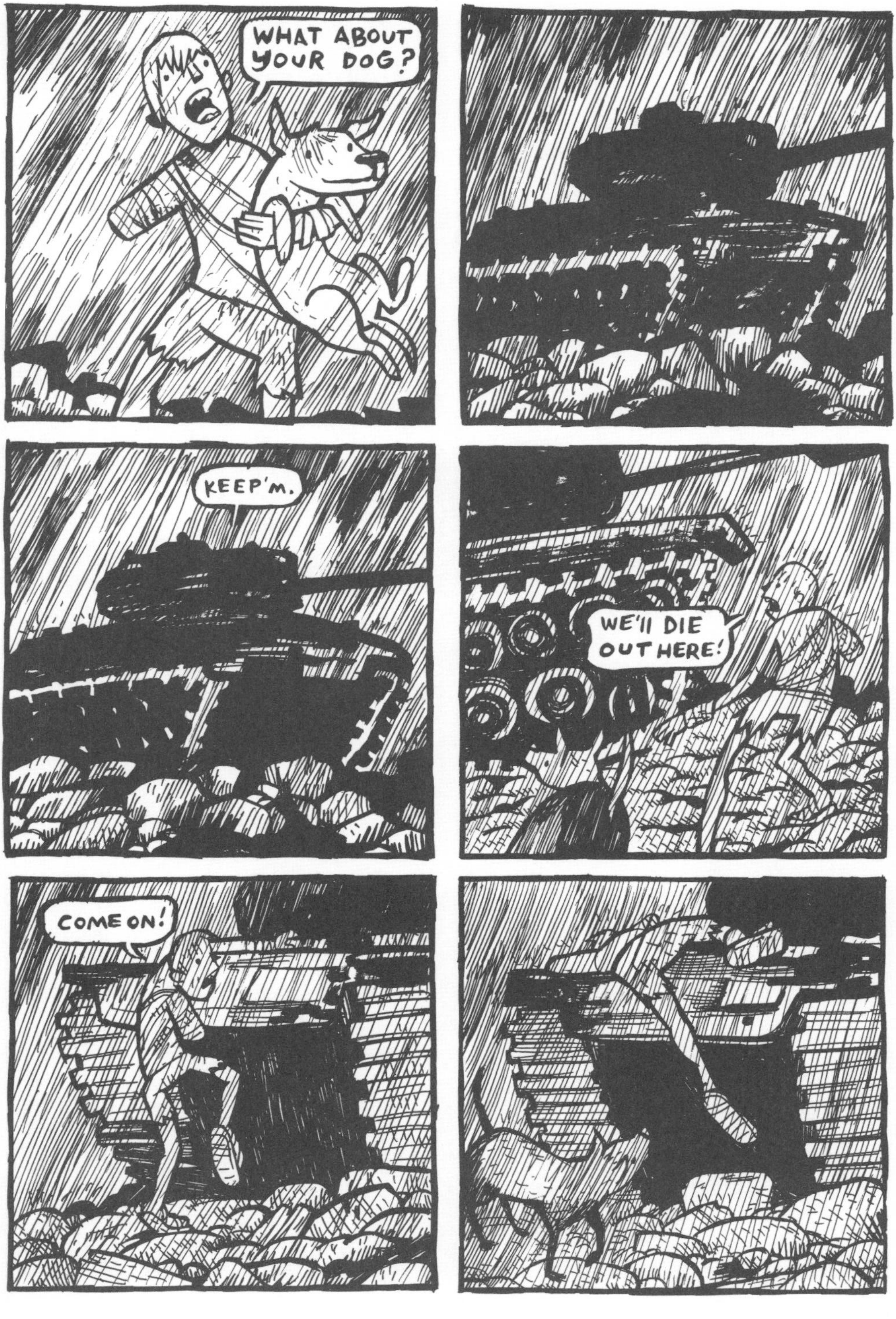
WHAT ABOUT YOUR DOG?
KEEP'M.
WE'll DIE OUT HERE!
COME ON!

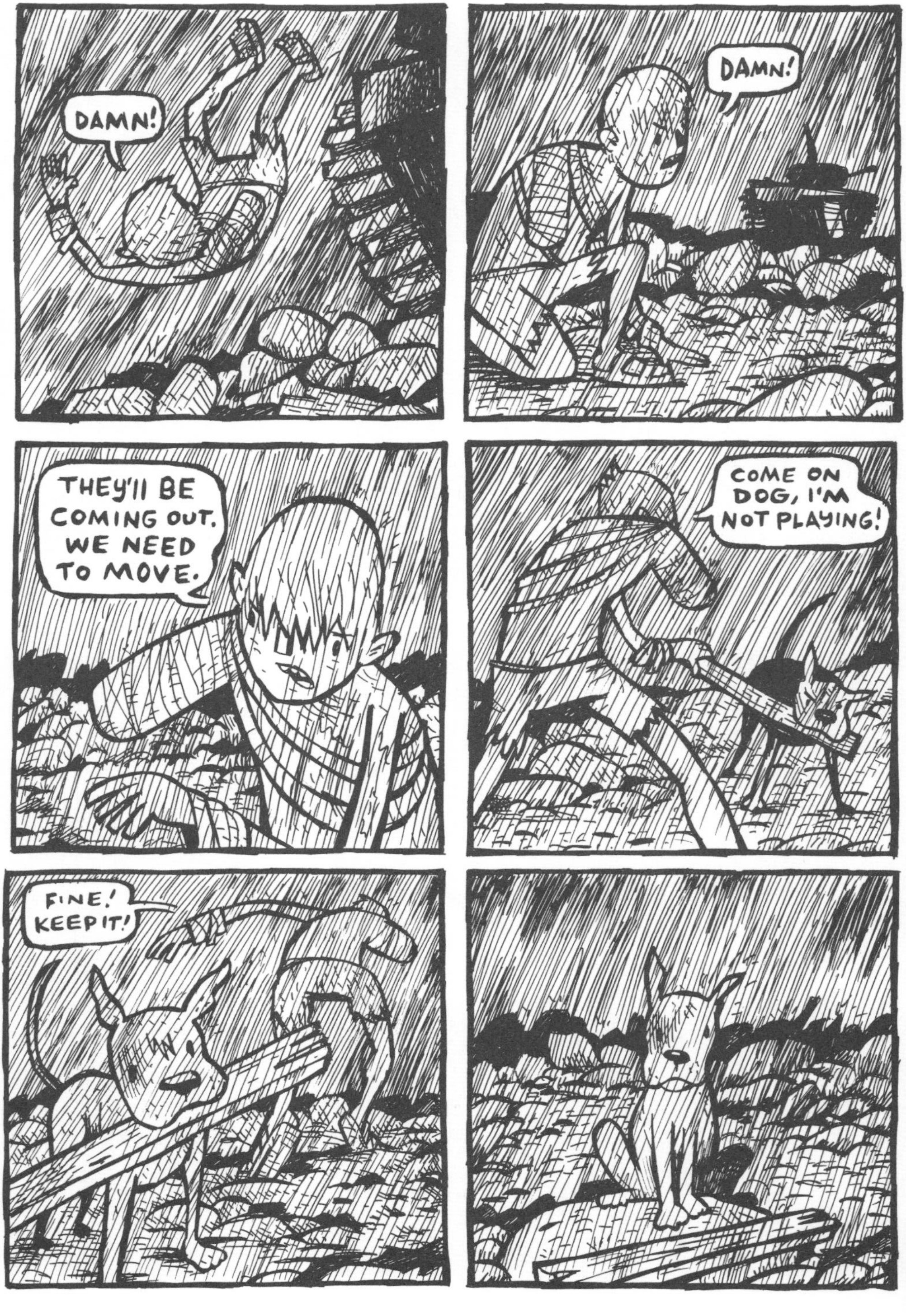
DAMN!
DAMN!
THEY'LL BE COMING OUT. WE NEED TO MOVE.
COME ON DOG, I'M NOT PLAYING!
FINE! KEEP IT!

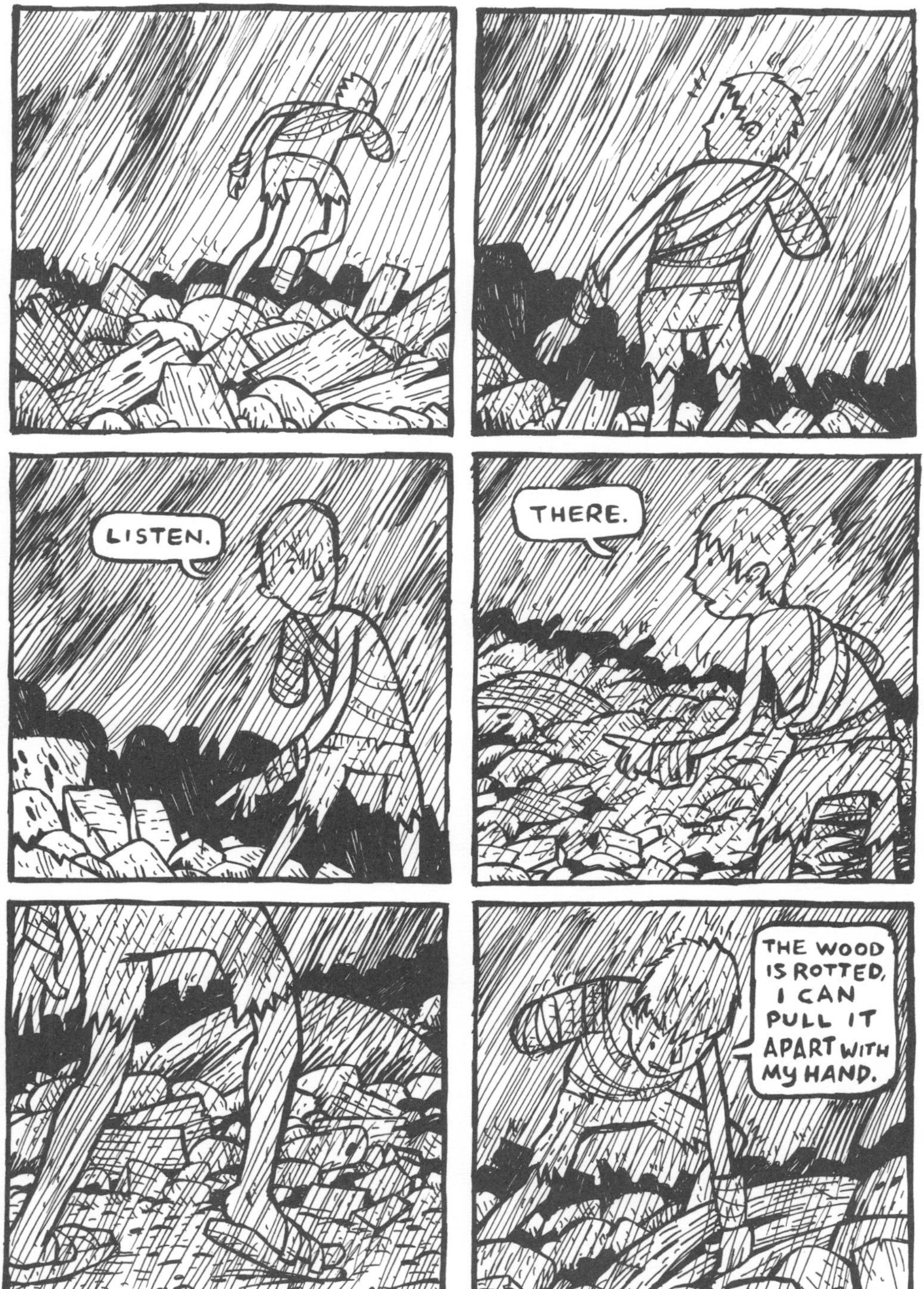
LISTEN.
THERE.
THE WOOD IS ROTTED, I CAN PULL IT APART WITH MY HAND.

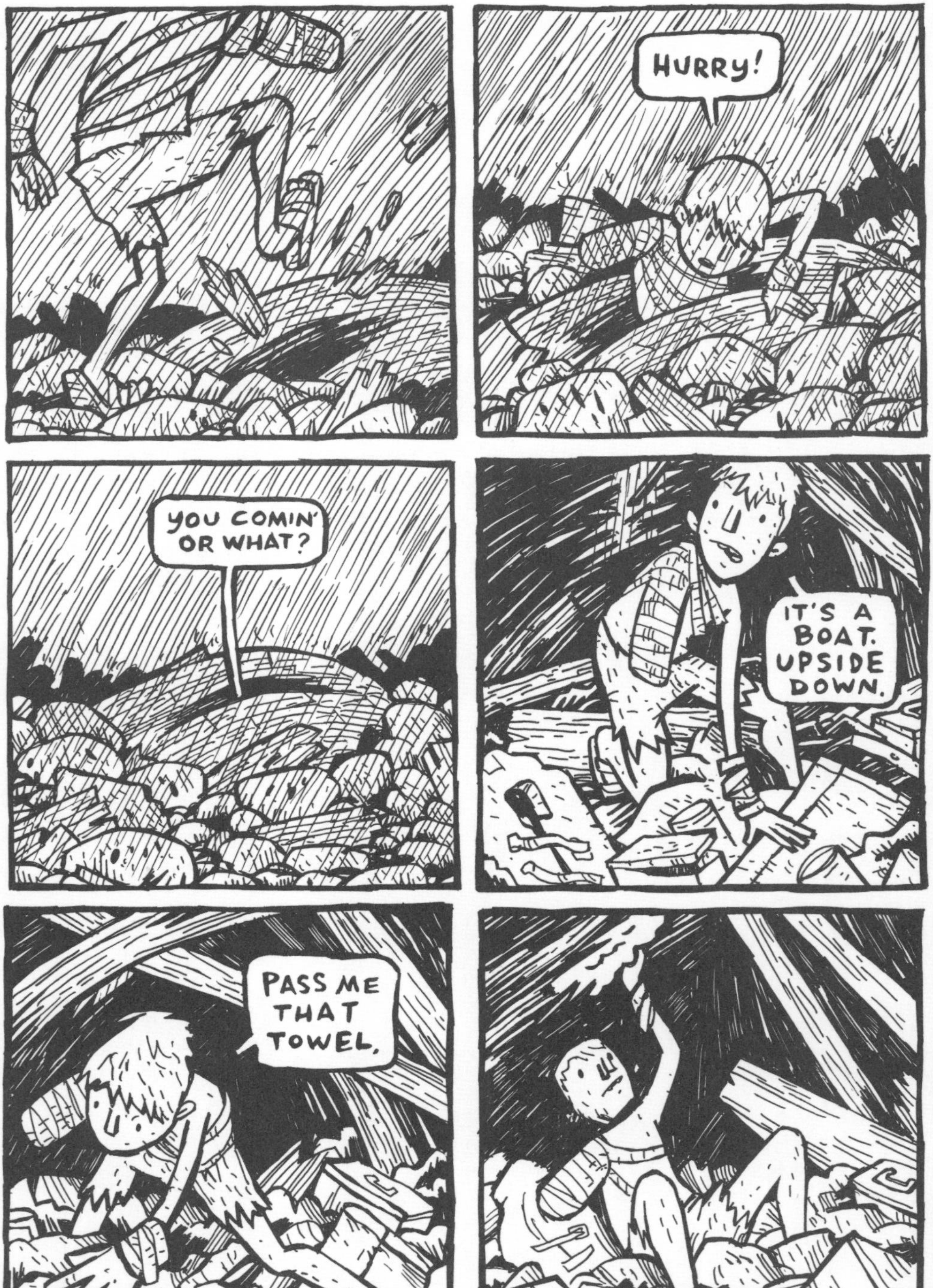
HURRY!
YOU COMIN' OR WHAT?
IT'S A BOAT. UPSIDE DOWN.
PASS ME THAT TOWEL.

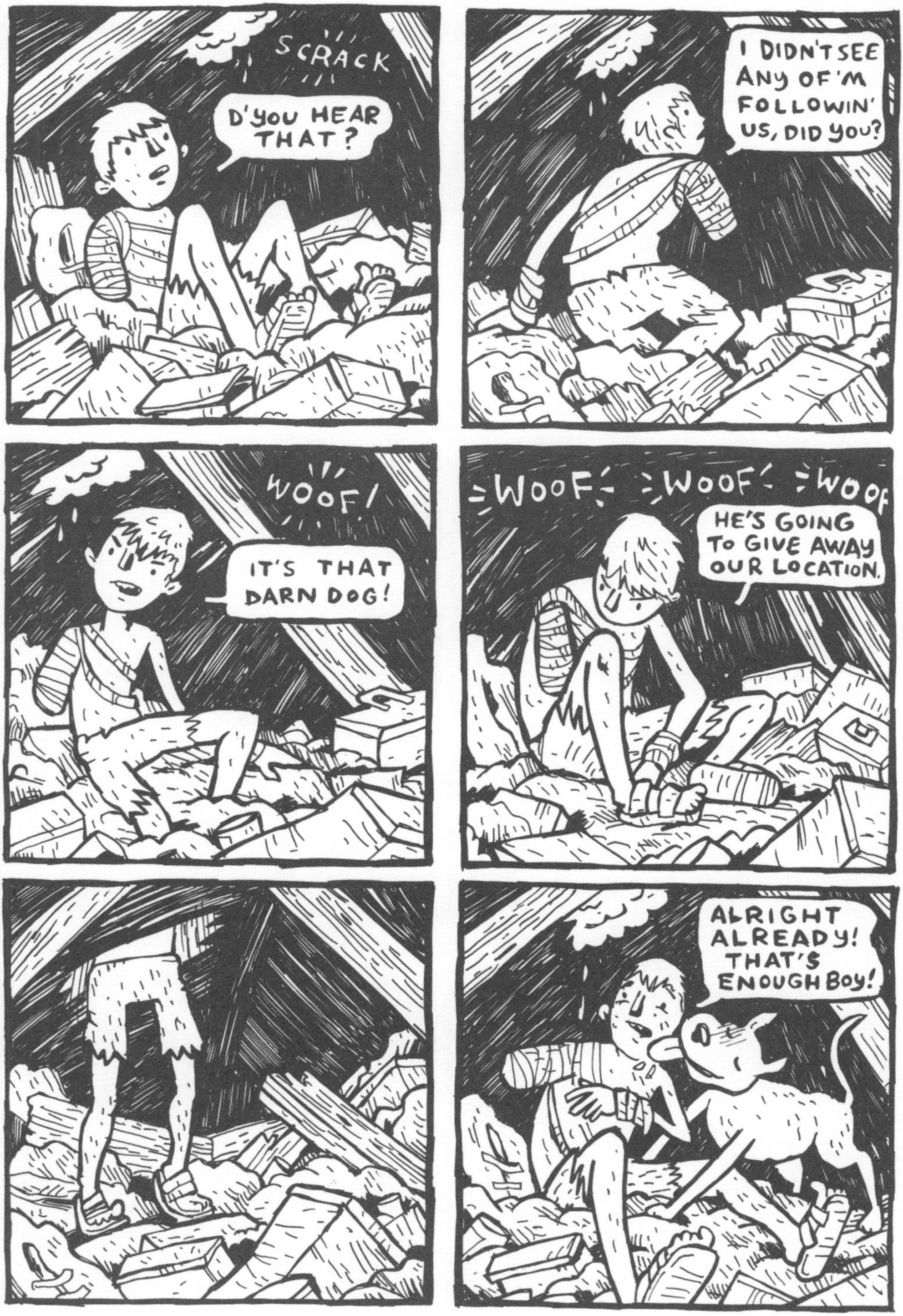
SCRACK
D'YOU HEAR THAT?
I DIDN'T SEE ANY OF 'M FOLLOWIN' US, DID YOU?
WOOF!
IT'S THAT DARN DOG!
WOOF WOOF WOOF
HE'S GOING TO GIVE AWAY OUR LOCATION.
ALRIGHT ALREADY! THAT'S ENOUGH BOY!

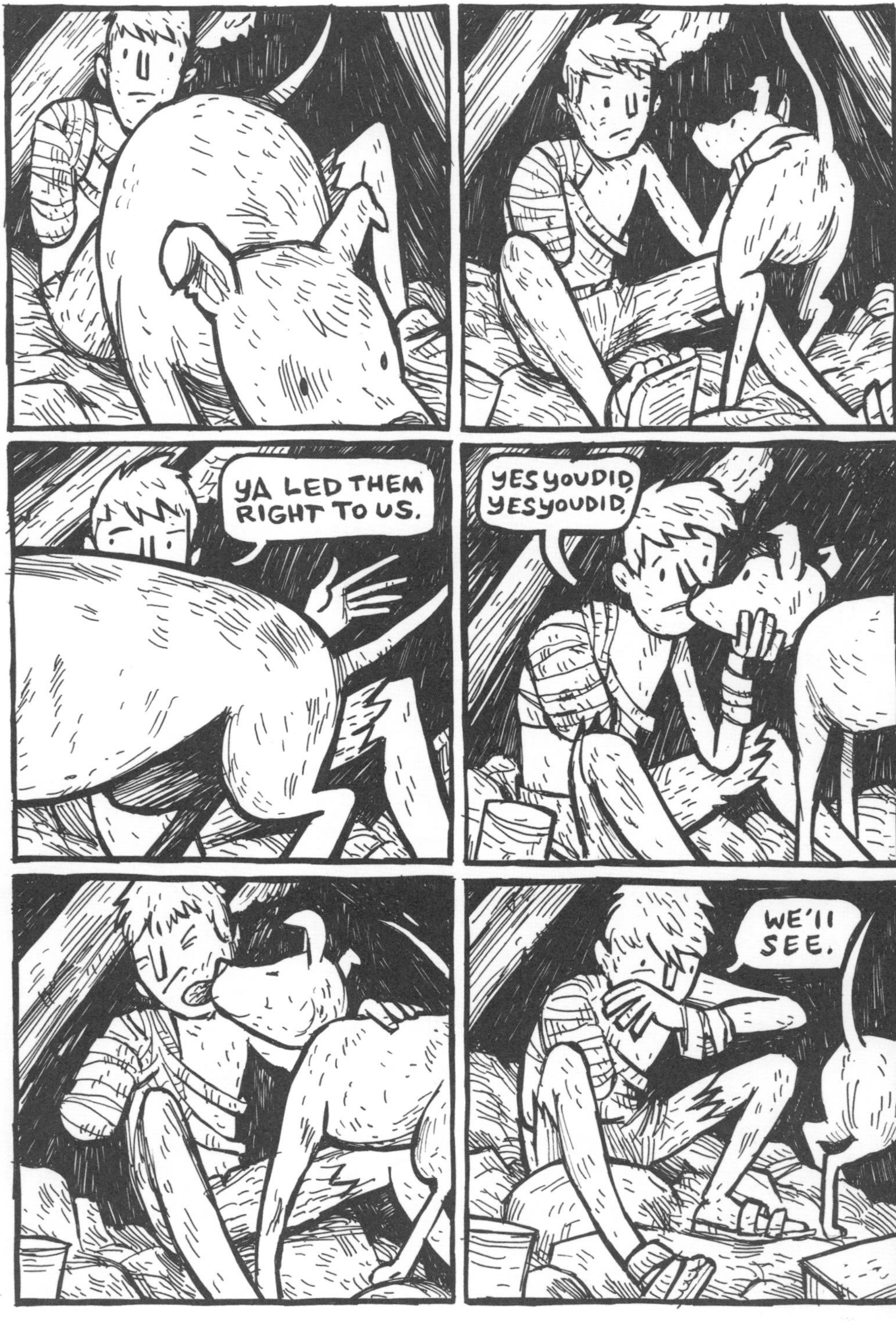
YA LED THEM RIGHT TO US.
YES YOU DID, YES YOU DID.
WE'll SEE.

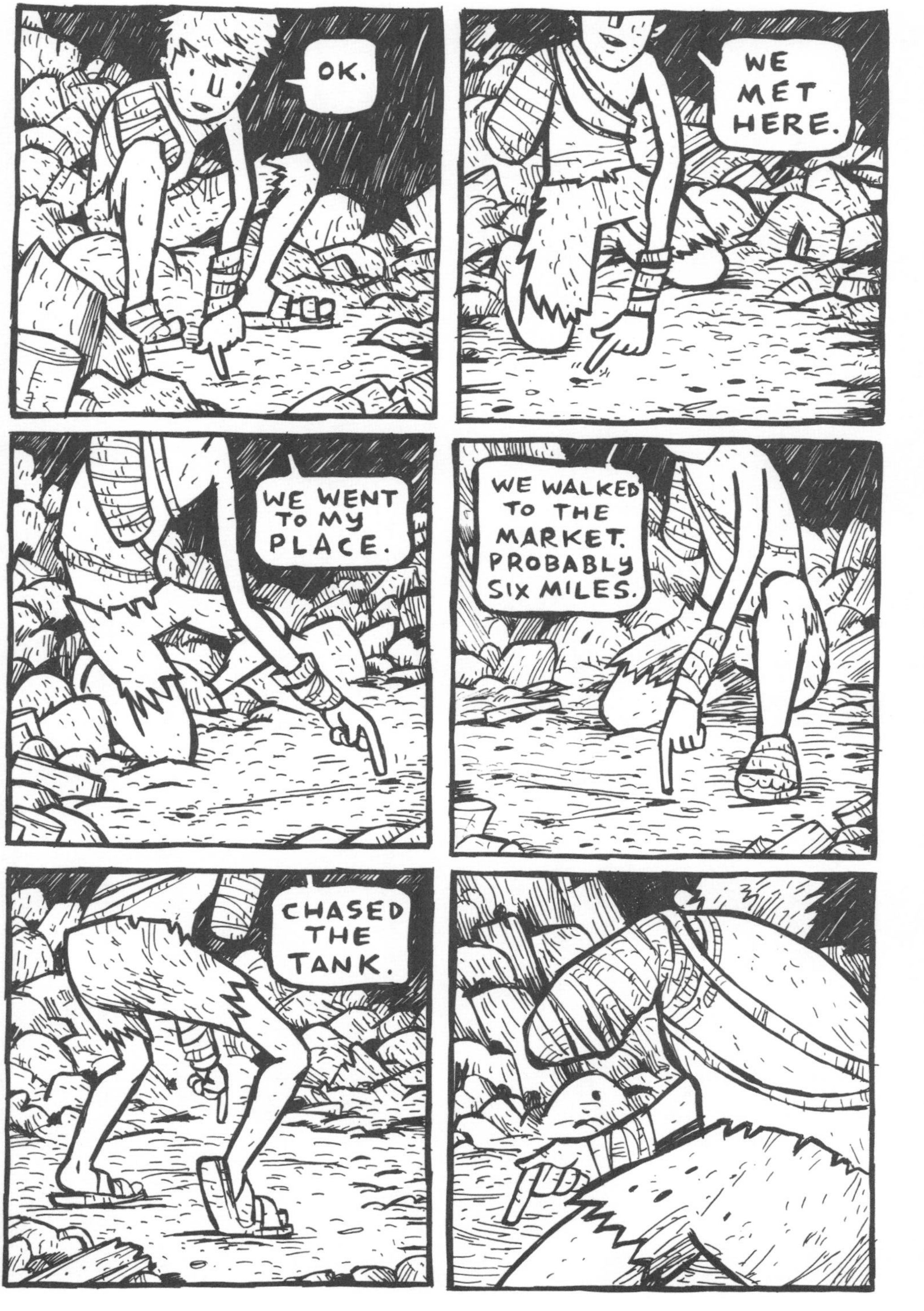
OK.
WE MET HERE.
WE WENT TO MY PLACE.
WE WALKED TO THE MARKET. PROBABLY SIX MILES.
CHASED THE TANK.

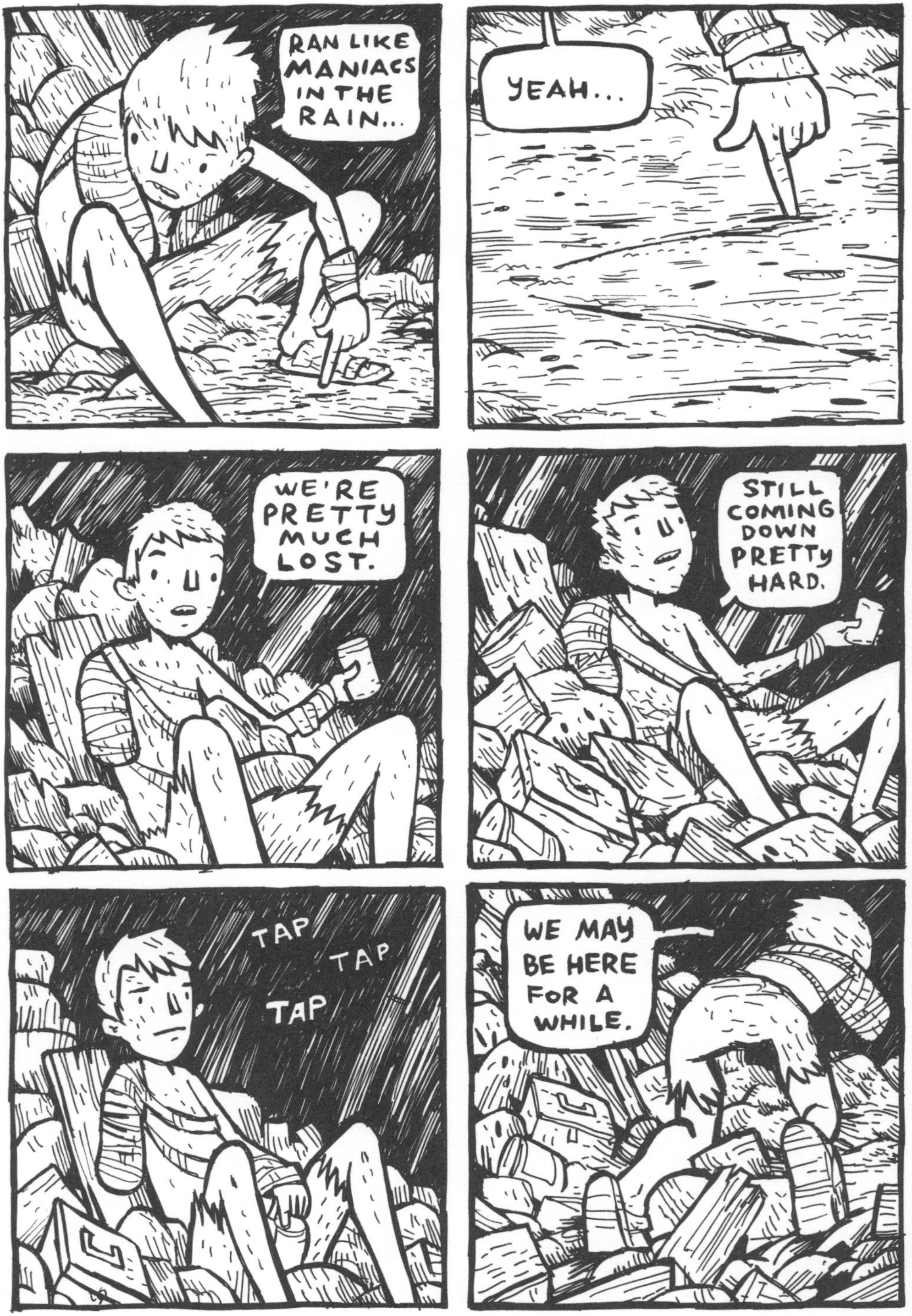
RAN LIKE MANIACS IN THE RAIN...
YEAH...
WE'RE PRETTY MUCH LOST.
STILL COMING DOWN PRETTY HARD.
TAP
TAP
TAP
WE MAY BE HERE FOR A WHILE.

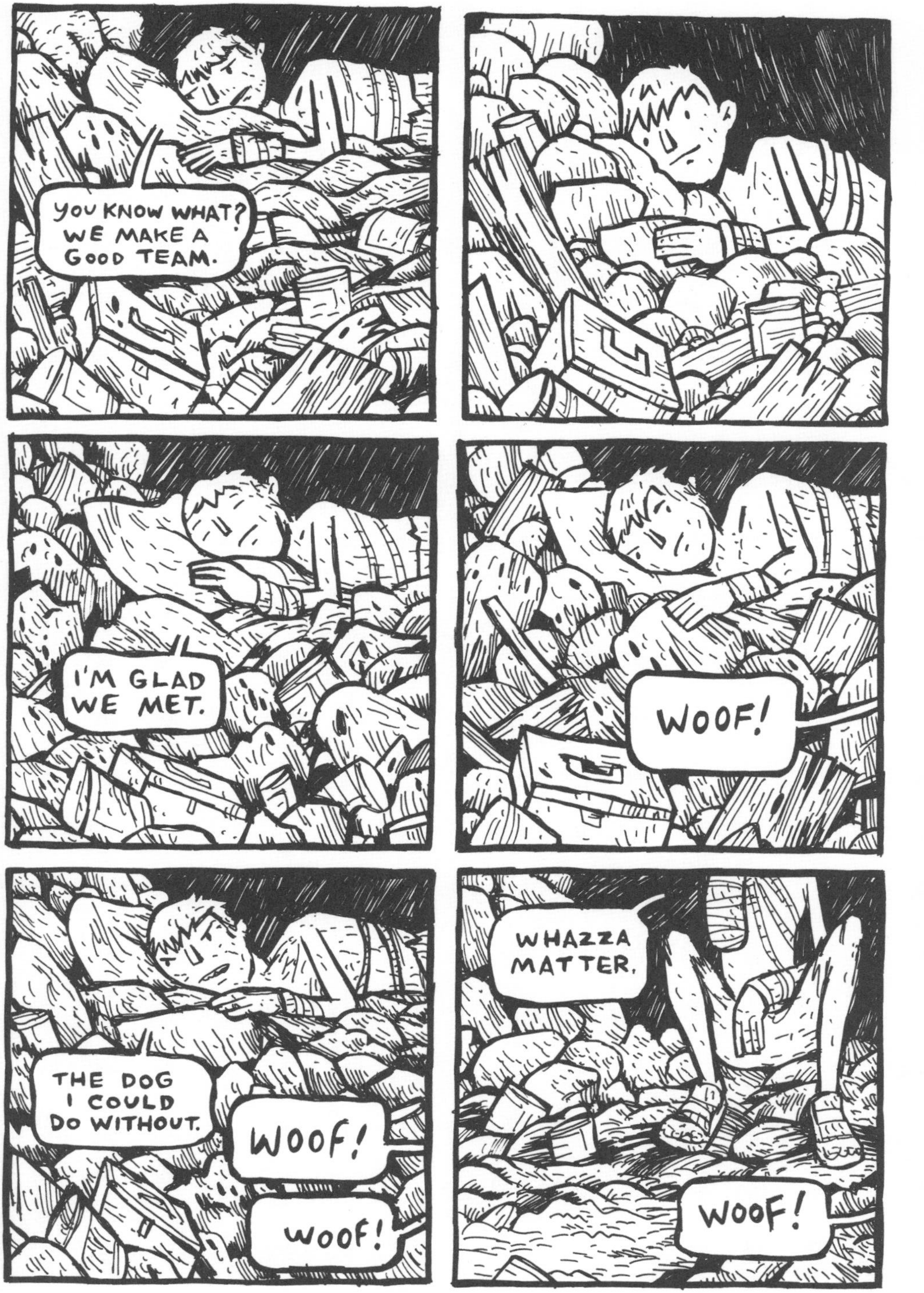
YOU KNOW WHAT? WE MAKE A GOOD TEAM.
I'M GLAD WE MET.
WOOF!
THE DOG I COULD DO WITHOUT.
WOOF!
WOOF!
WHAZZA MATTER.
WOOF!

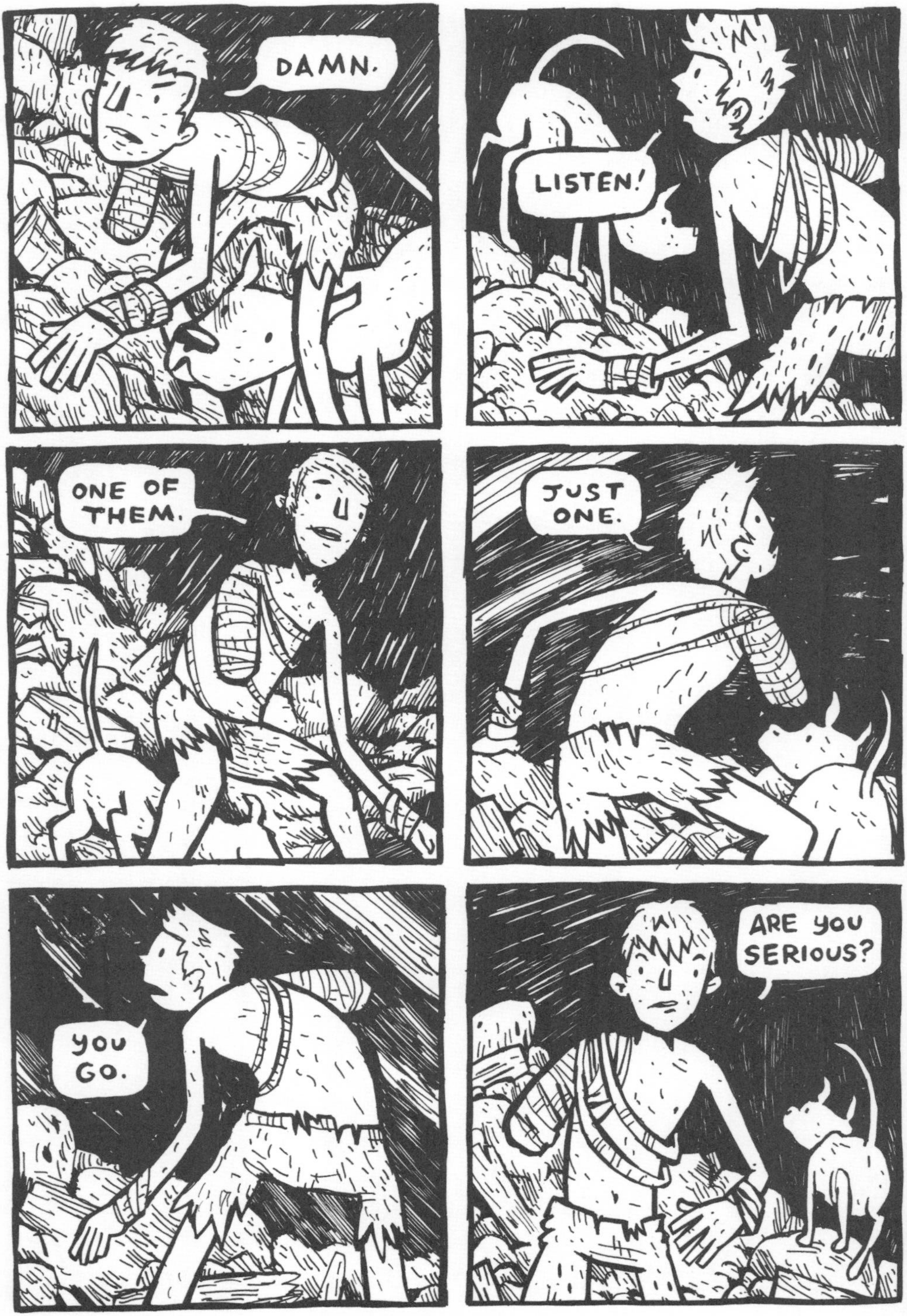
DAMN.
LISTEN!
ONE OF THEM.
JUST ONE.
YOU GO.
ARE YOU SERIOUS?

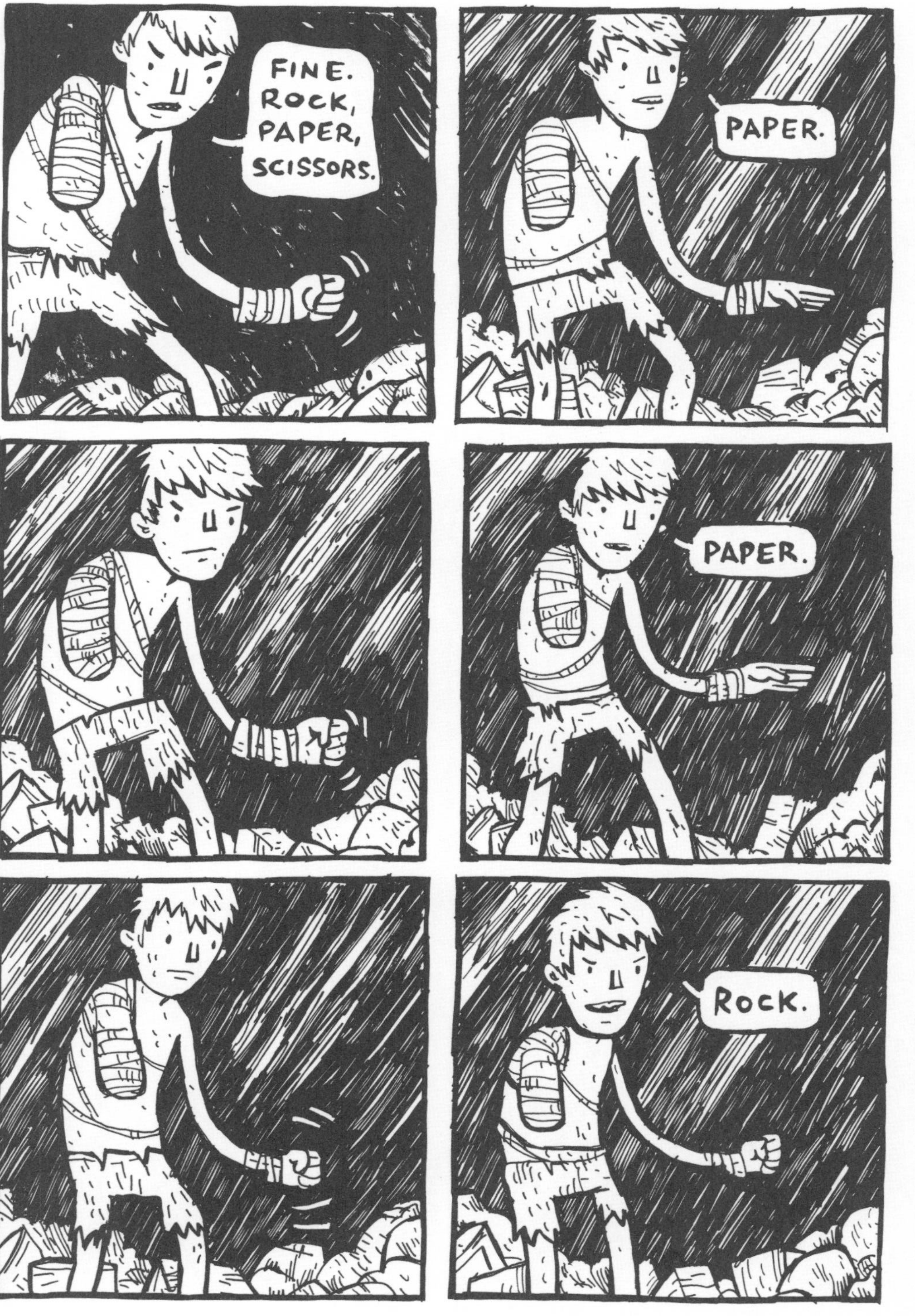
FINE. ROCK, PAPER, SCISSORS.
PAPER.
PAPER.
ROCK.

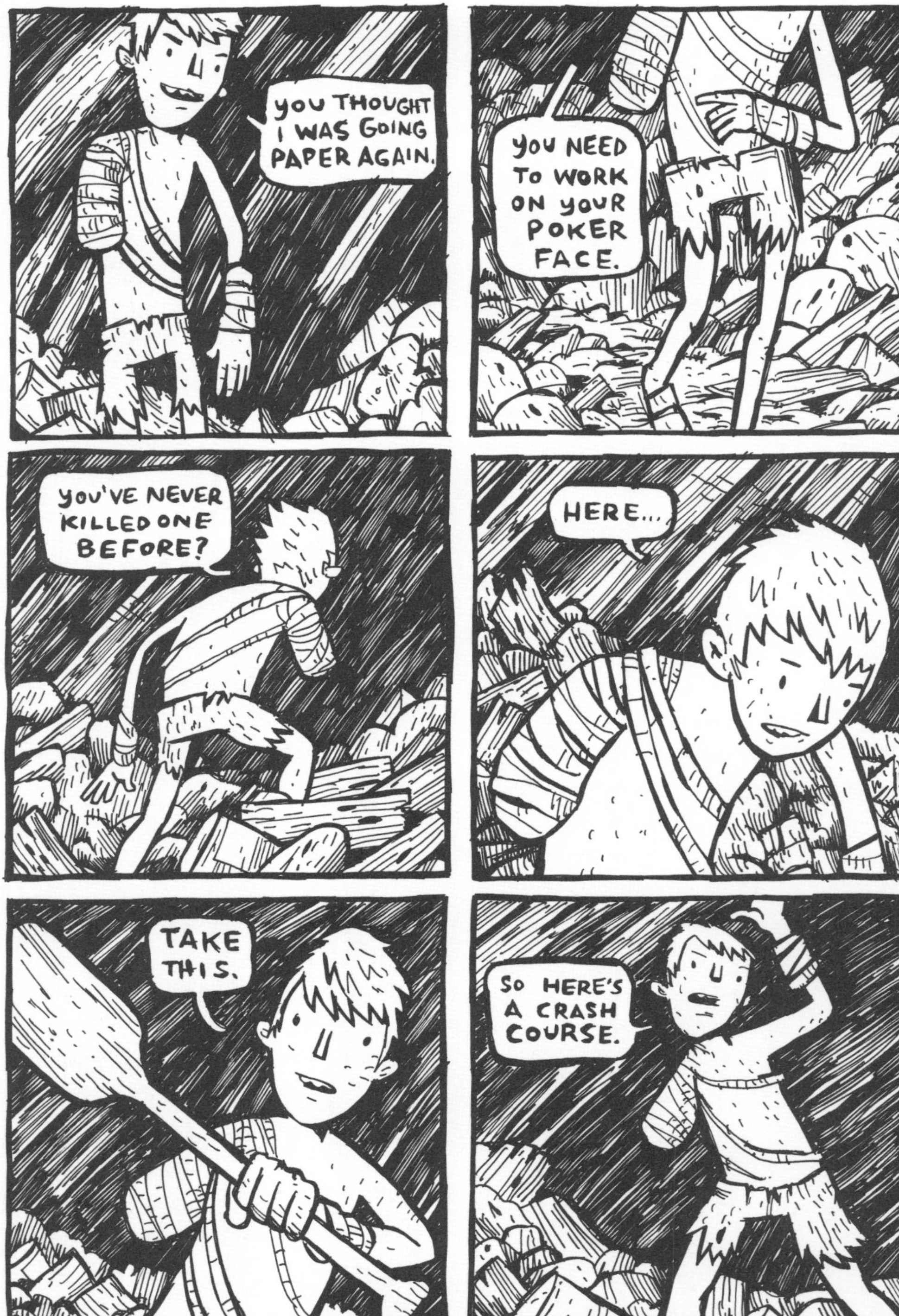
YOU THOUGHT I WAS GOING PAPER AGAIN.
YOU NEED TO WORK ON YOUR POKER FACE.
YOU'VE NEVER KILLED ONE BEFORE?
HERE...
TAKE THIS.
SO HERE'S A CRASH COURSE.

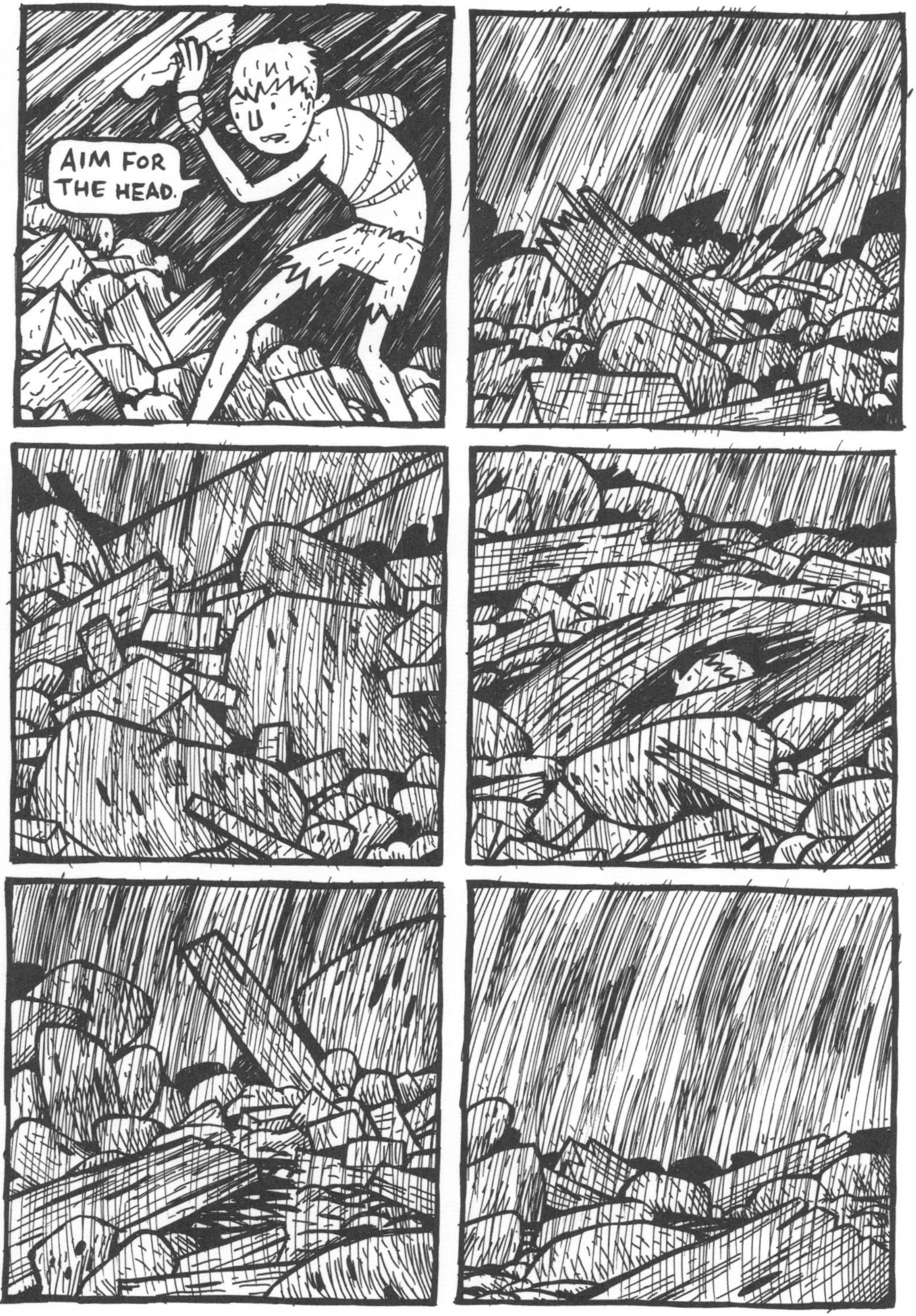
AIM FOR THE HEAD.

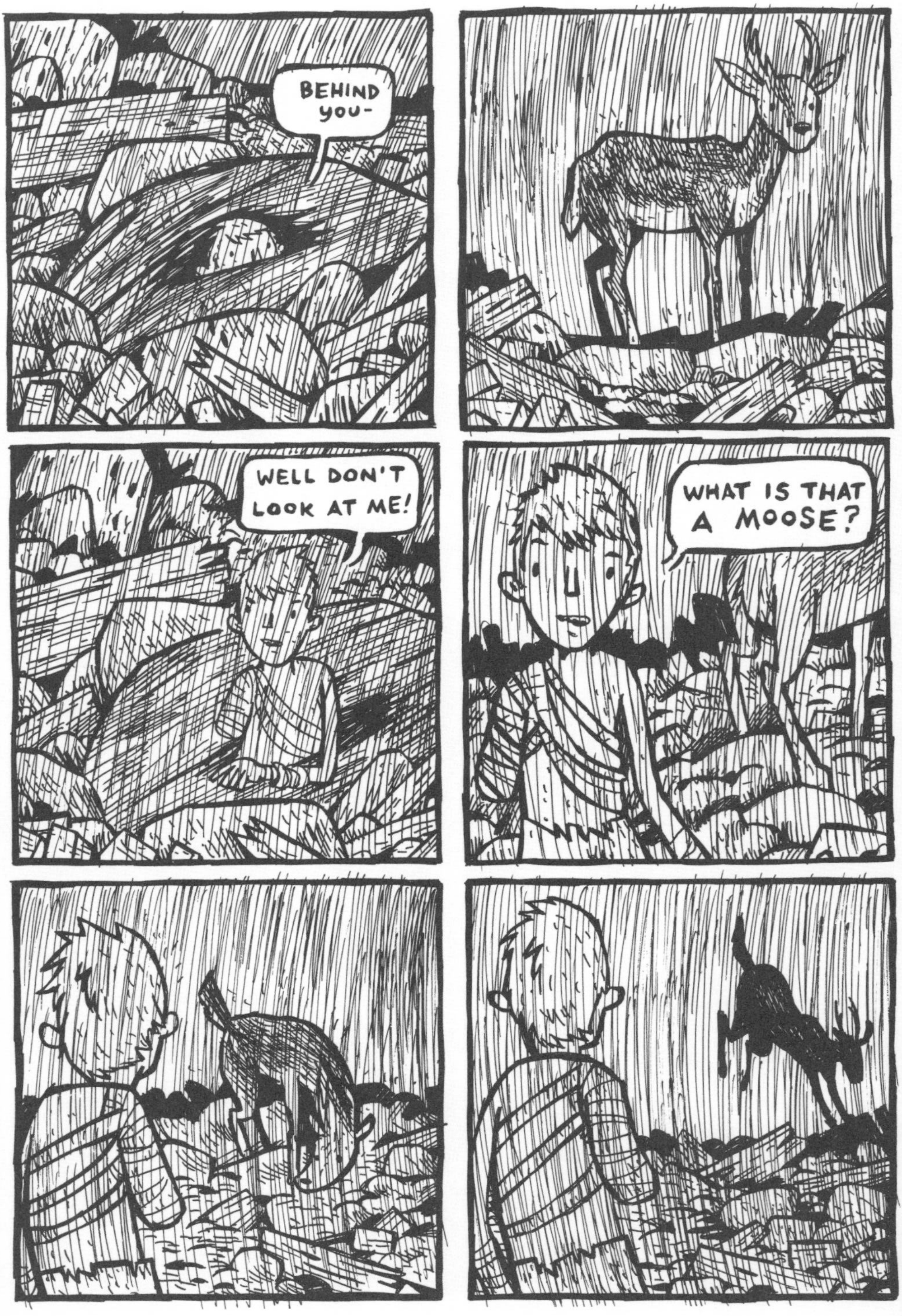
BEHIND YOU-
WELL DON'T LOOK AT ME!
WHAT IS THAT A MOOSE?

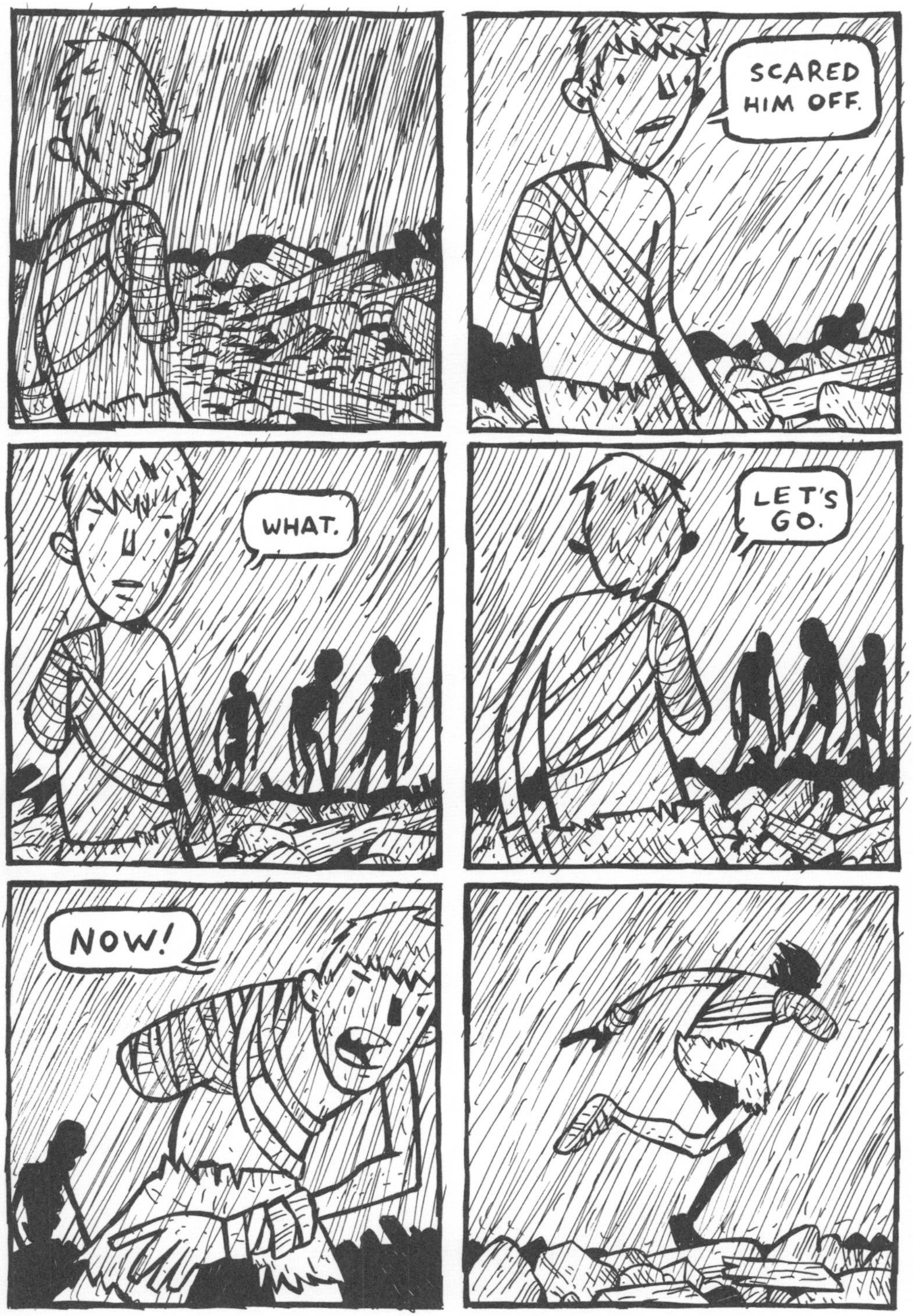
SCARED HIM OFF.
WHAT.
LET'S GO.
NOW!

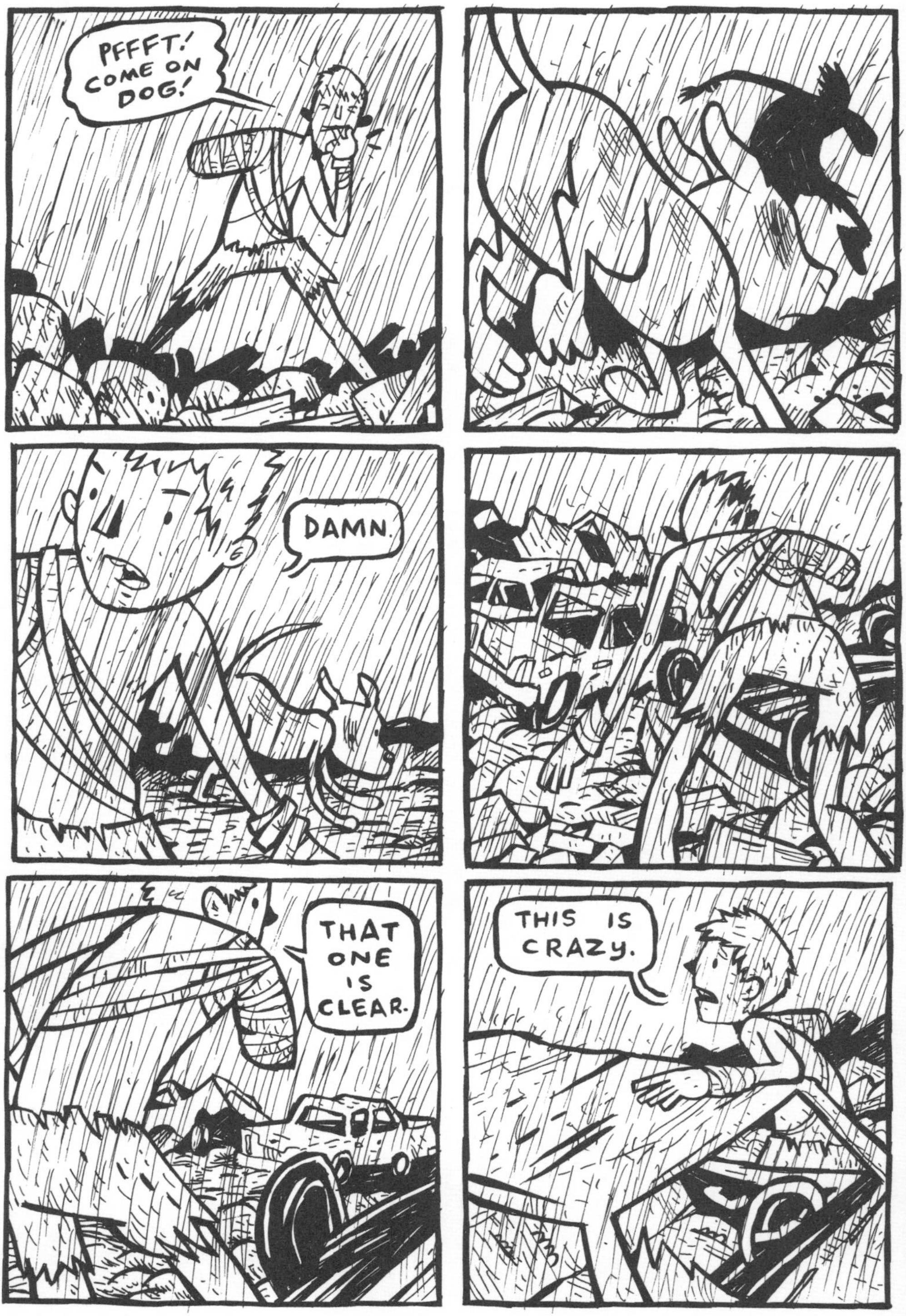
PFFFT! COME ON DOG!
DAMN.
THAT ONE IS CLEAR.
THIS IS CRAZY.

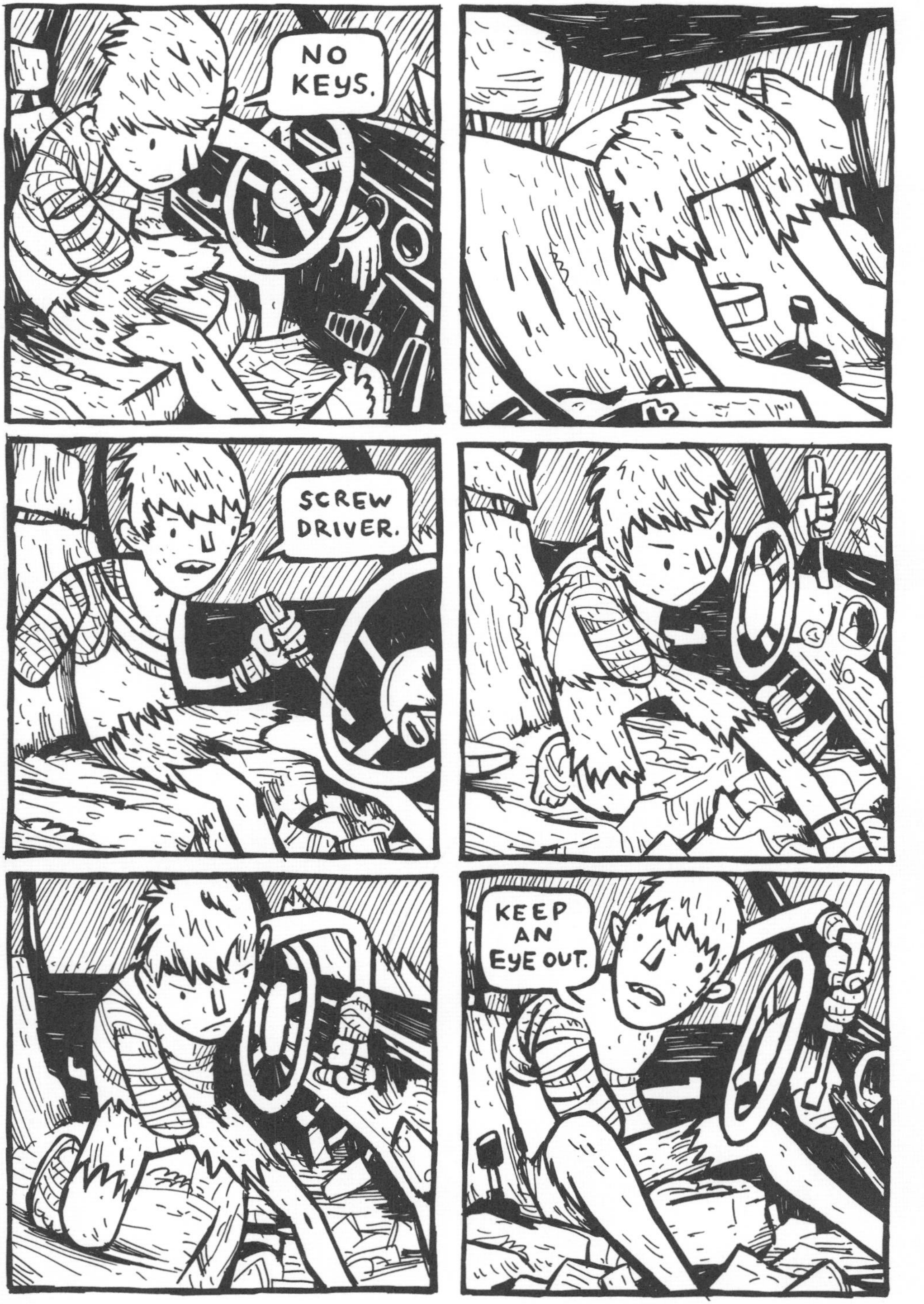
NO KEYS.
SCREW DRIVER.
KEEP AN EYE OUT.

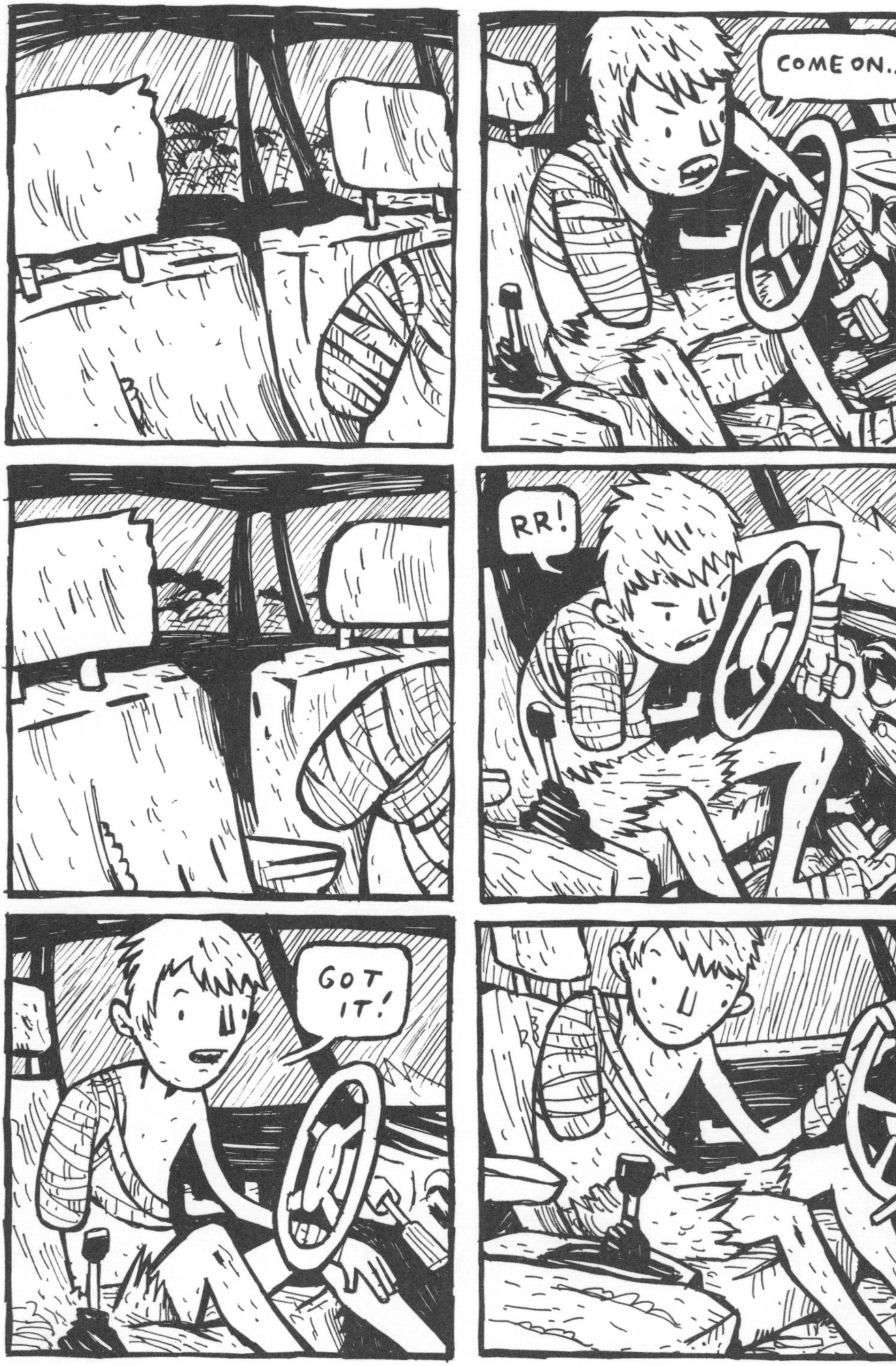
COME ON...
RR!
GOT IT!

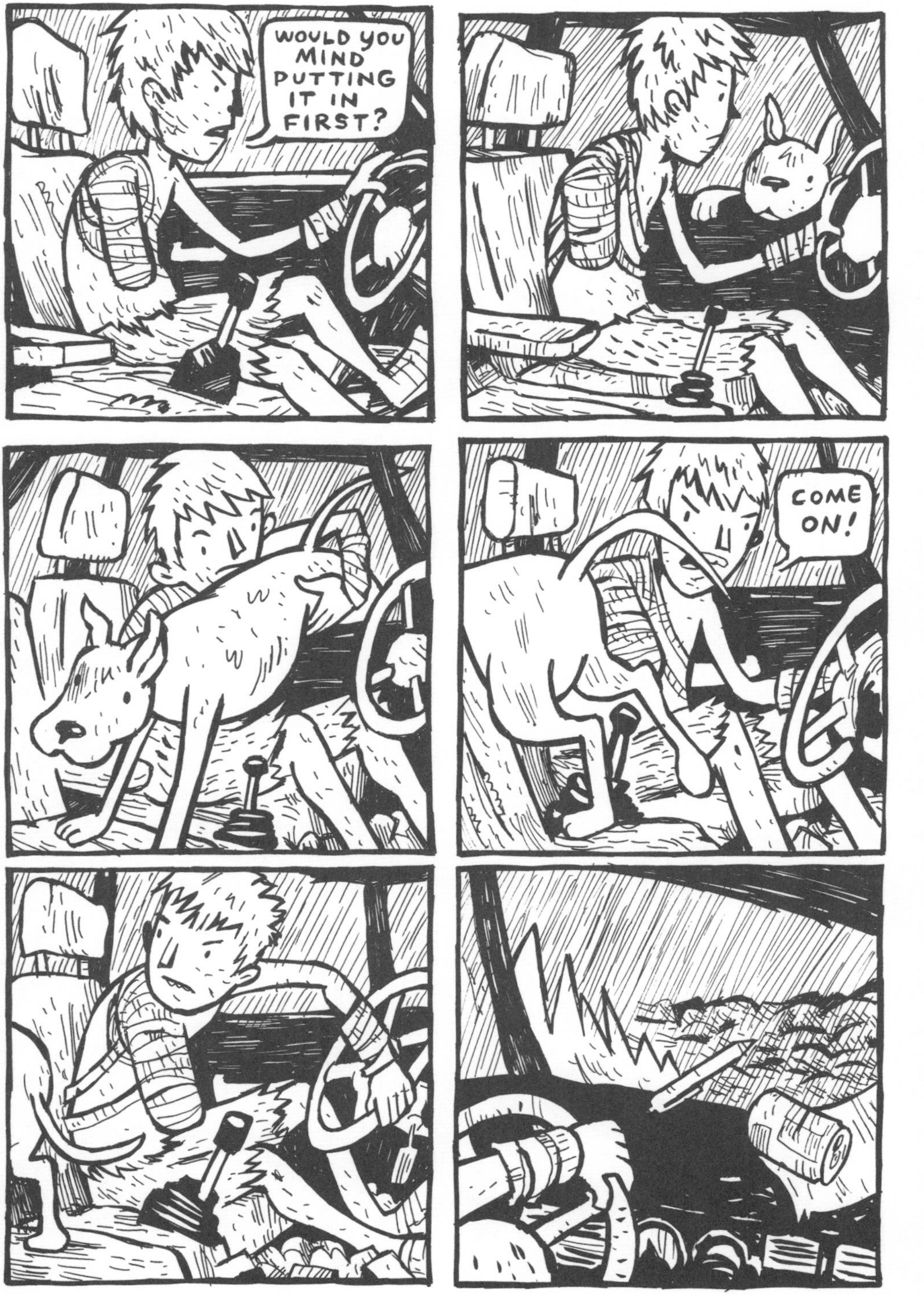
WOULD YOU MIND PUTTING IT IN FIRST?
COME ON!

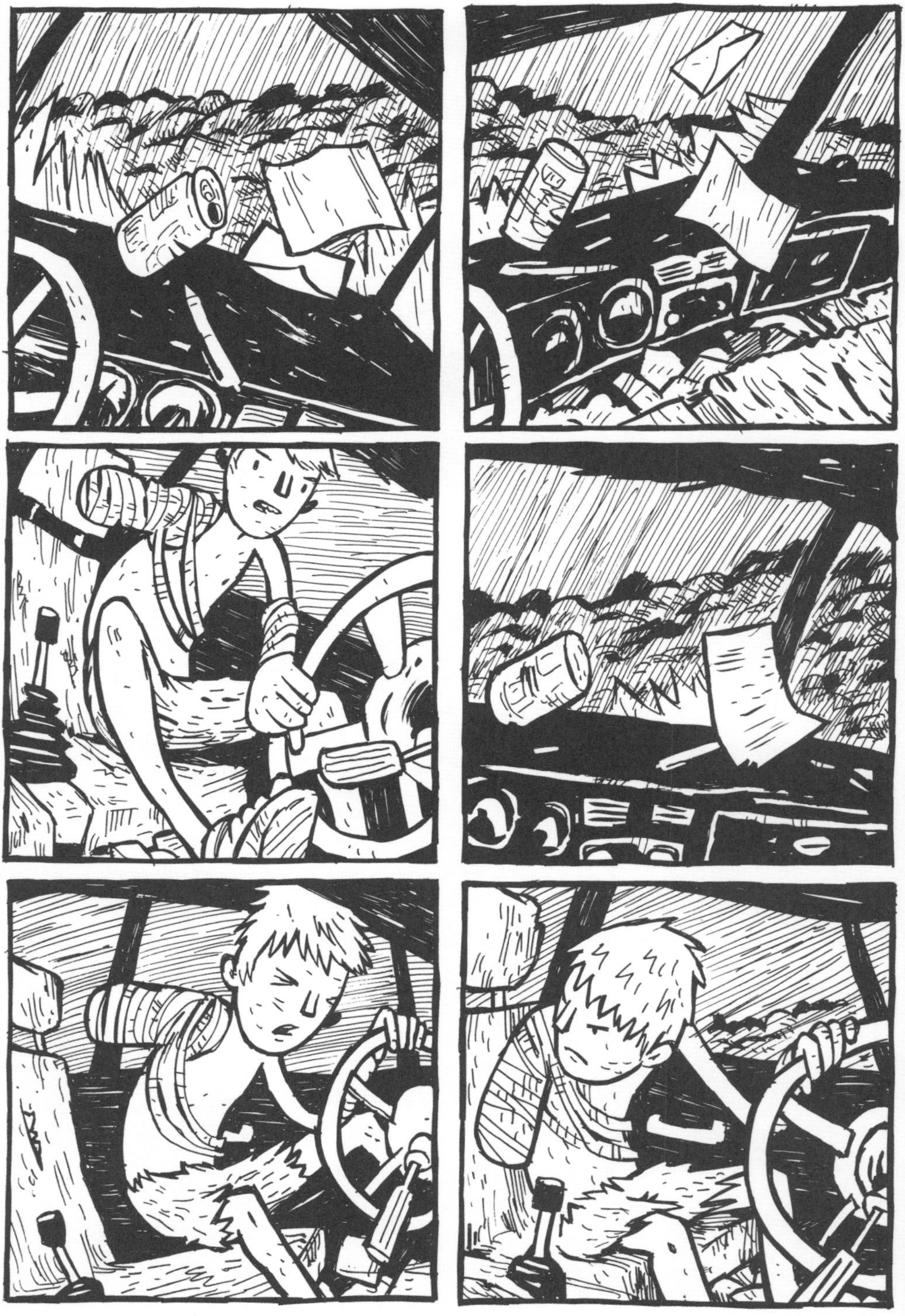

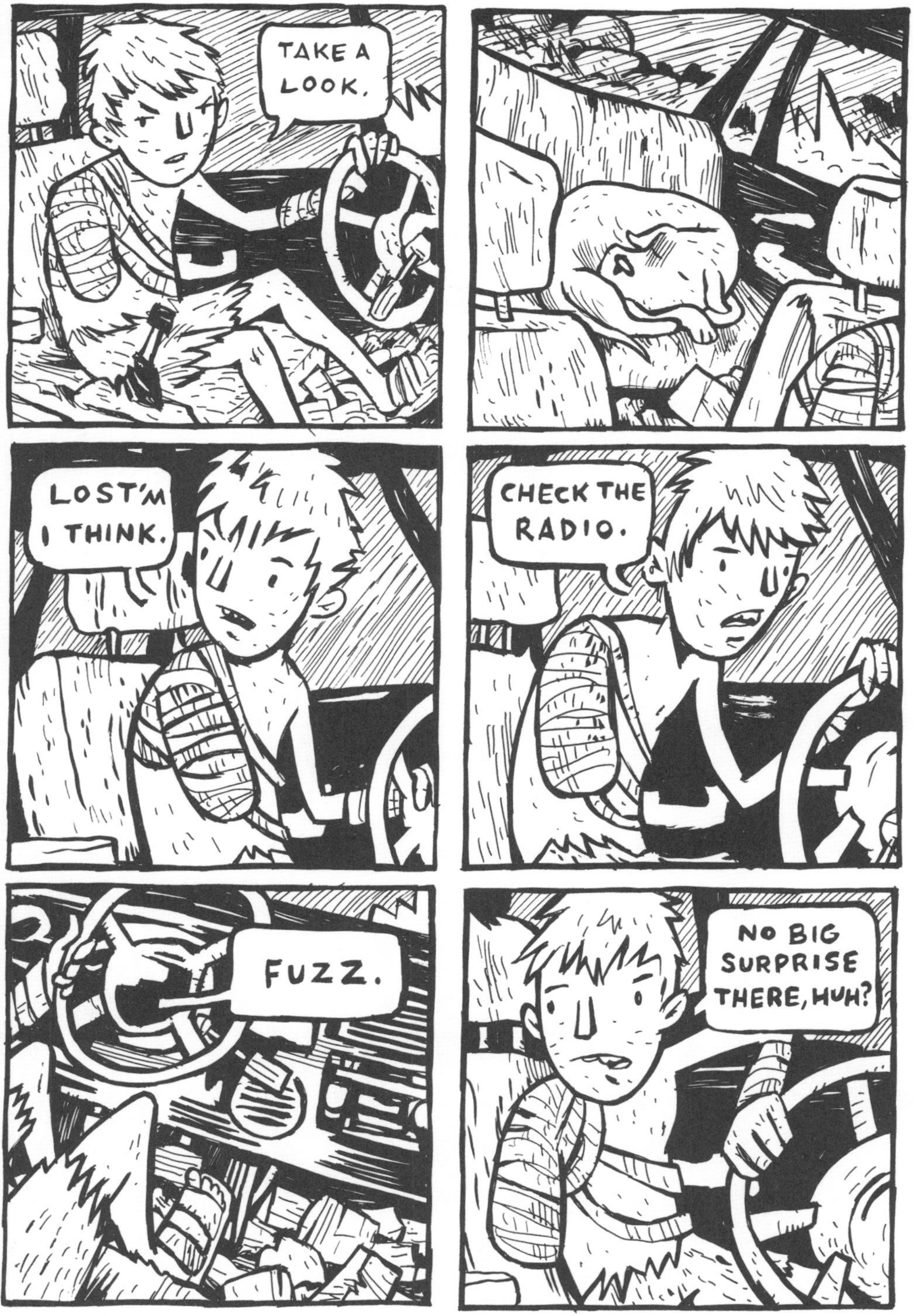
TAKE A LOOK.
LOST'M I THINK.
CHECK THE RADIO.
FUZZ.
NO BIG SURPRISE THERE, HUH?

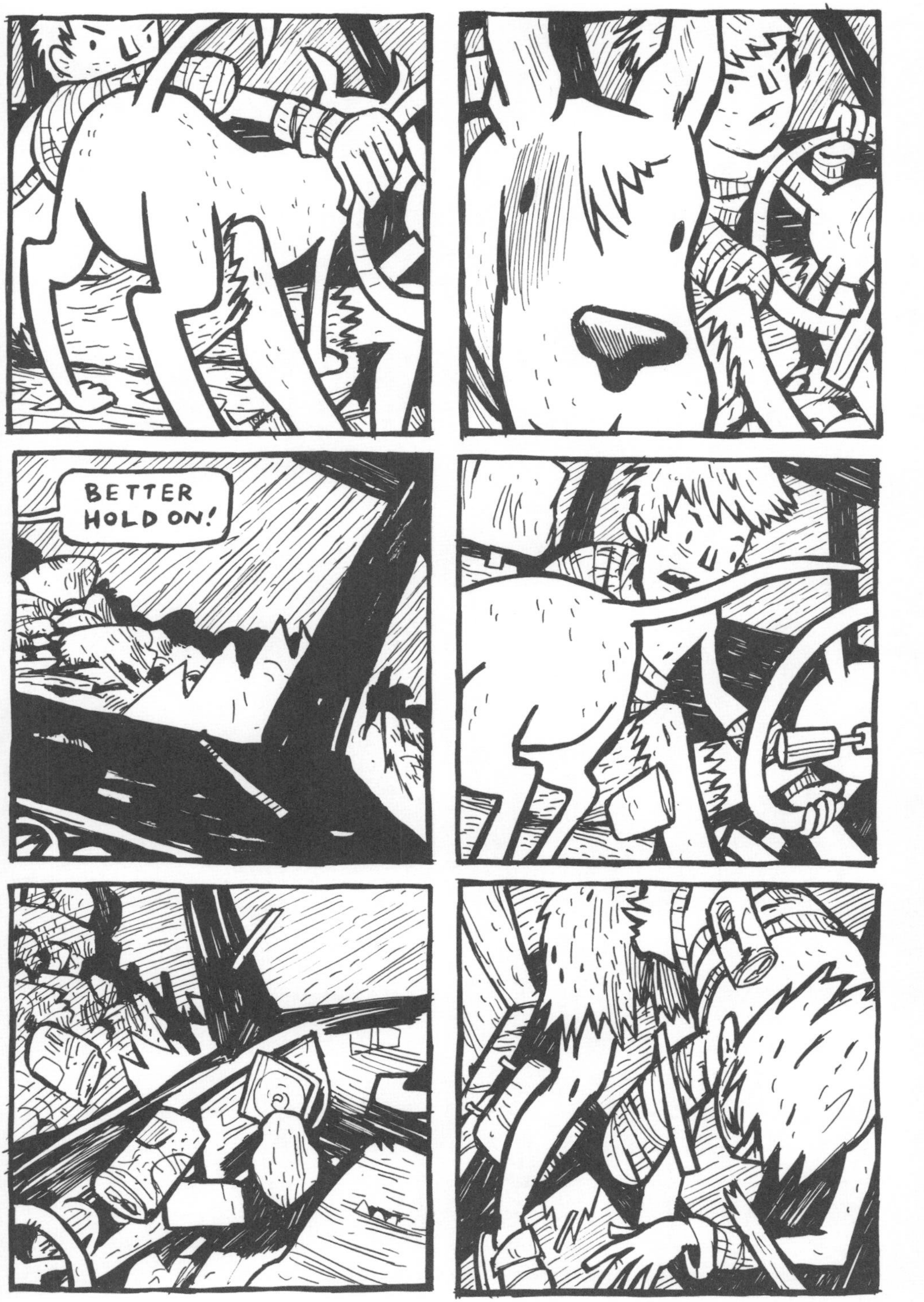
BETTER HOLD ON!

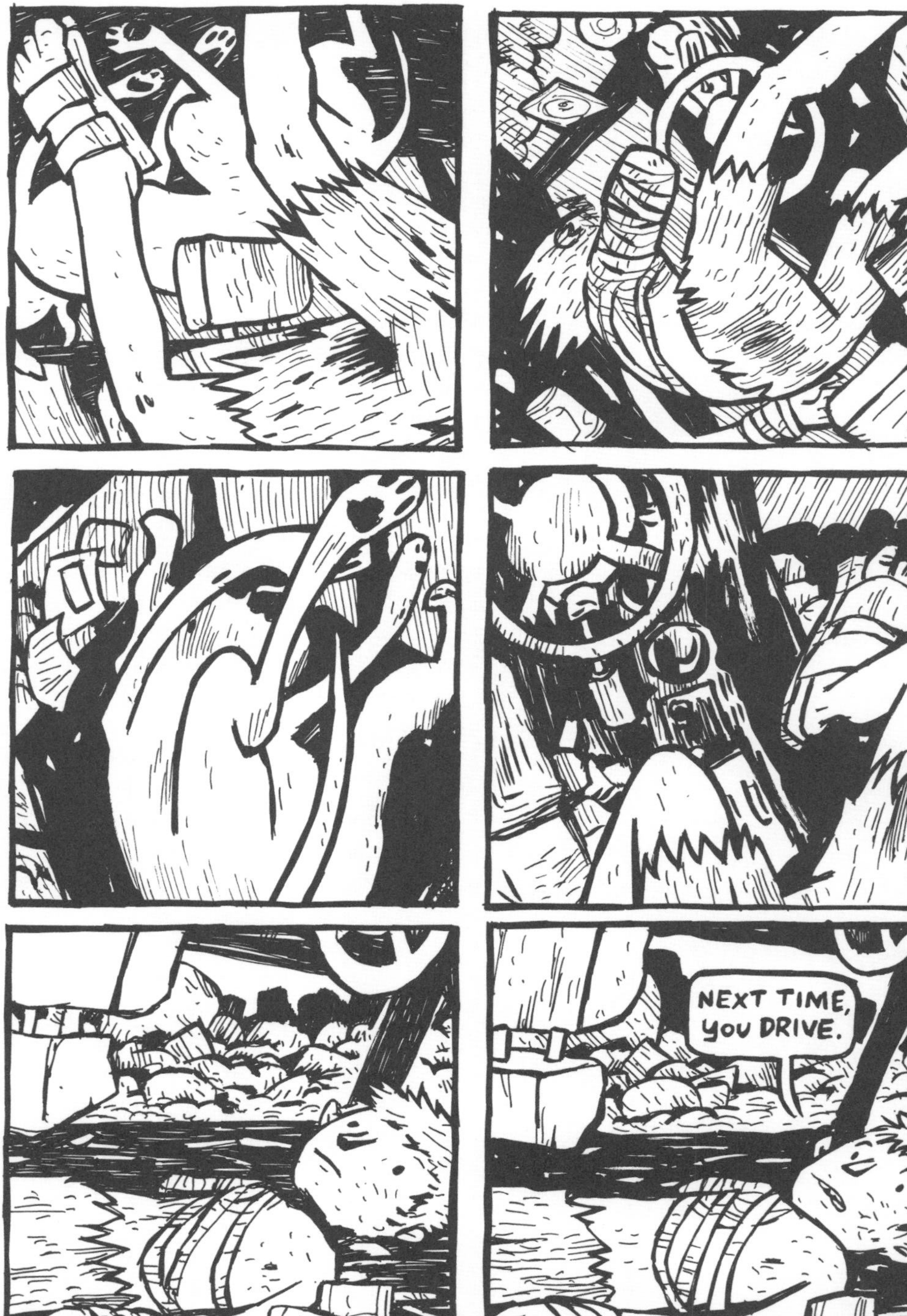
NEXT TIME, YOU DRIVE.

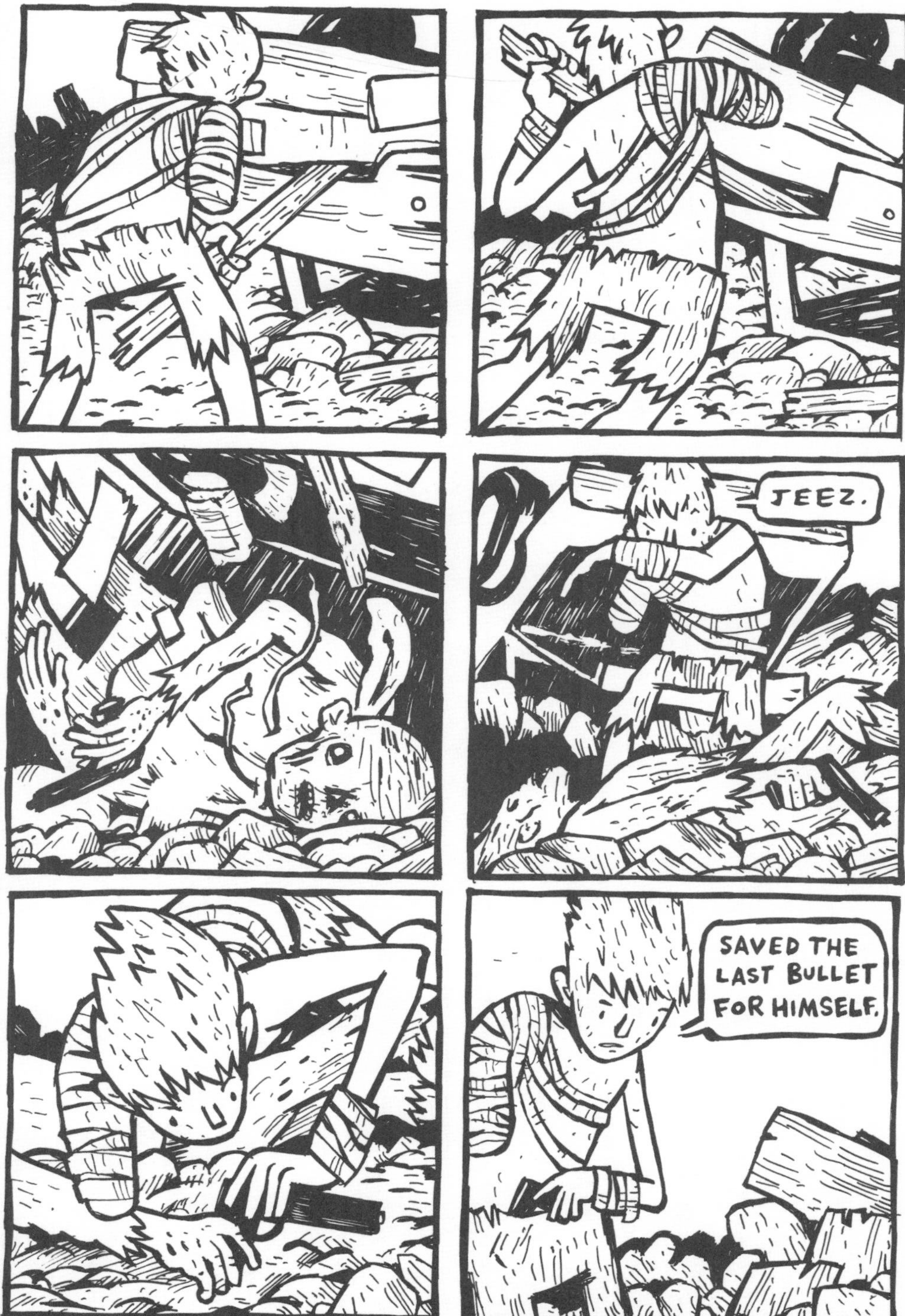
JEEZ.
SAVED THE LAST BULLET FOR HIMSELF.

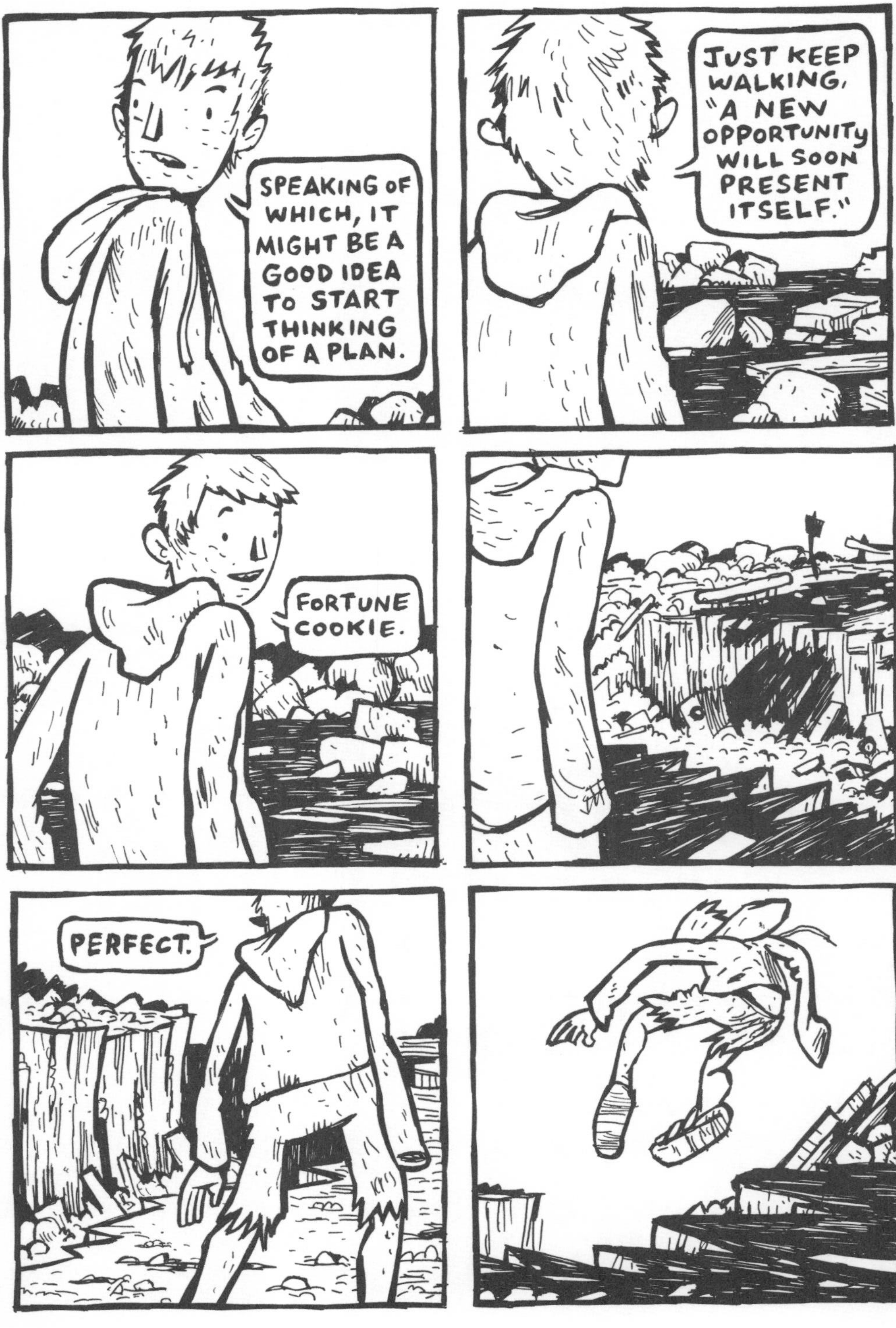

SPEAKING OF WHICH, IT MIGHT BE A GOOD IDEA TO START THINKING OF A PLAN.
JUST KEEP WALKING, "A NEW OPPORTUNITY WILL SOON PRESENT ITSELF."
FORTUNE COOKIE.
PERFECT.

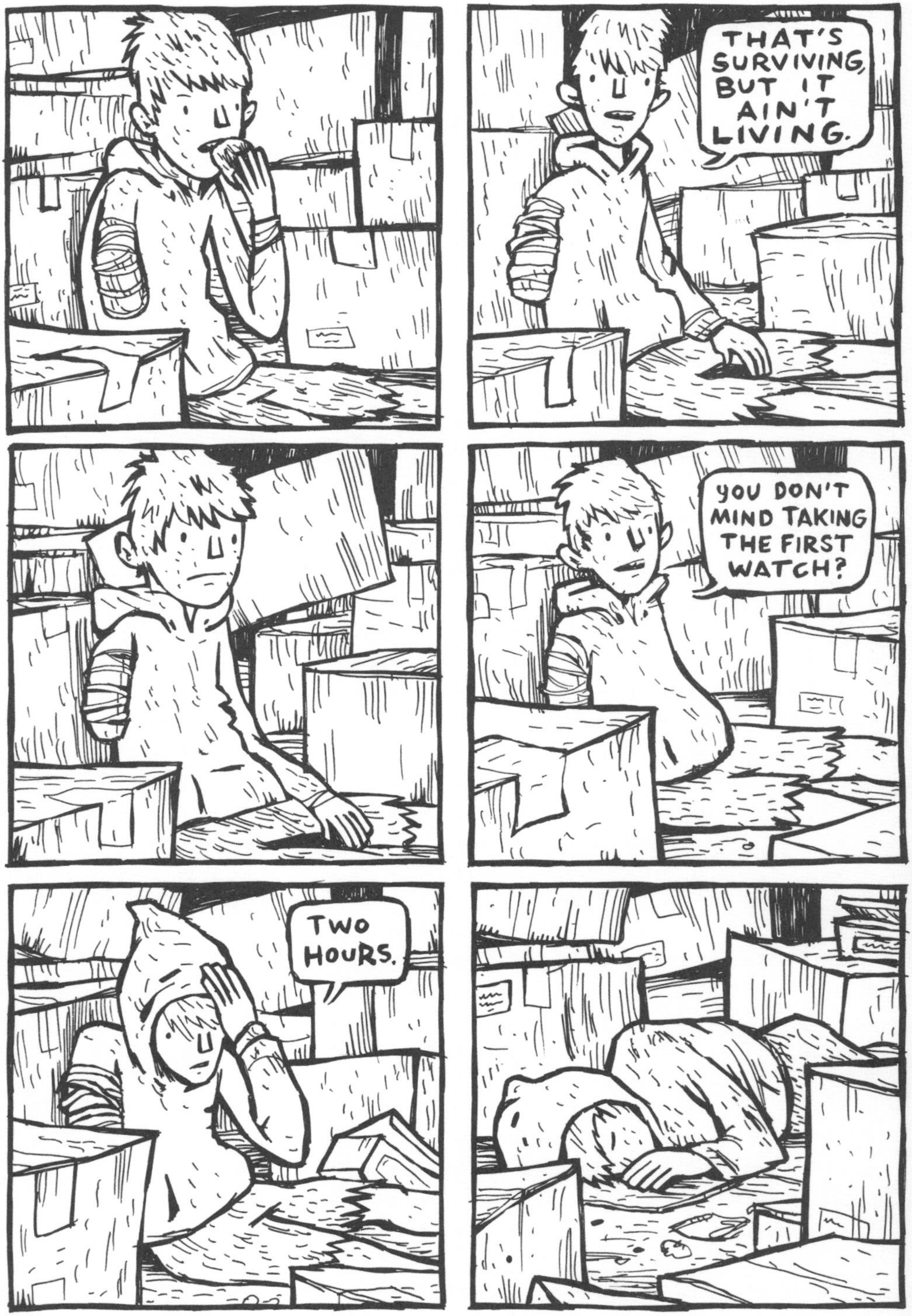
THAT'S SURVIVING, BUT IT AIN'T LIVING.
YOU DON'T MIND TAKING THE FIRST WATCH?
TWO HOURS.

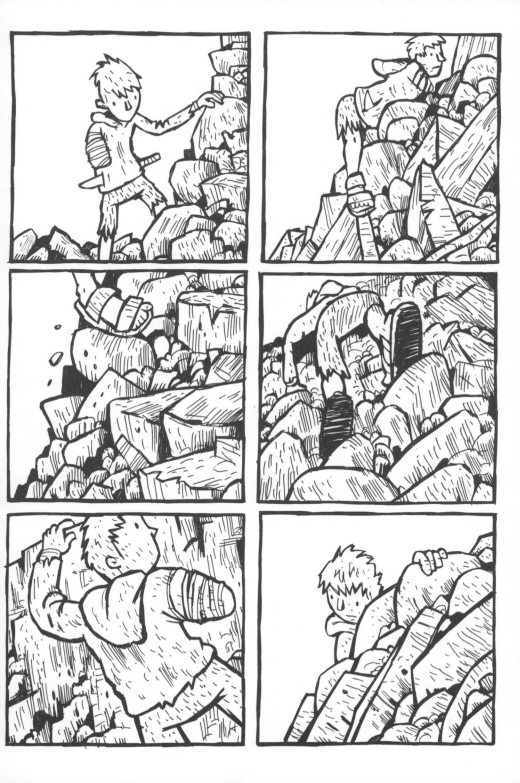

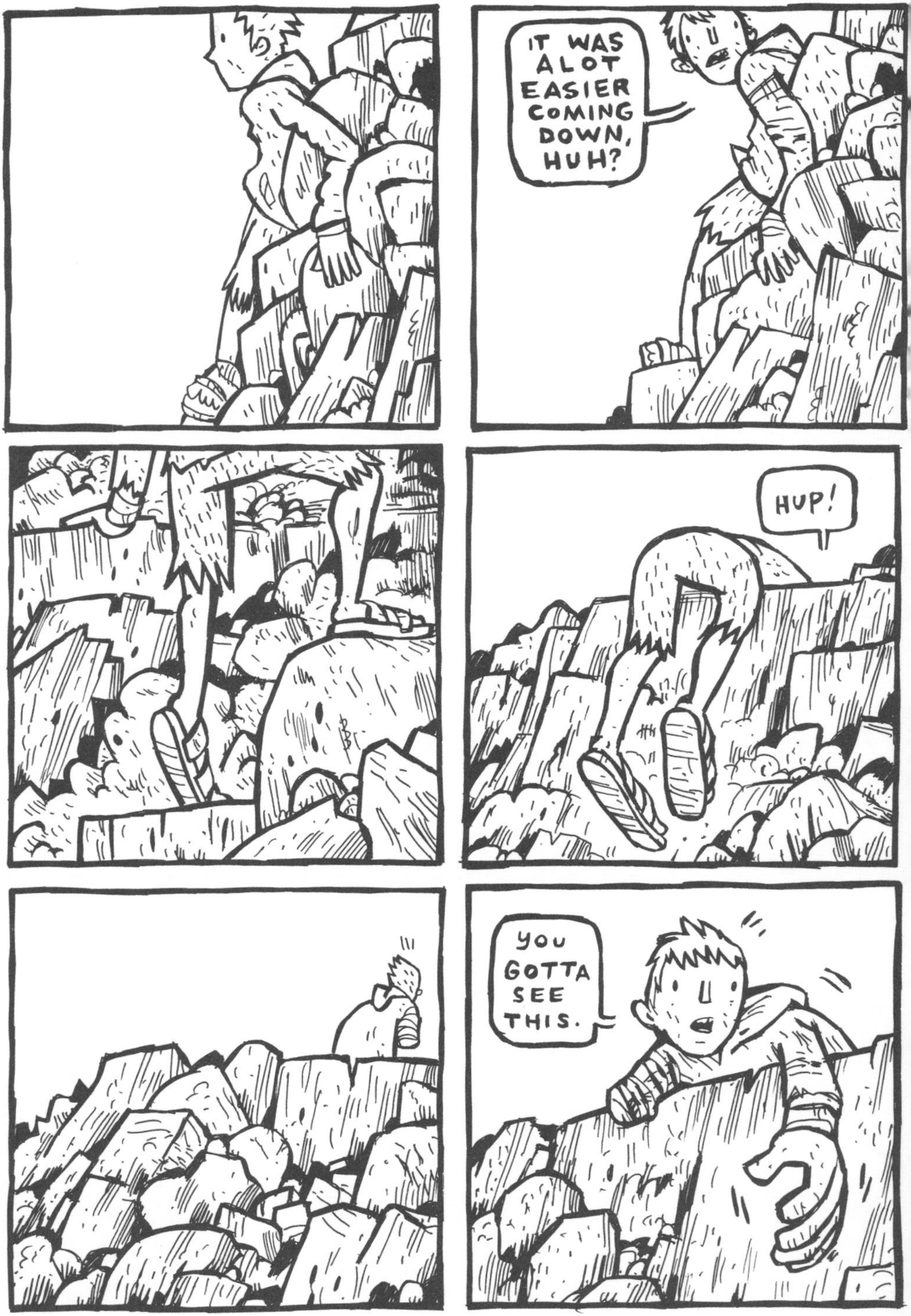
IT WAS ALOT EASIER COMING DOWN, HUH?
HUP!
YOU GOTTA SEE THIS.

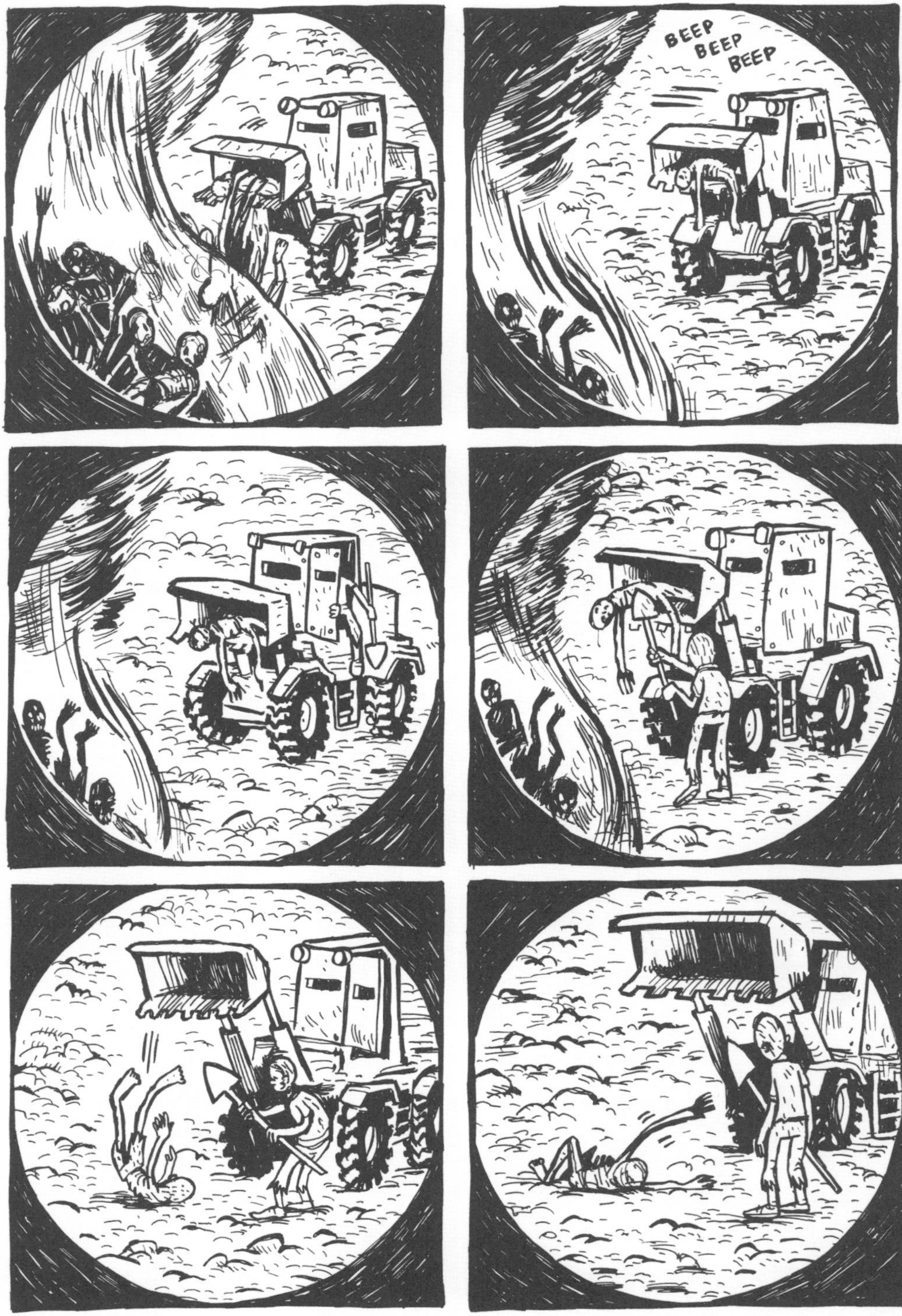
BEEP
BEEP
BEEP

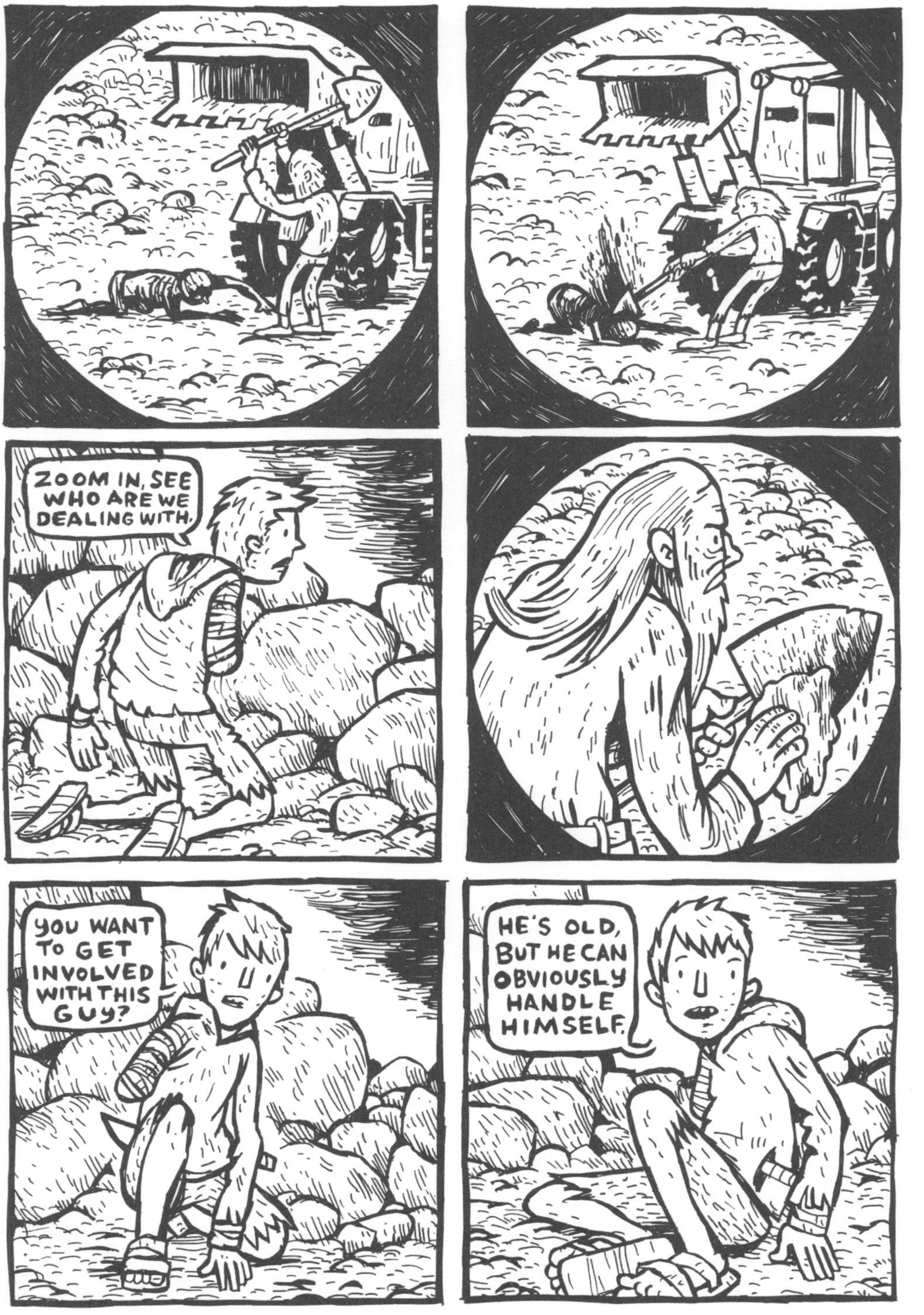
ZOOM IN, SEE WHO ARE WE DEALING WITH.
YOU WANT TO GET INVOLVED WITH THIS GUY?
HE'S OLD, BUT HE CAN OBVIOUSLY HANDLE HIMSELF.

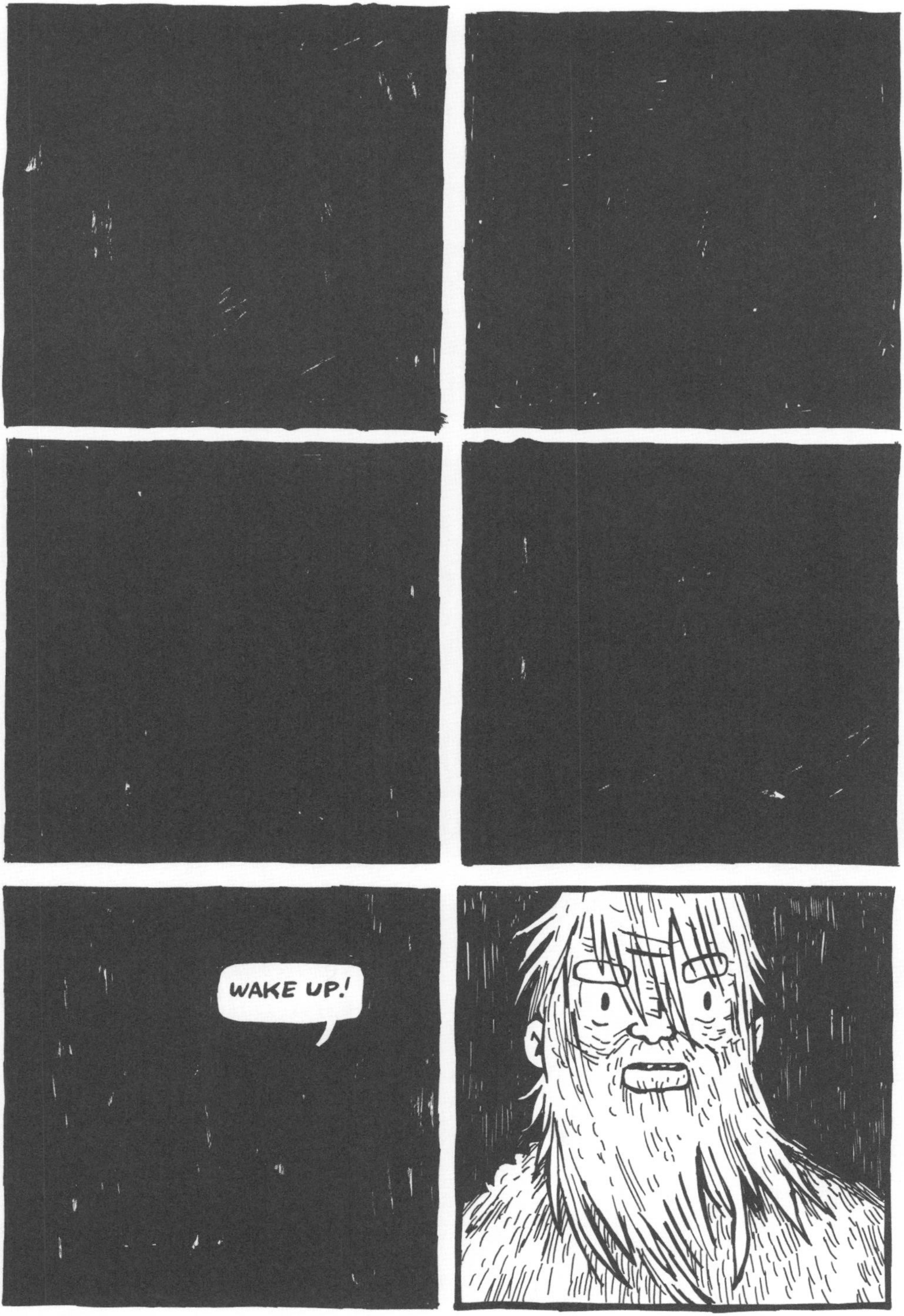
WAKE UP!

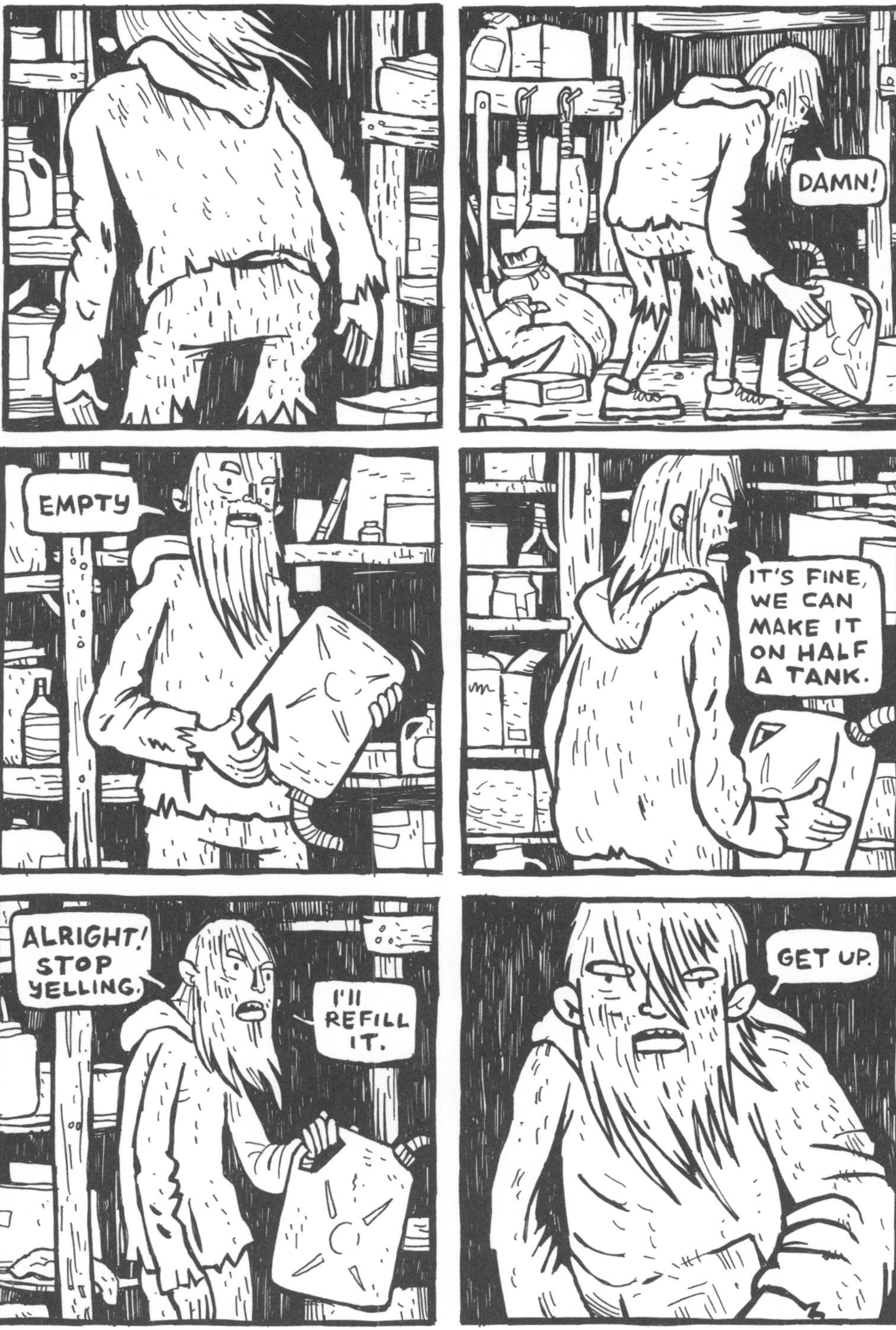
DAMN!
EMPTY
IT'S FINE, WE CAN MAKE IT ON HALF A TANK.
ALRIGHT! STOP YELLING.
I'll REFILL IT.
GET UP.

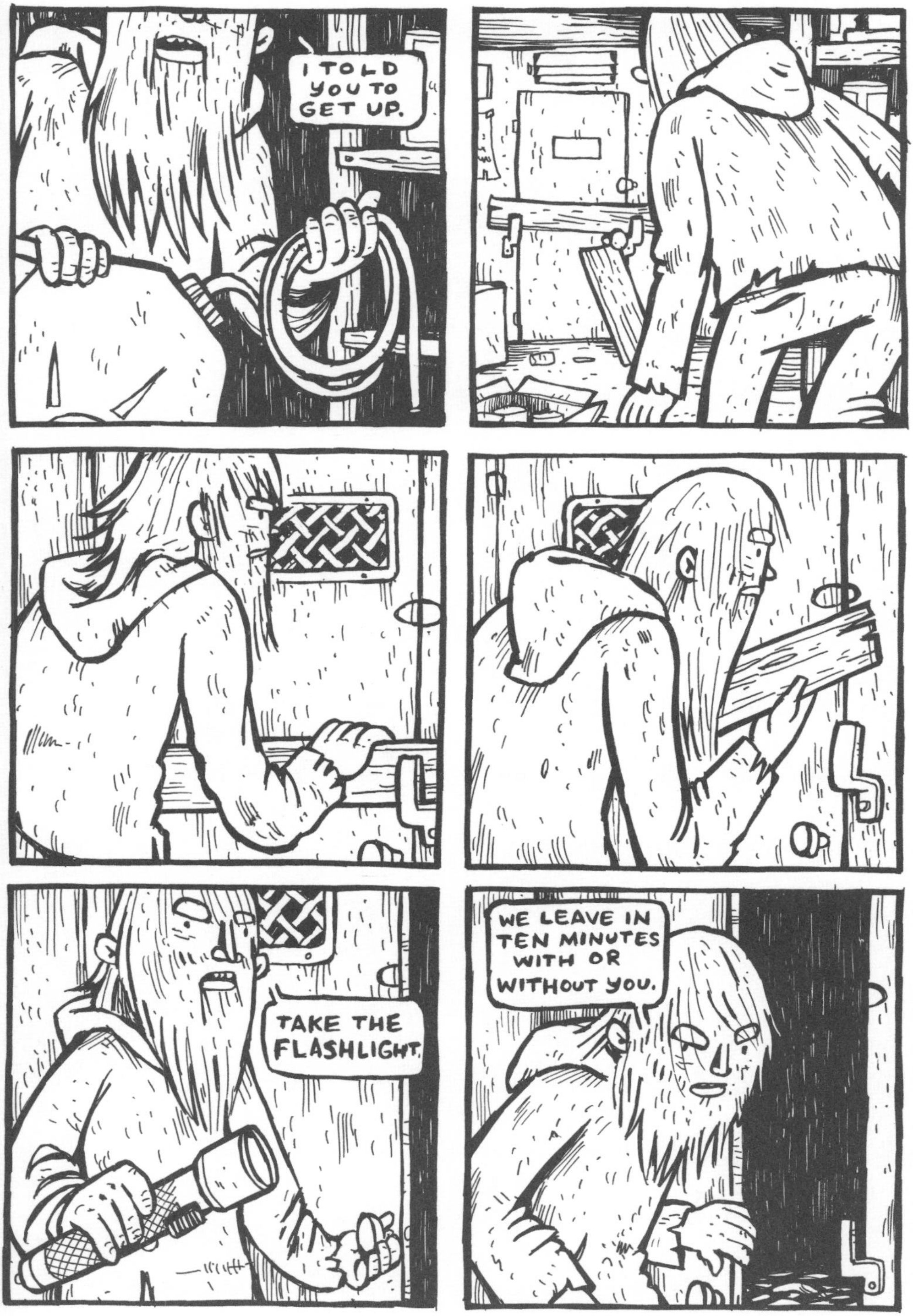
I TOLD YOU TO GET UP.
TAKE THE FLASHLIGHT.
WE LEAVE IN TEN MINUTES WITH OR WITHOUT YOU.

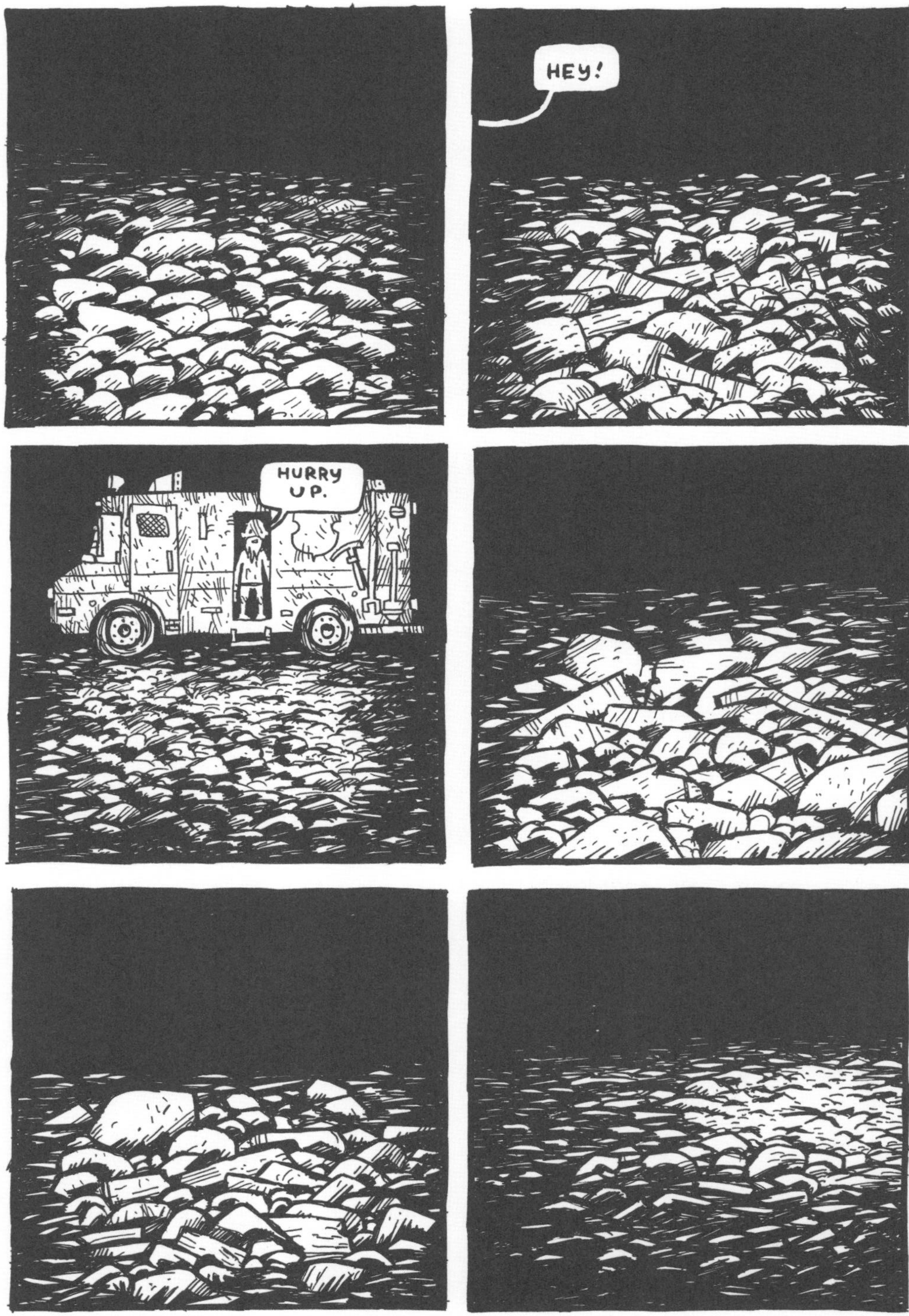
HEY!
HURRY UP.

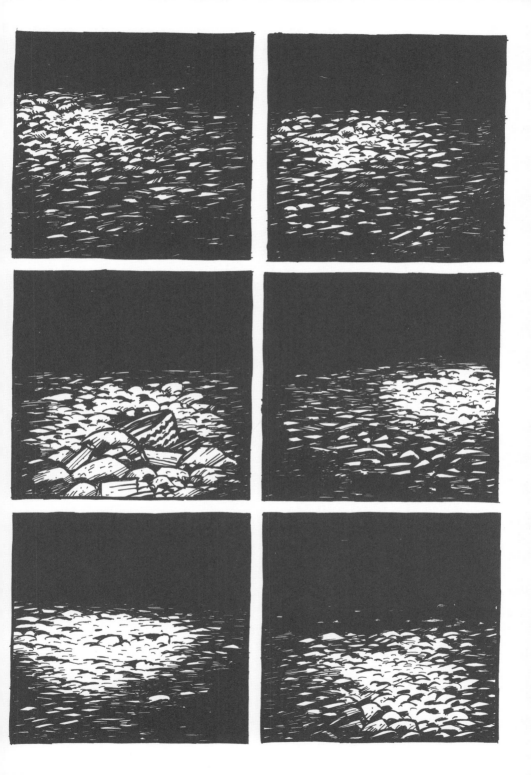

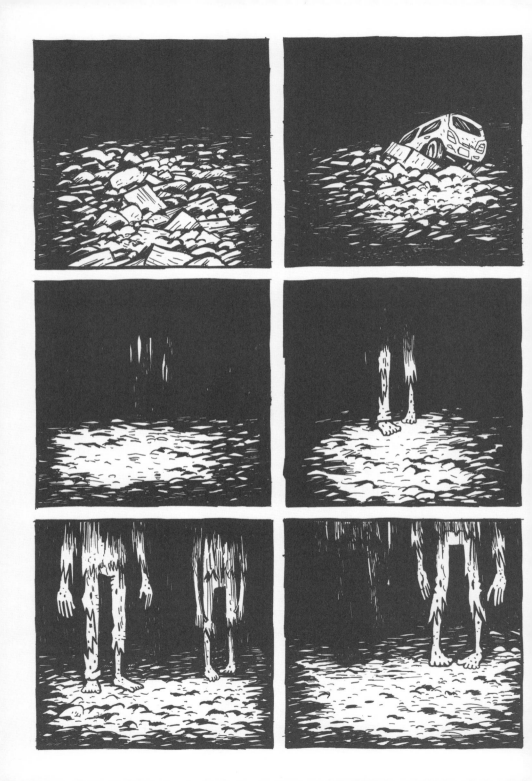

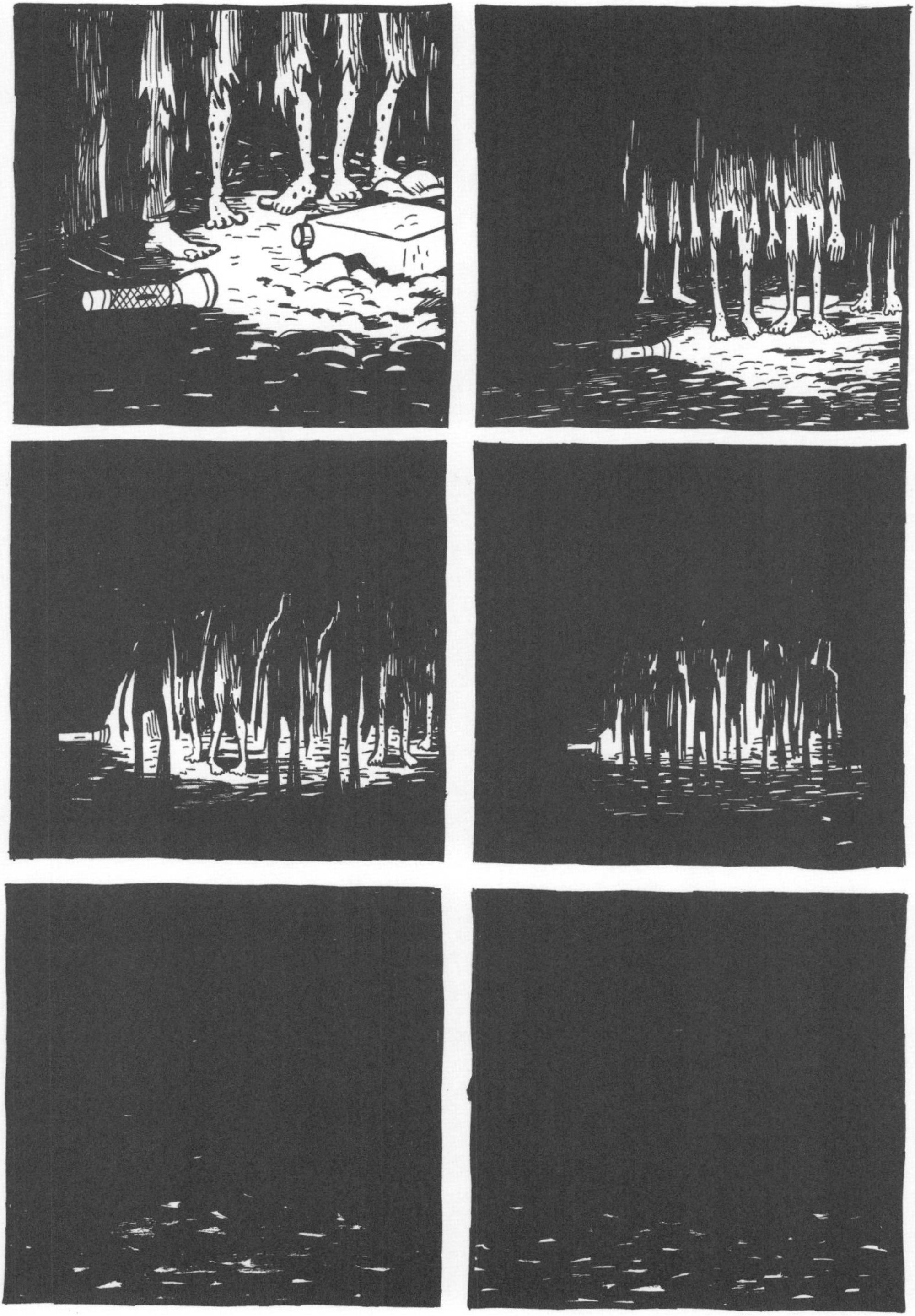

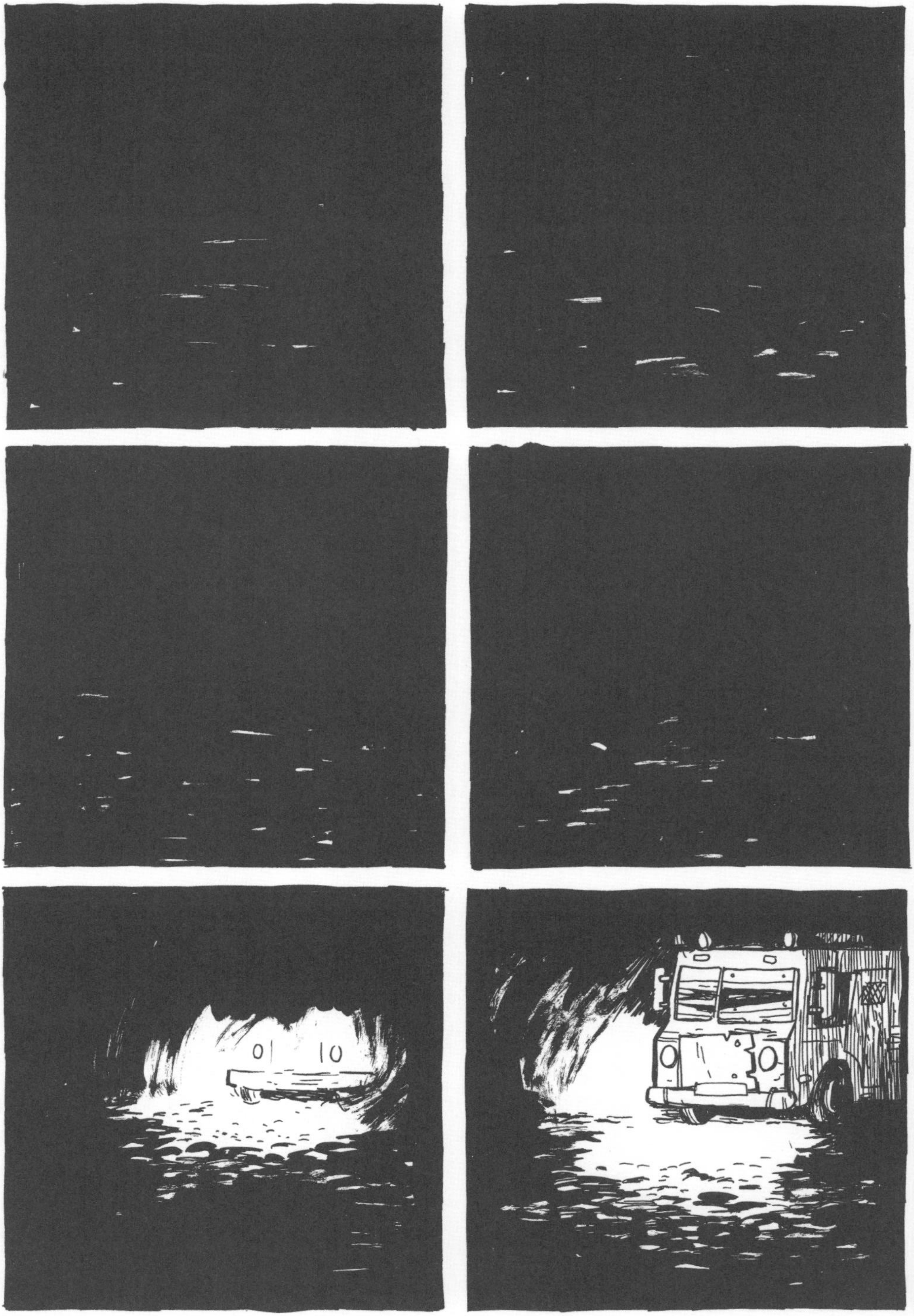

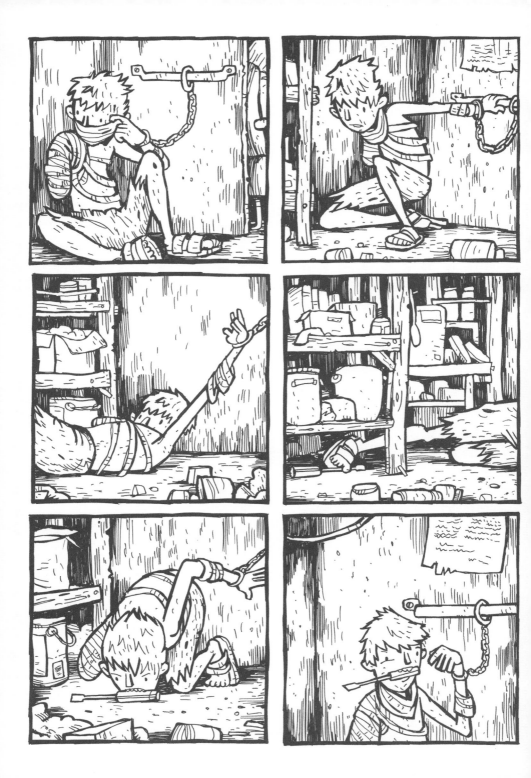

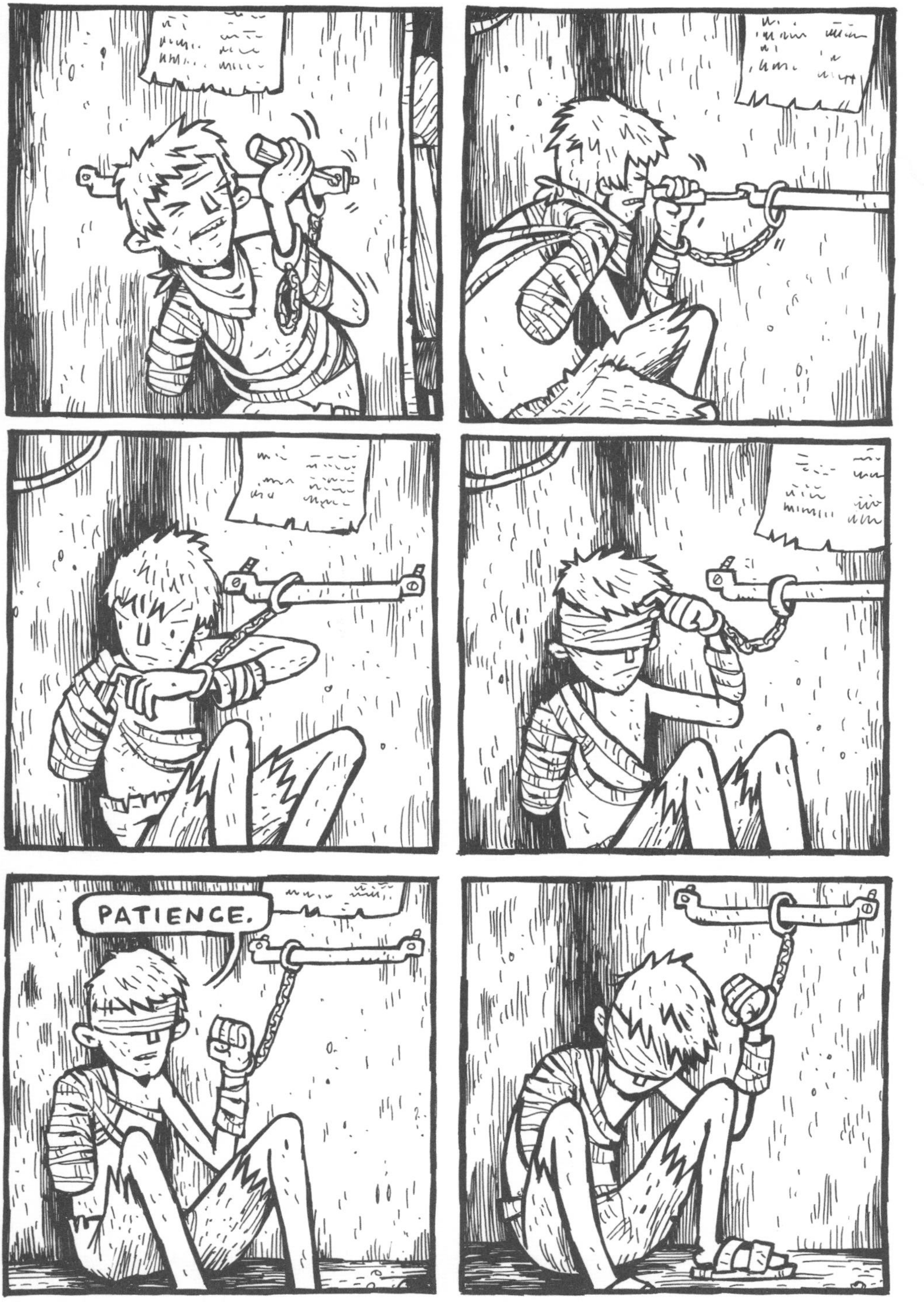
PATIENCE.

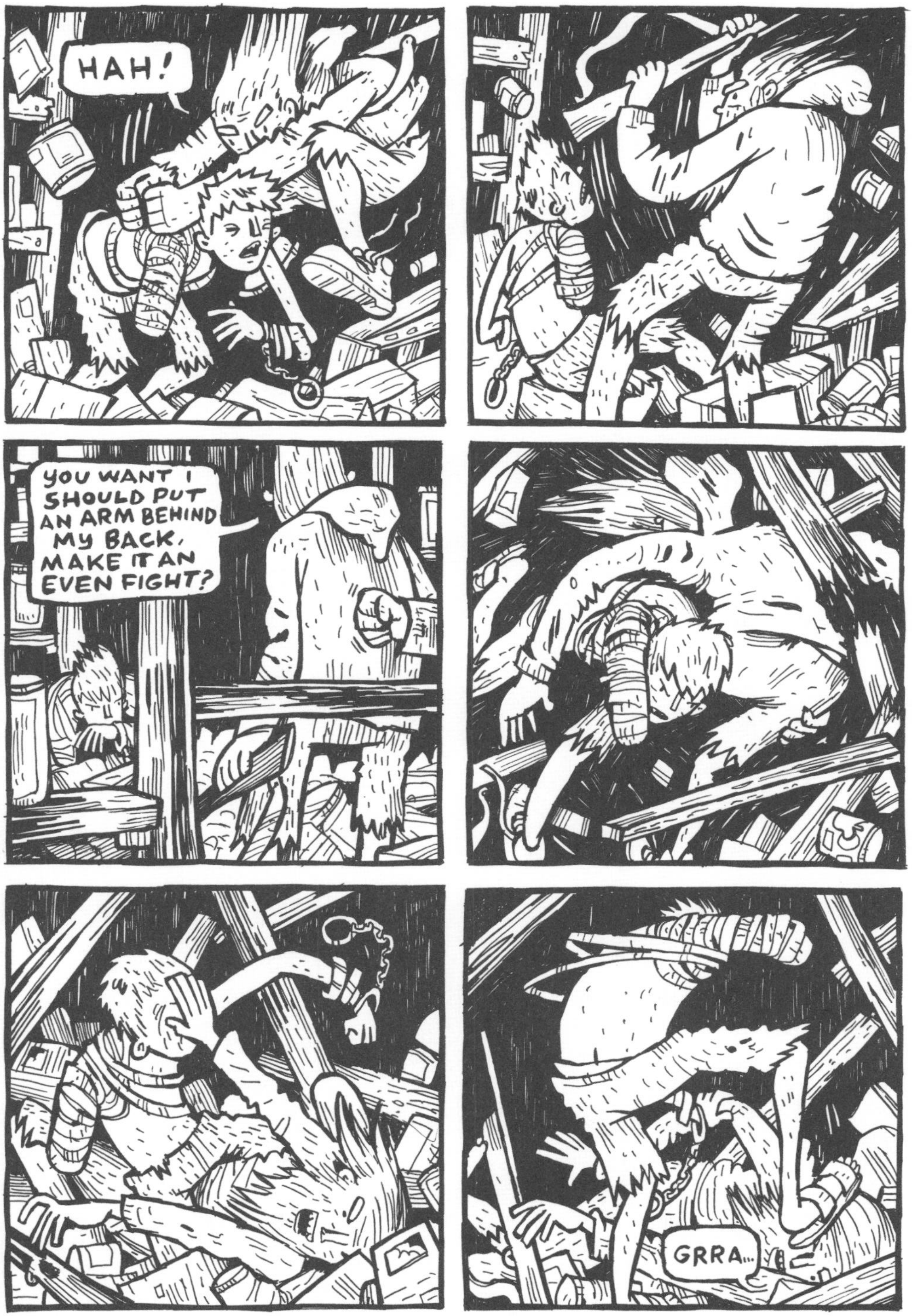
HAH!
YOU WANT I SHOULD PUT AN ARM BEHIND MY BACK, MAKE IT AN EVEN FIGHT?
GRRA...

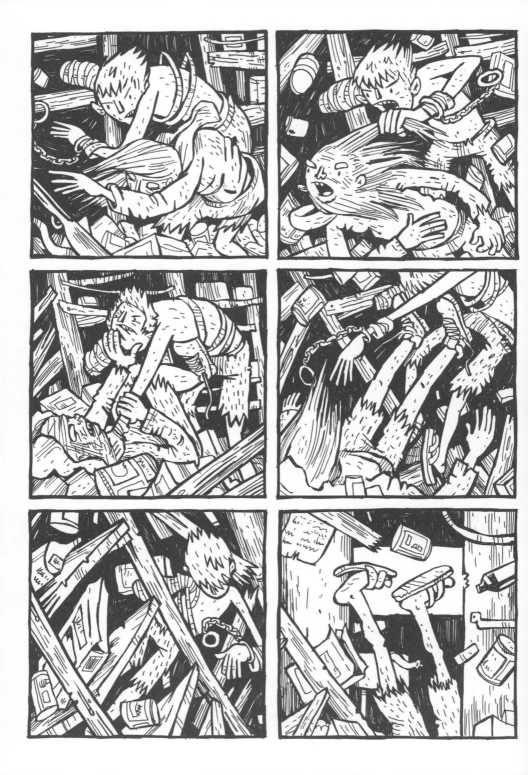

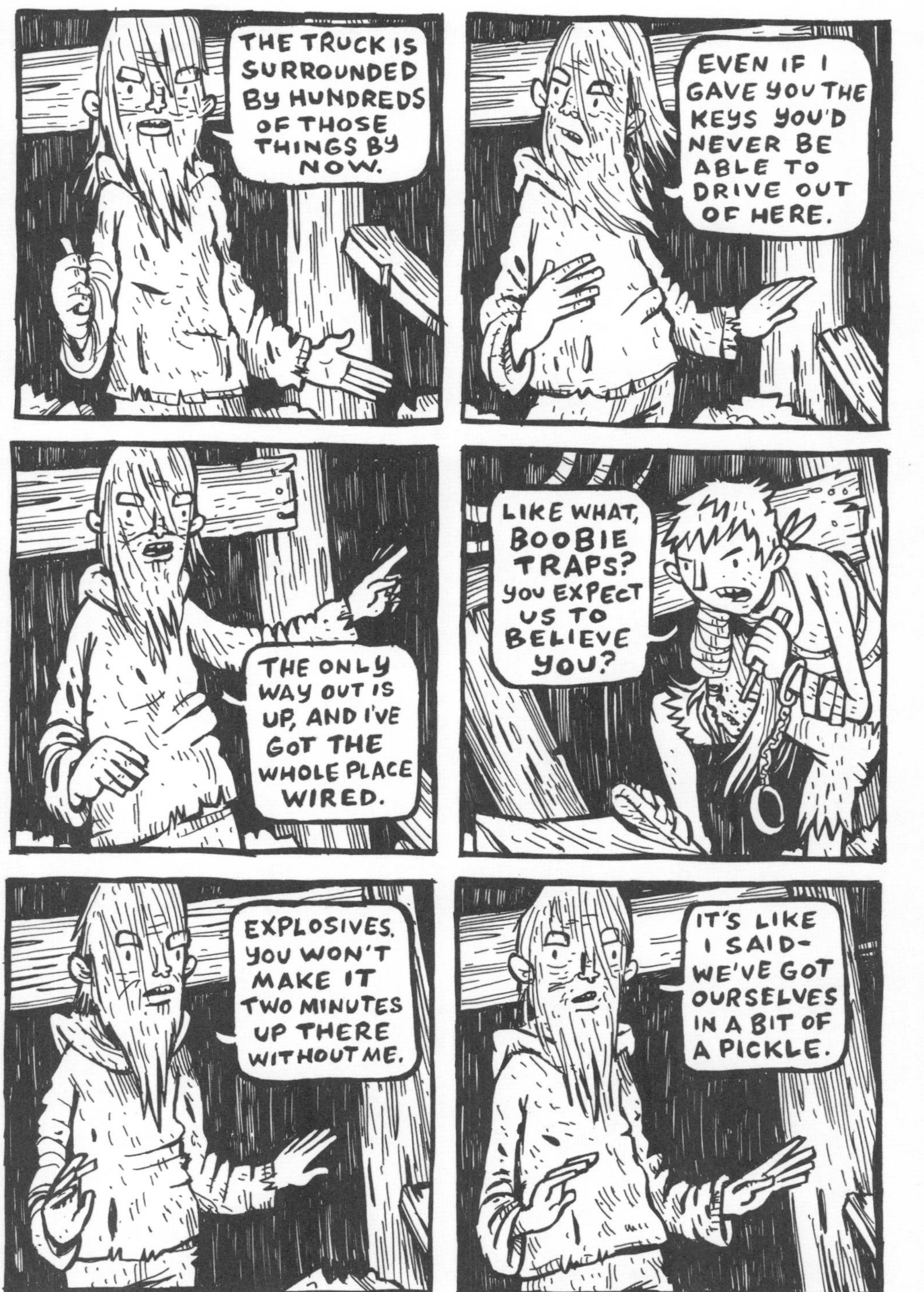
THE TRUCK IS SURROUNDED BY HUNDREDS OF THOSE THINGS BY NOW.
EVEN IF I GAVE YOU THE KEYS YOU'D NEVER BE ABLE TO DRIVE OUT OF HERE.
THE ONLY WAY OUT IS UP, AND I'VE GOT THE WHOLE PLACE WIRED.
LIKE WHAT, BOOBIE TRAPS? YOU EXPECT US TO BELIEVE YOU?
EXPLOSIVES. YOU WON'T MAKE IT TWO MINUTES UP THERE WITHOUT ME.
IT'S LIKE I SAID- WE'VE GOT OURSELVES IN A BIT OF A PICKLE.

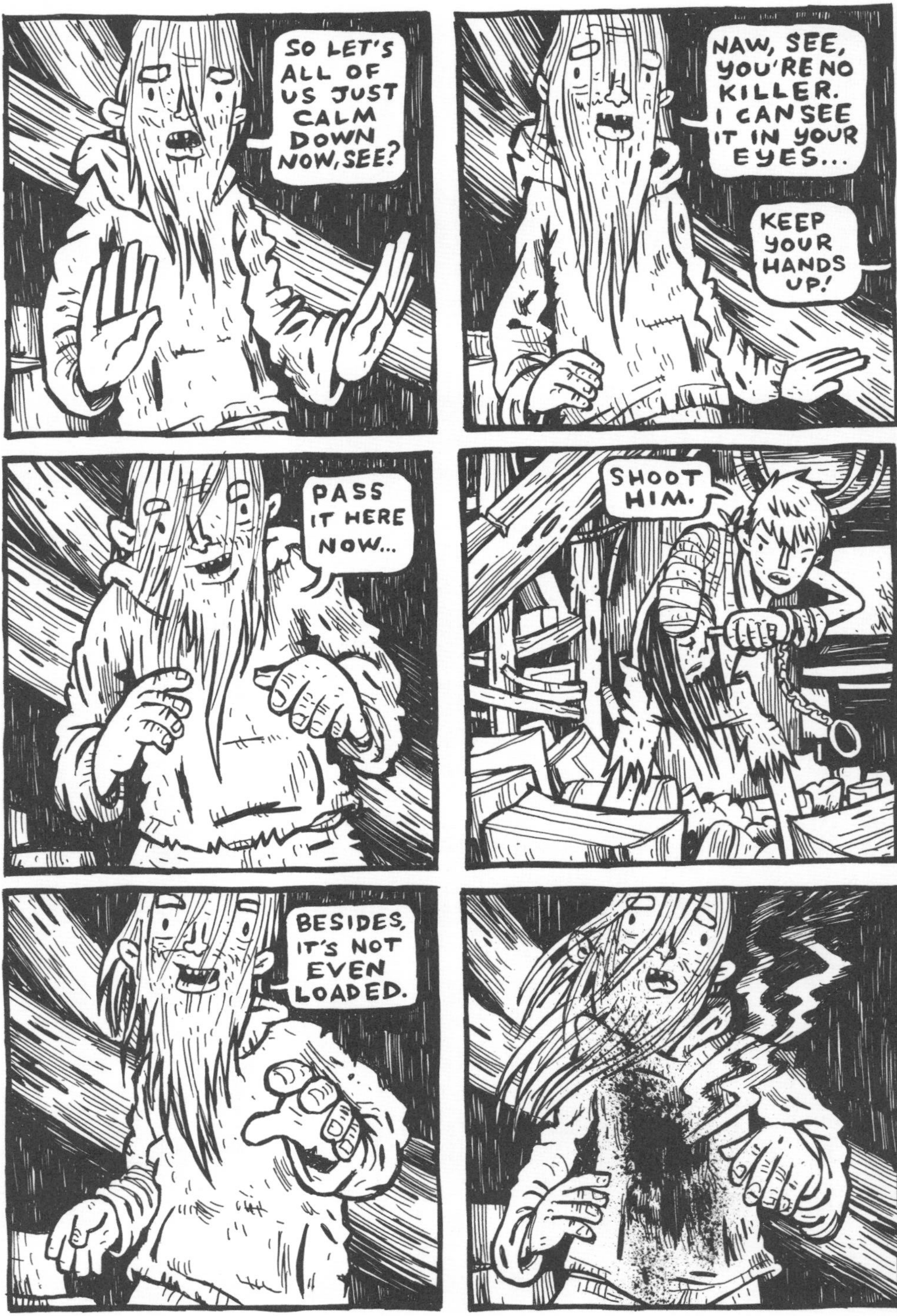
SO LET'S ALL OF US JUST CALM DOWN NOW, SEE?
NAW, SEE, YOU'RE NO KILLER. I CAN SEE IT IN YOUR EYES...
KEEP YOUR HANDS UP!
PASS IT HERE NOW...
SHOOT HIM.
BESIDES, IT'S NOT EVEN LOADED.

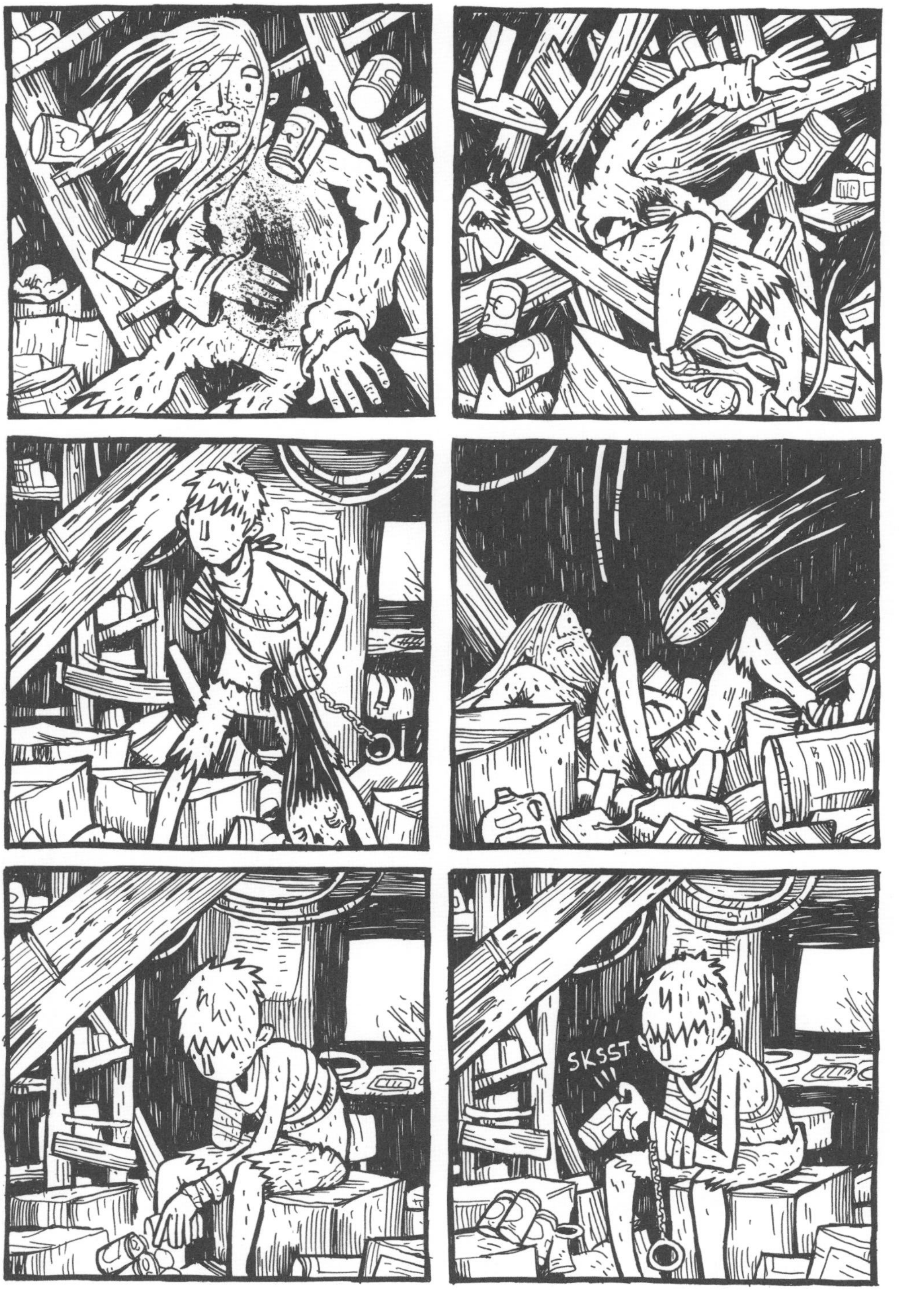
SKSST

OR MAYBE SOMETHING WORSE.

TRUST ME— I'VE SEEN WORSE.

CAN'T SEE ANYTHING. SMELLS TERRIBLE.

THAT FLASHLIGHT WOULD HAVE BEEN USEFUL...

...

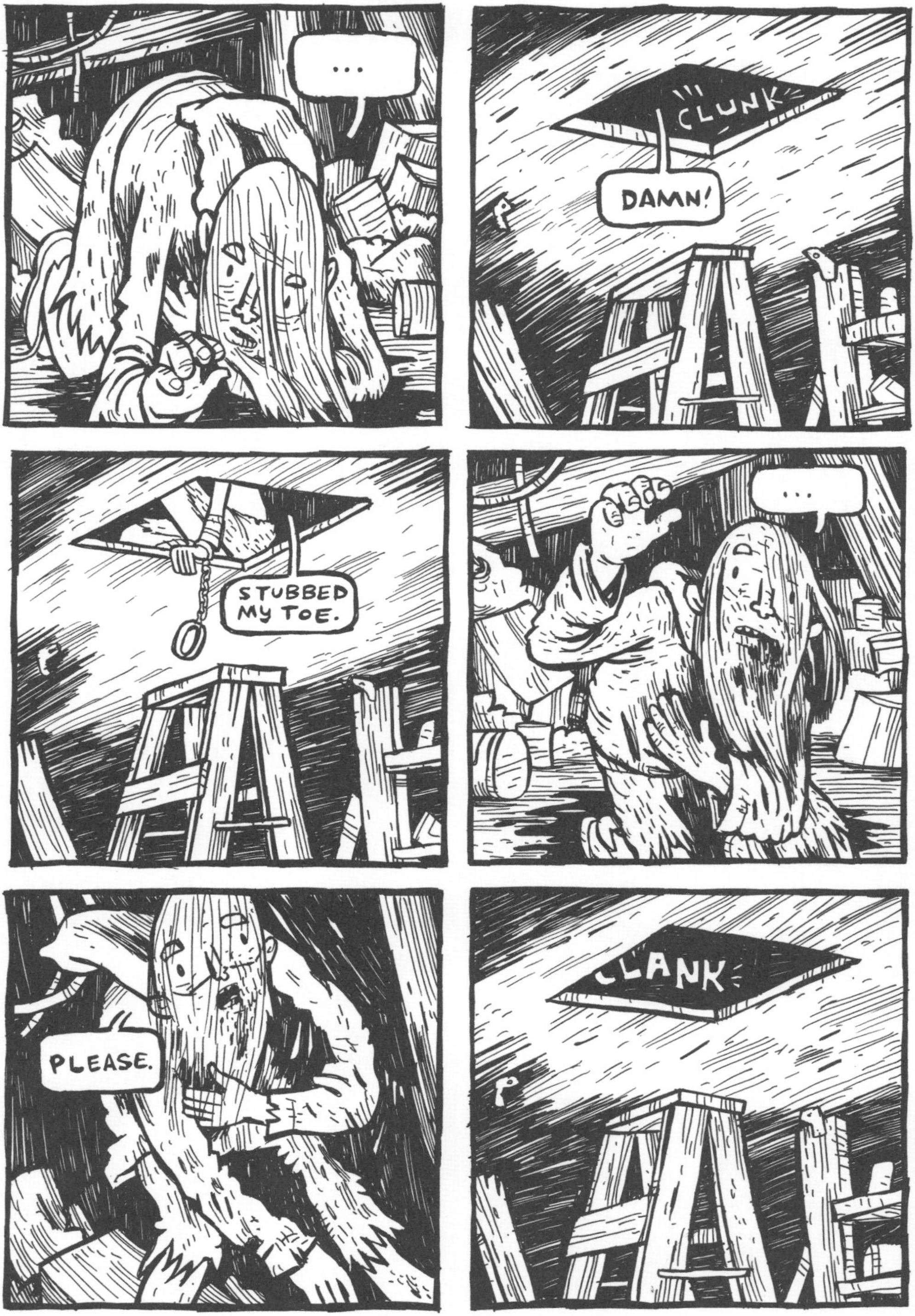
...
CLUNK
DAMN!
STUBBED MY TOE.
...
PLEASE.
CLANK

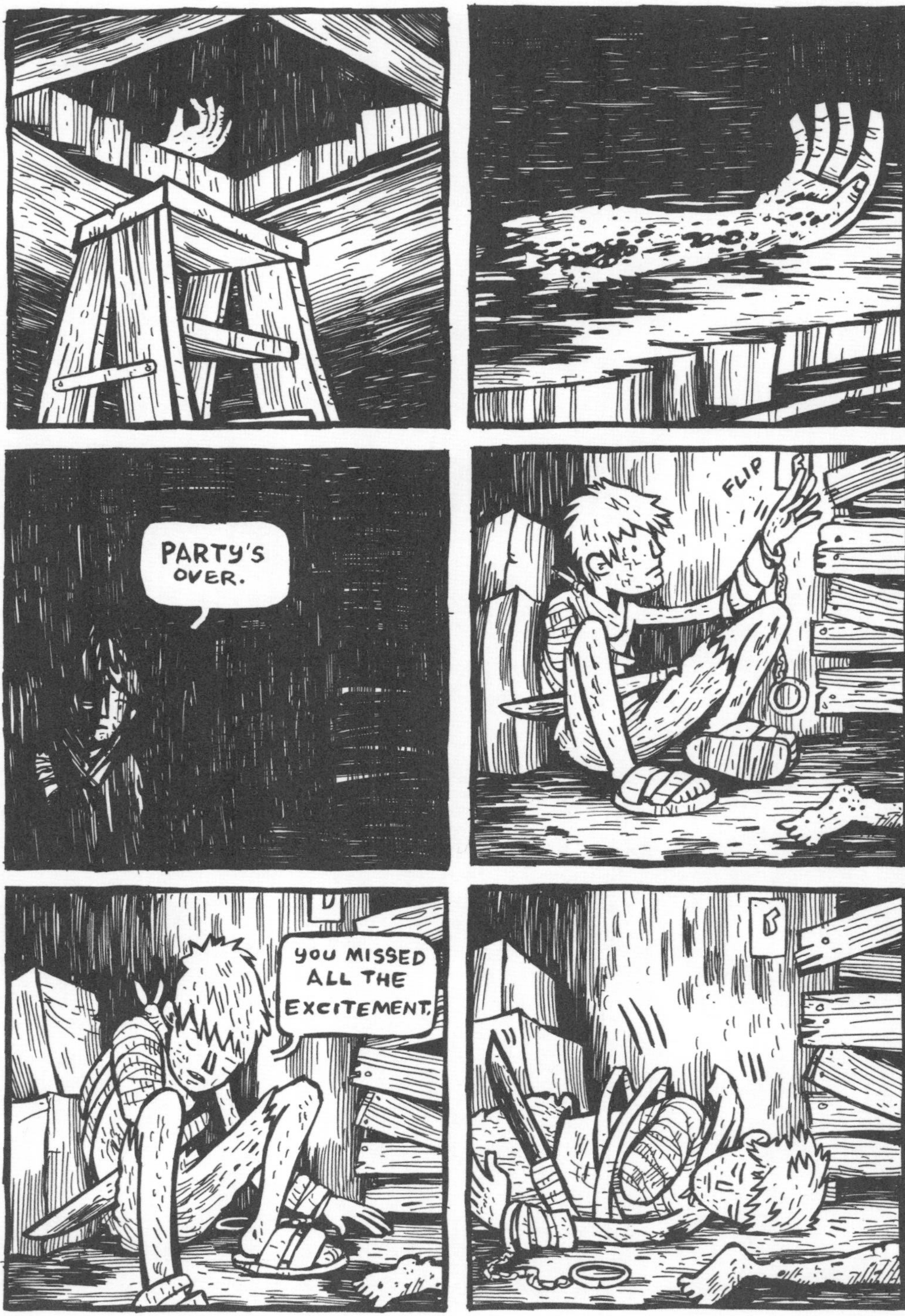
PARTY'S OVER.
FLIP
YOU MISSED ALL THE EXCITEMENT.

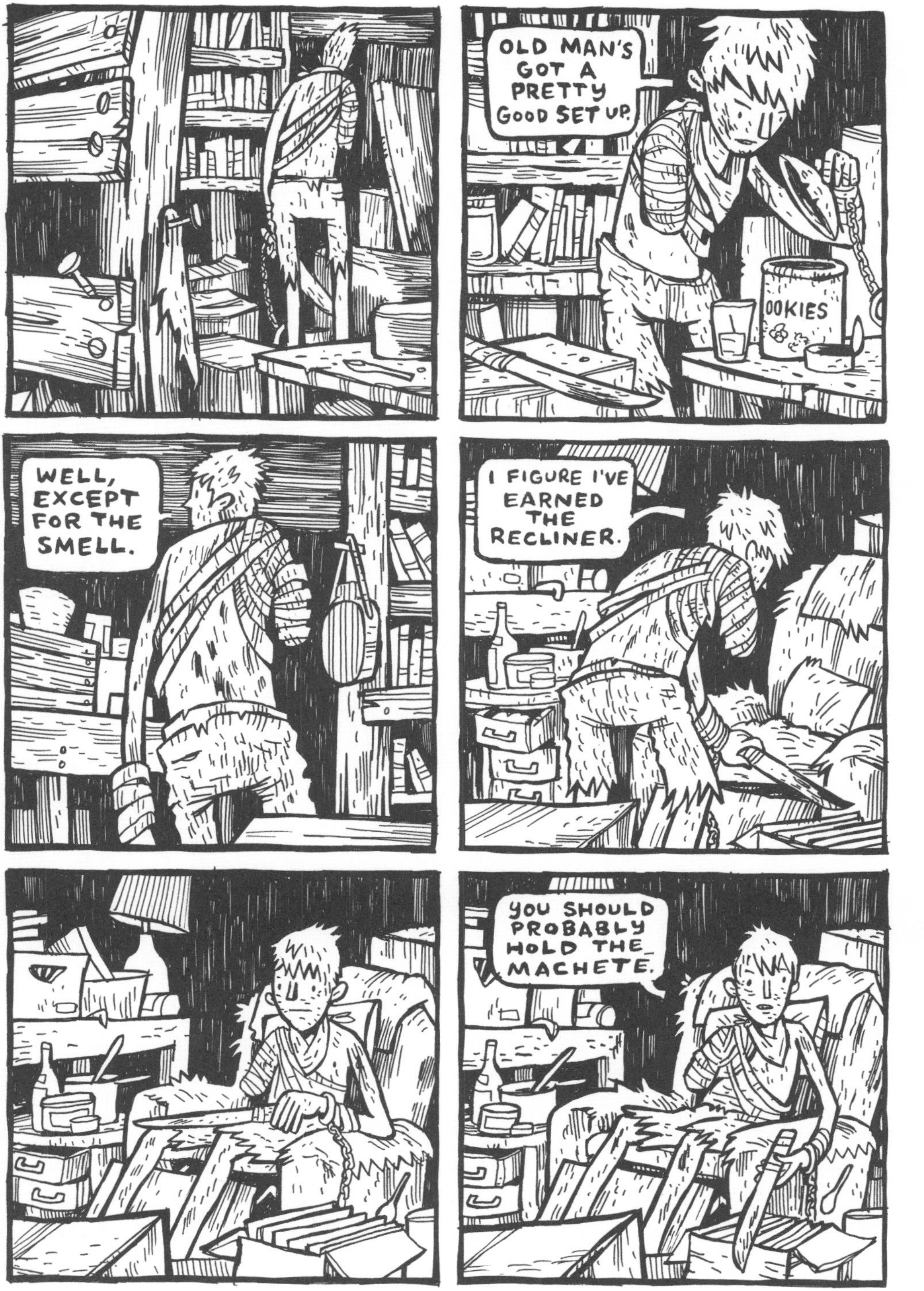
OLD MAN'S GOT A PRETTY GOOD SET UP.
OOKIES
WELL, EXCEPT FOR THE SMELL.
I FIGURE I'VE EARNED THE RECLINER.
YOU SHOULD PROBABLY HOLD THE MACHETE.

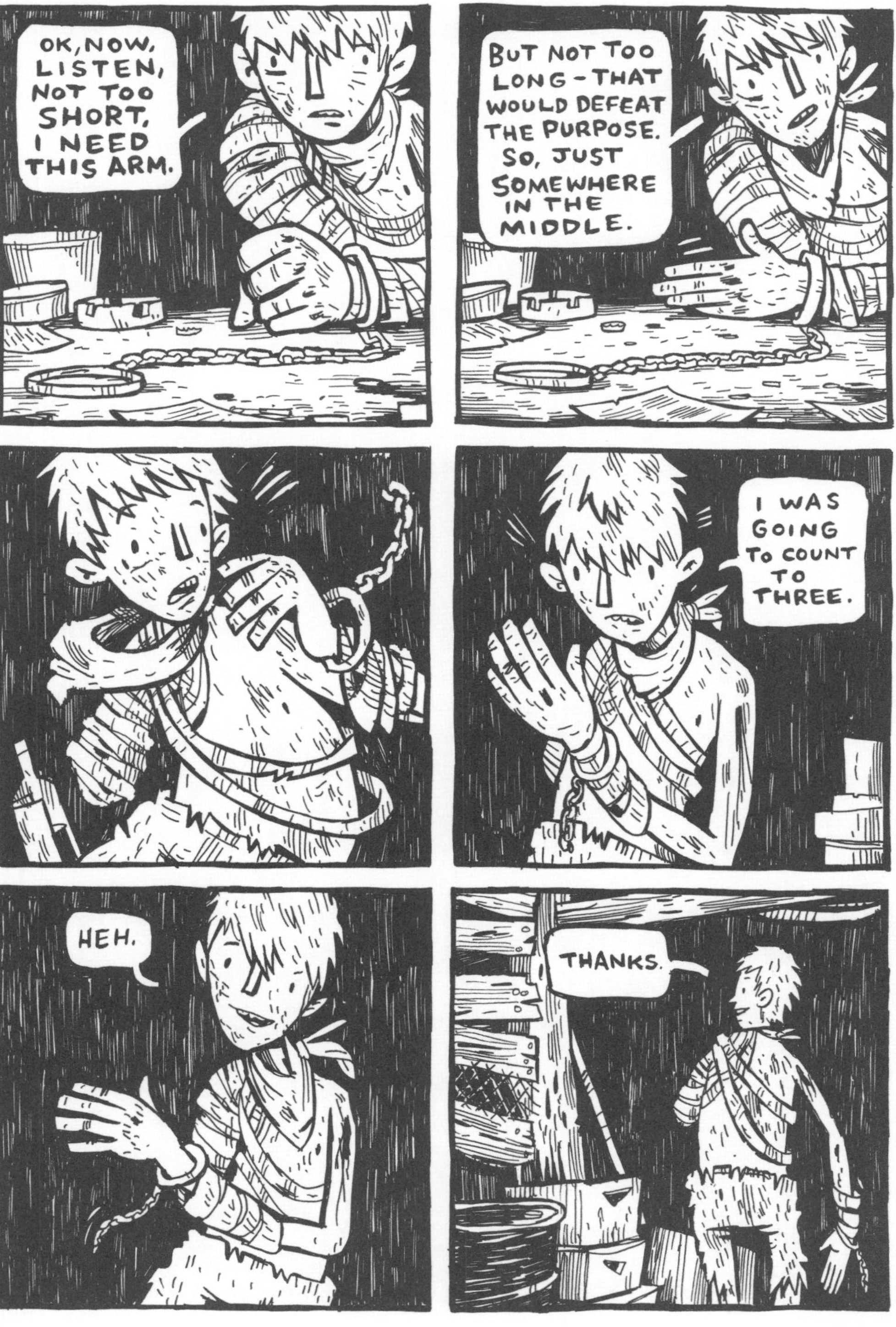
OK, NOW, LISTEN, NOT TOO SHORT, I NEED THIS ARM.
BUT NOT TOO LONG - THAT WOULD DEFEAT THE PURPOSE. SO, JUST SOMEWHERE IN THE MIDDLE.
I WAS GOING TO COUNT TO THREE.
HEH.
THANKS.

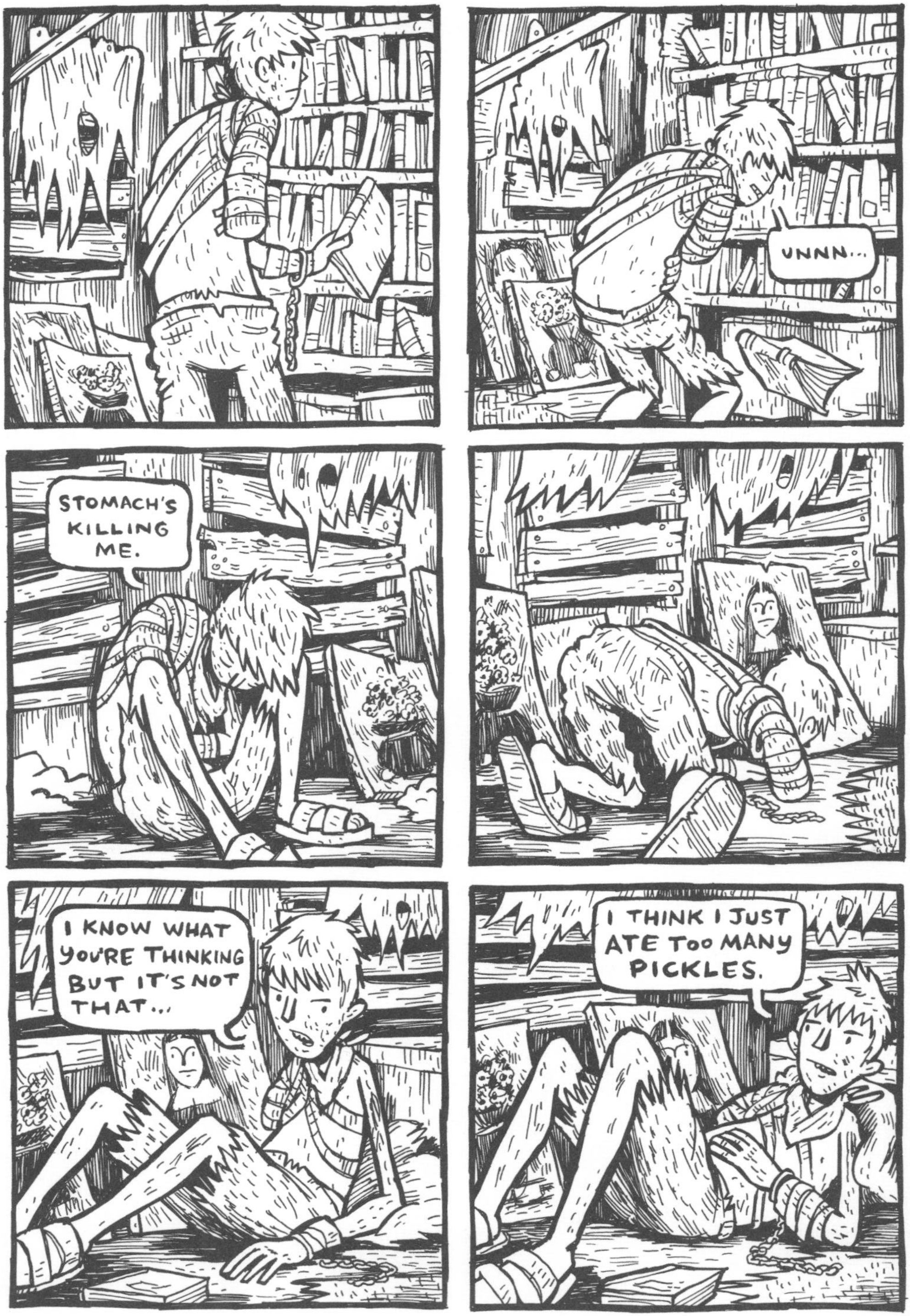
UNNN...
STOMACH'S KILLING ME.
I KNOW WHAT YOU'RE THINKING BUT IT'S NOT THAT...
I THINK I JUST ATE TOO MANY PICKLES.

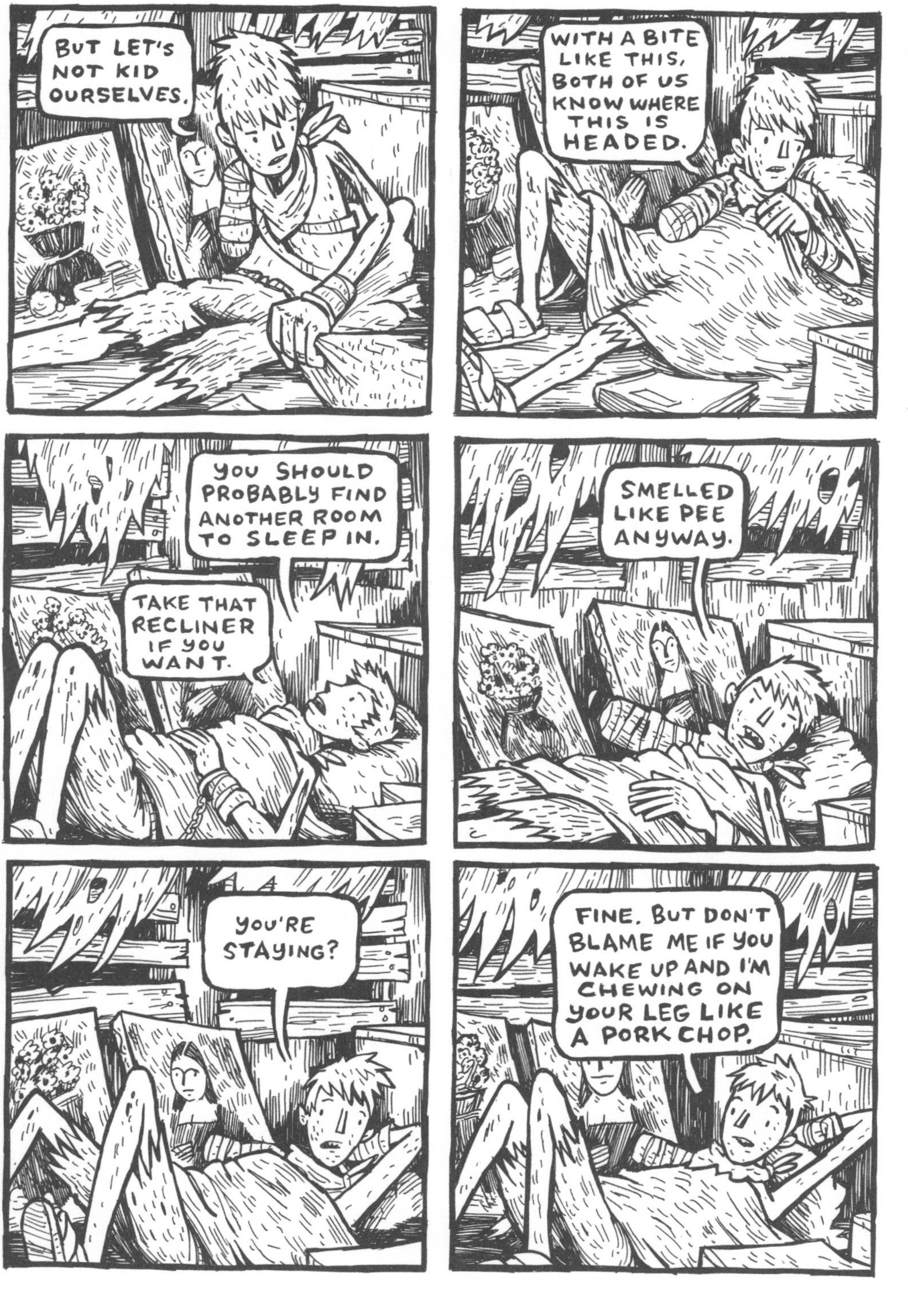
BUT LET'S NOT KID OURSELVES.
WITH A BITE LIKE THIS, BOTH OF US KNOW WHERE THIS IS HEADED.
YOU SHOULD PROBABLY FIND ANOTHER ROOM TO SLEEP IN.
TAKE THAT RECLINER IF YOU WANT.
SMELLED LIKE PEE ANYWAY.
YOU'RE STAYING?
FINE. BUT DON'T BLAME ME IF YOU WAKE UP AND I'M CHEWING ON YOUR LEG LIKE A PORK CHOP.

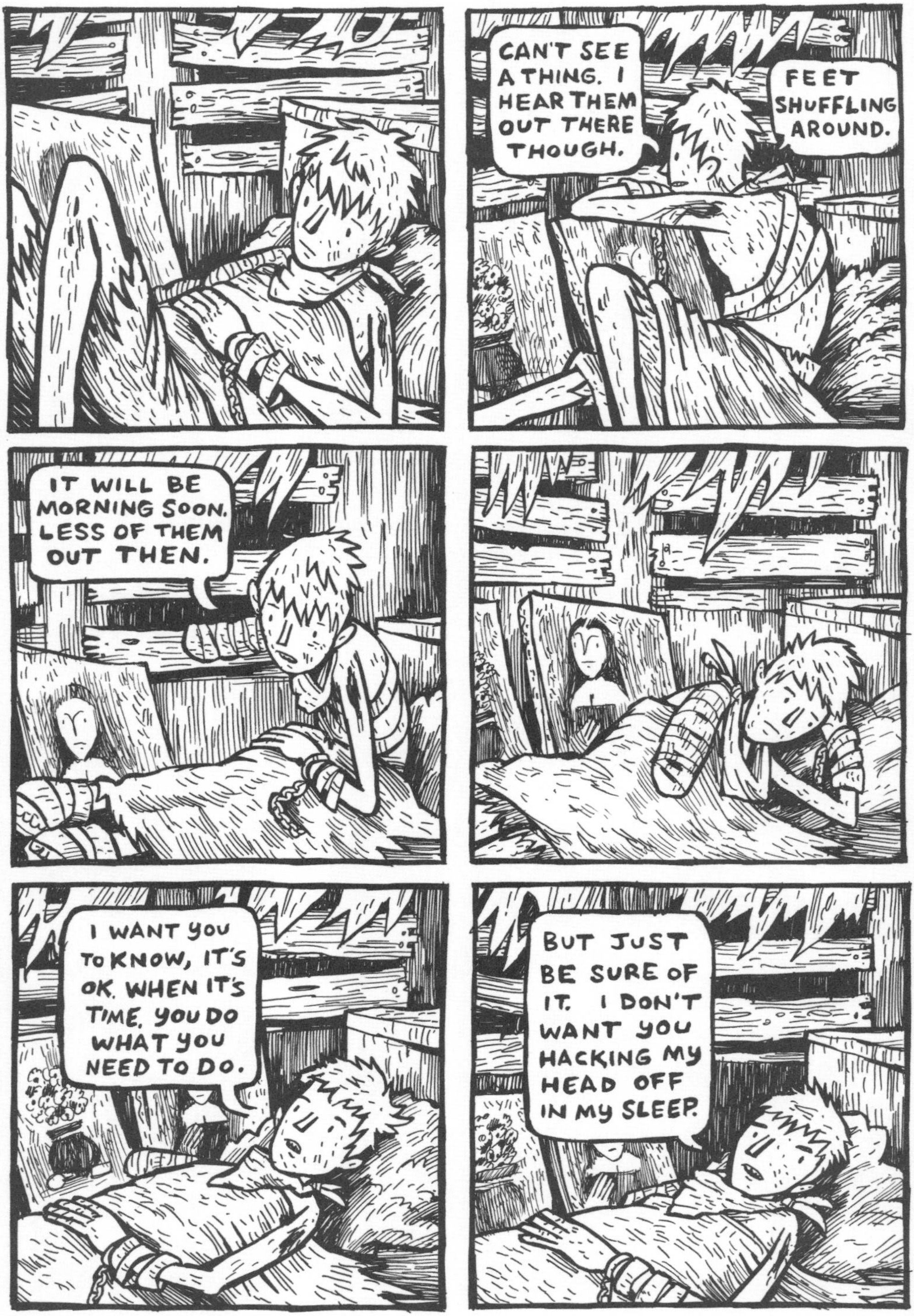
CAN'T SEE A THING. I HEAR THEM OUT THERE THOUGH.
FEET SHUFFLING AROUND.
IT WILL BE MORNING SOON. LESS OF THEM OUT THEN.
I WANT YOU TO KNOW, IT'S OK. WHEN IT'S TIME, YOU DO WHAT YOU NEED TO DO.
BUT JUST BE SURE OF IT. I DON'T WANT YOU HACKING MY HEAD OFF IN MY SLEEP.

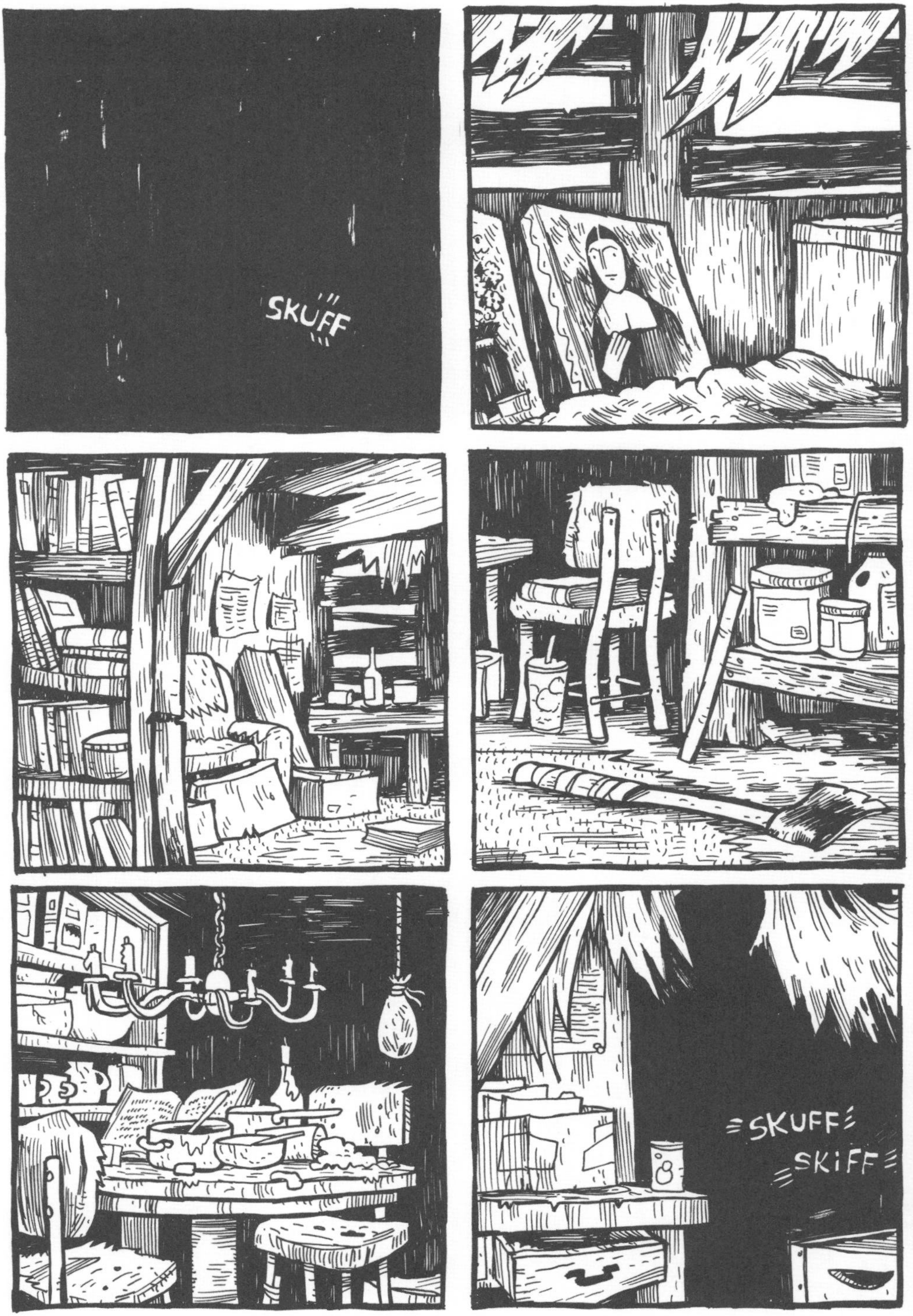

SKUFF
SKUFF
SKIFF

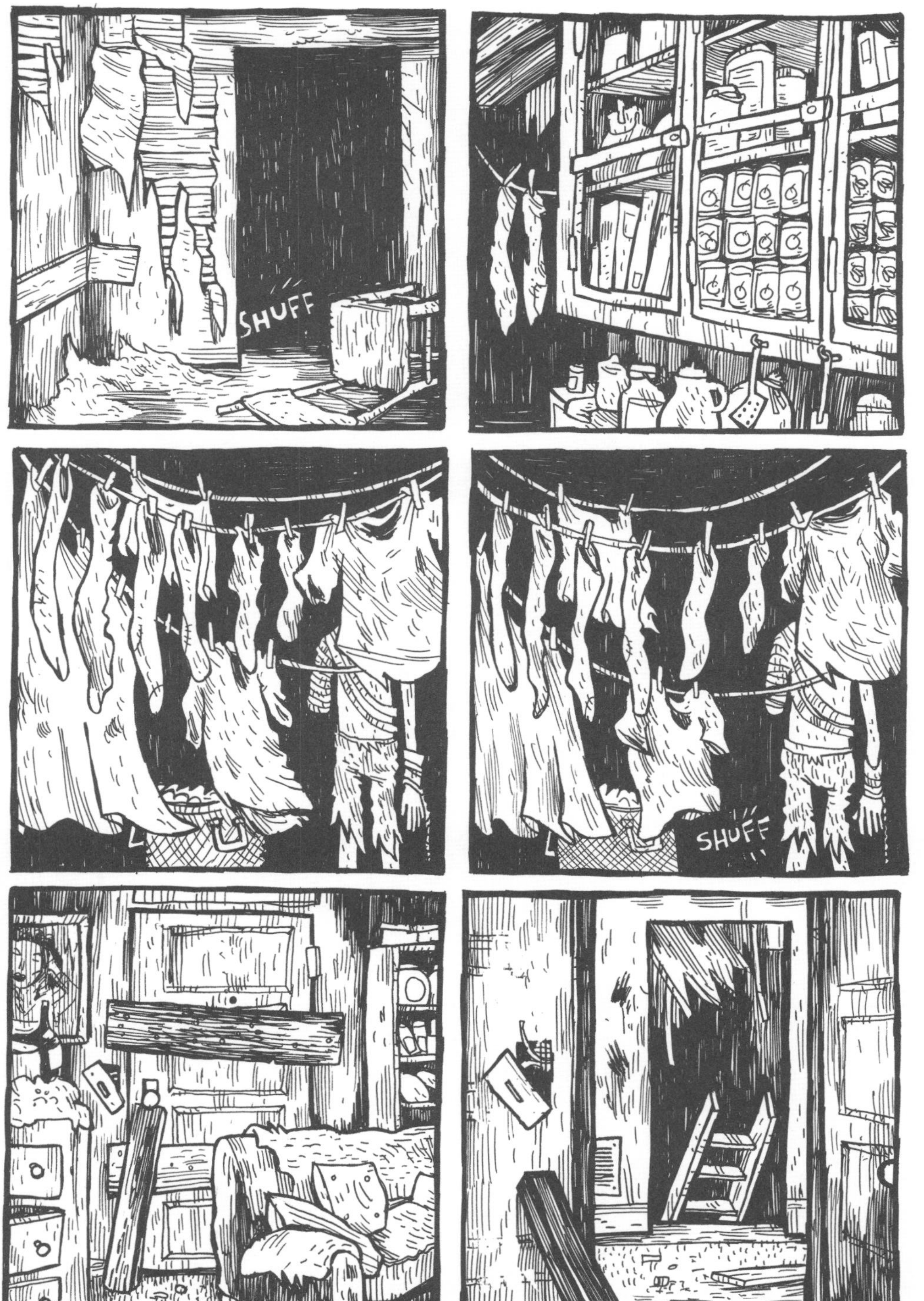
SHUFF
SHUFF

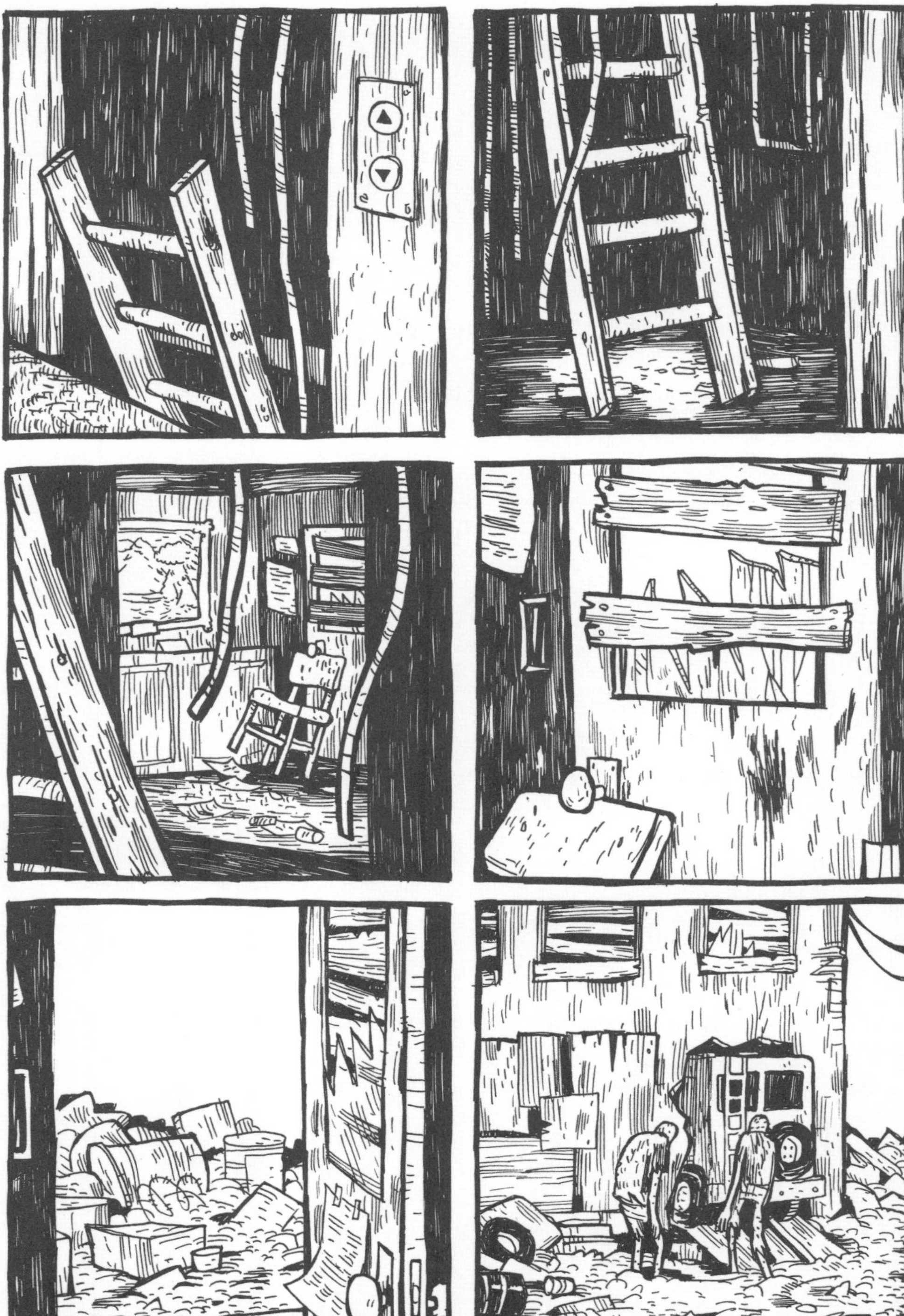

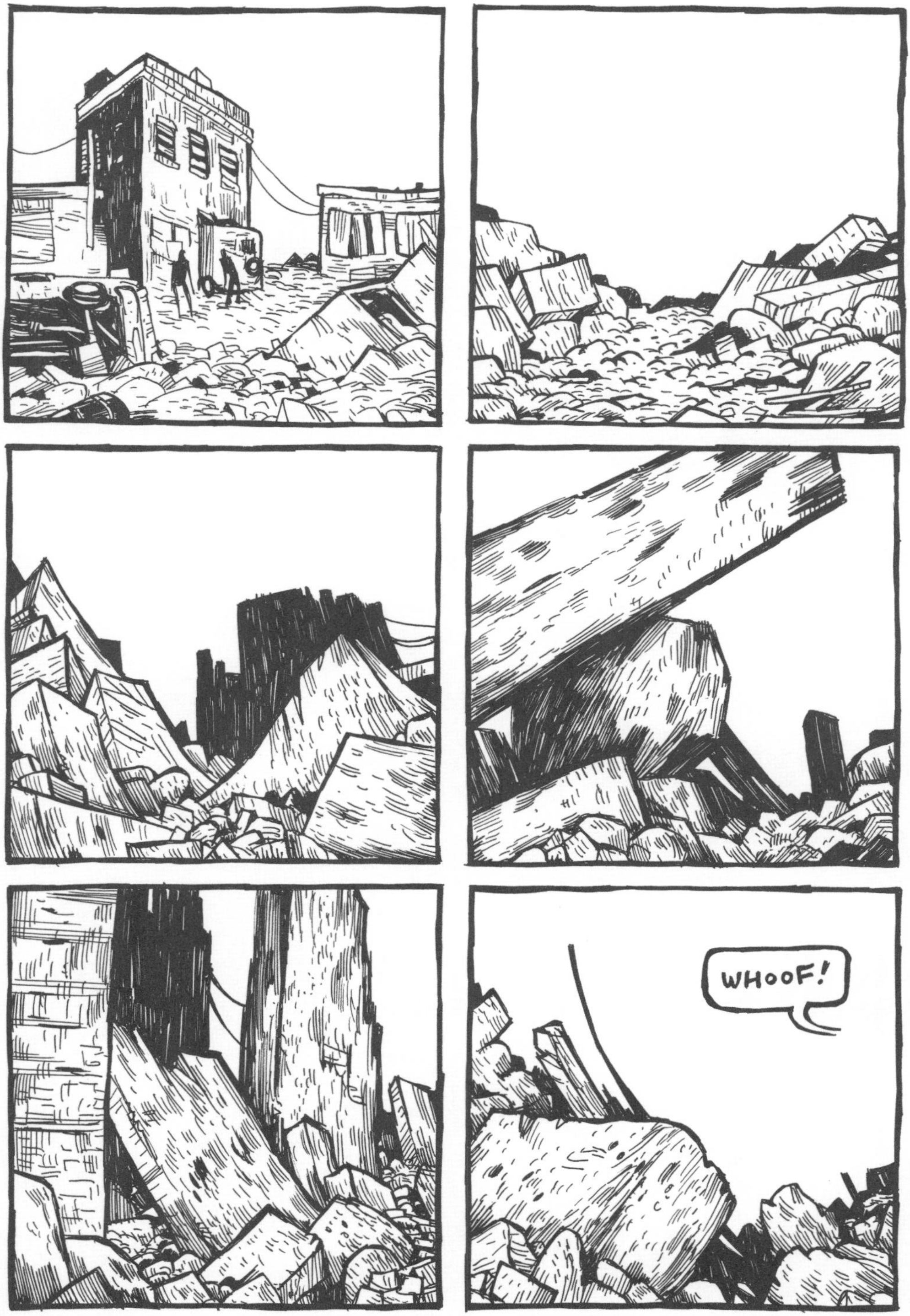
WHOOF!

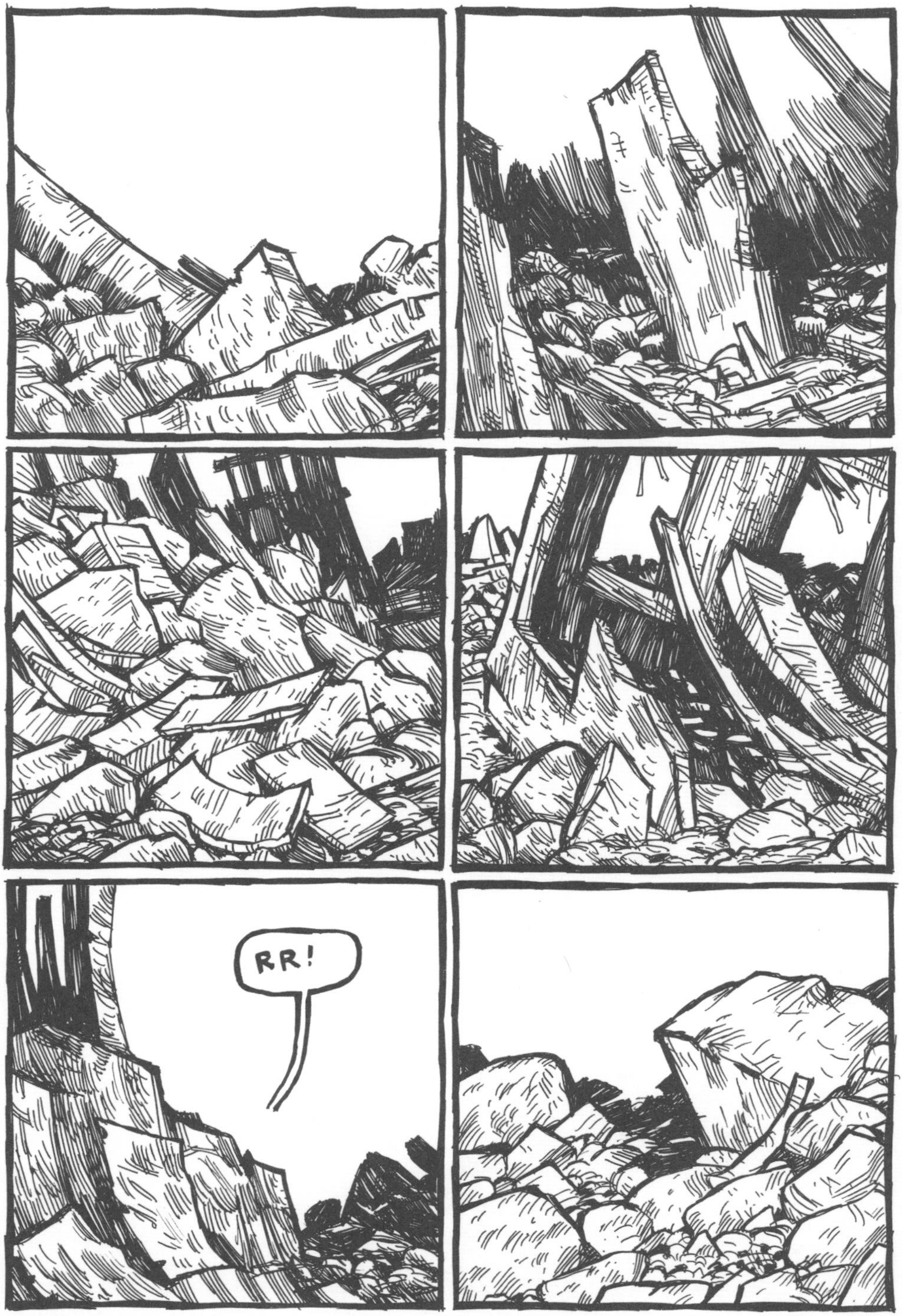
RR!

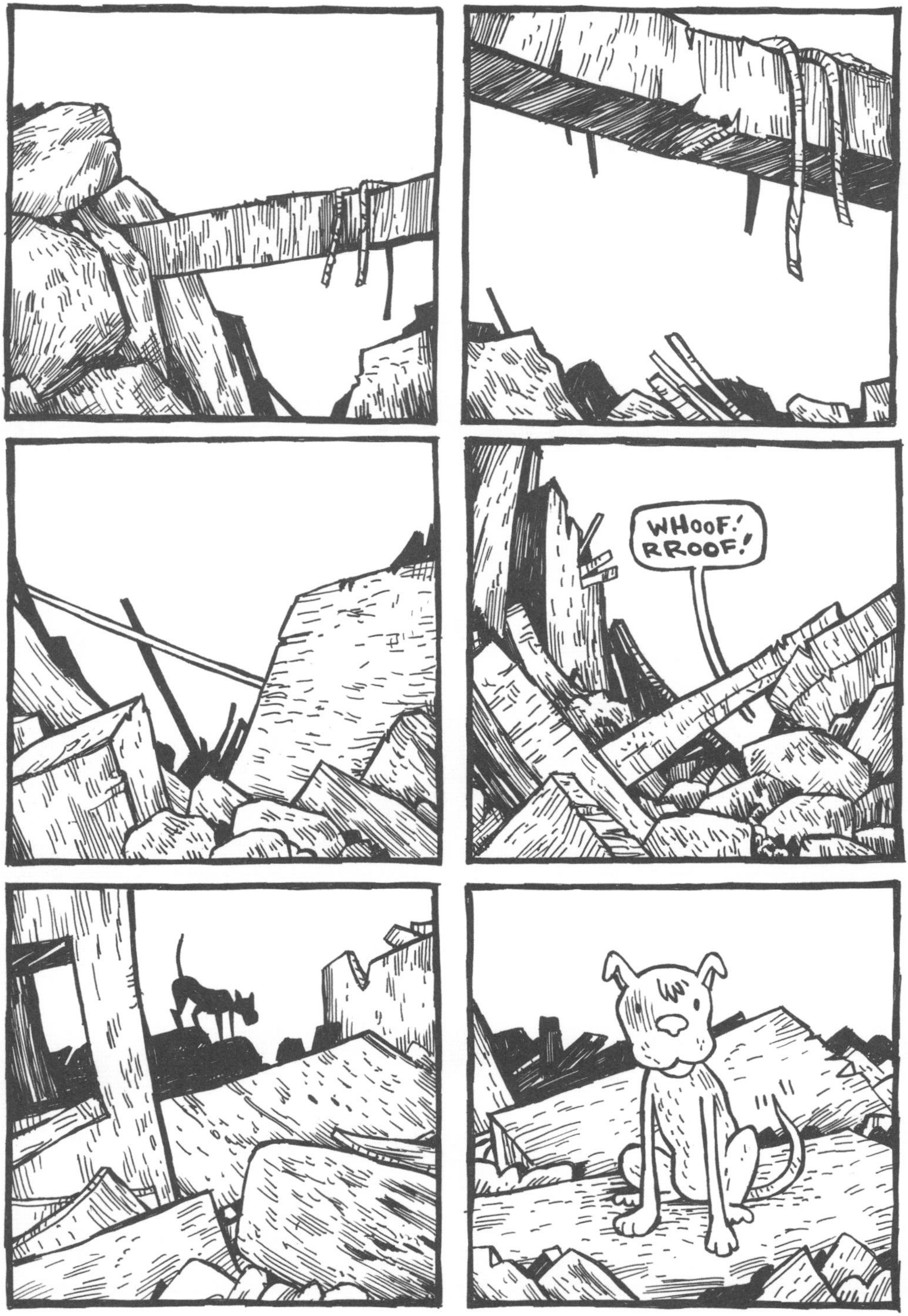
WHOOF! RROOF!

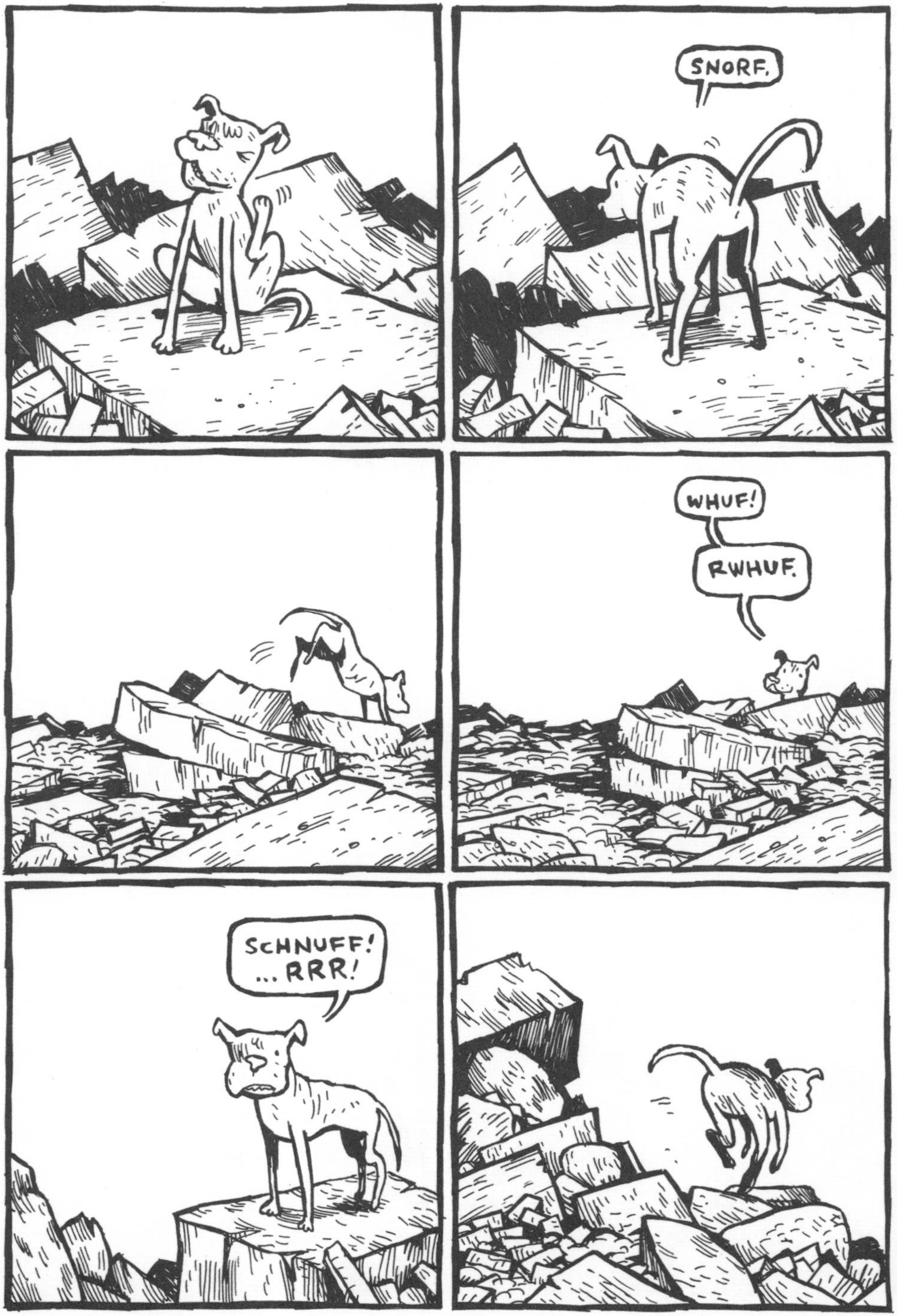
SNORF.
WHUF!
RWHUF.
SCHNUFF! ...RRR!

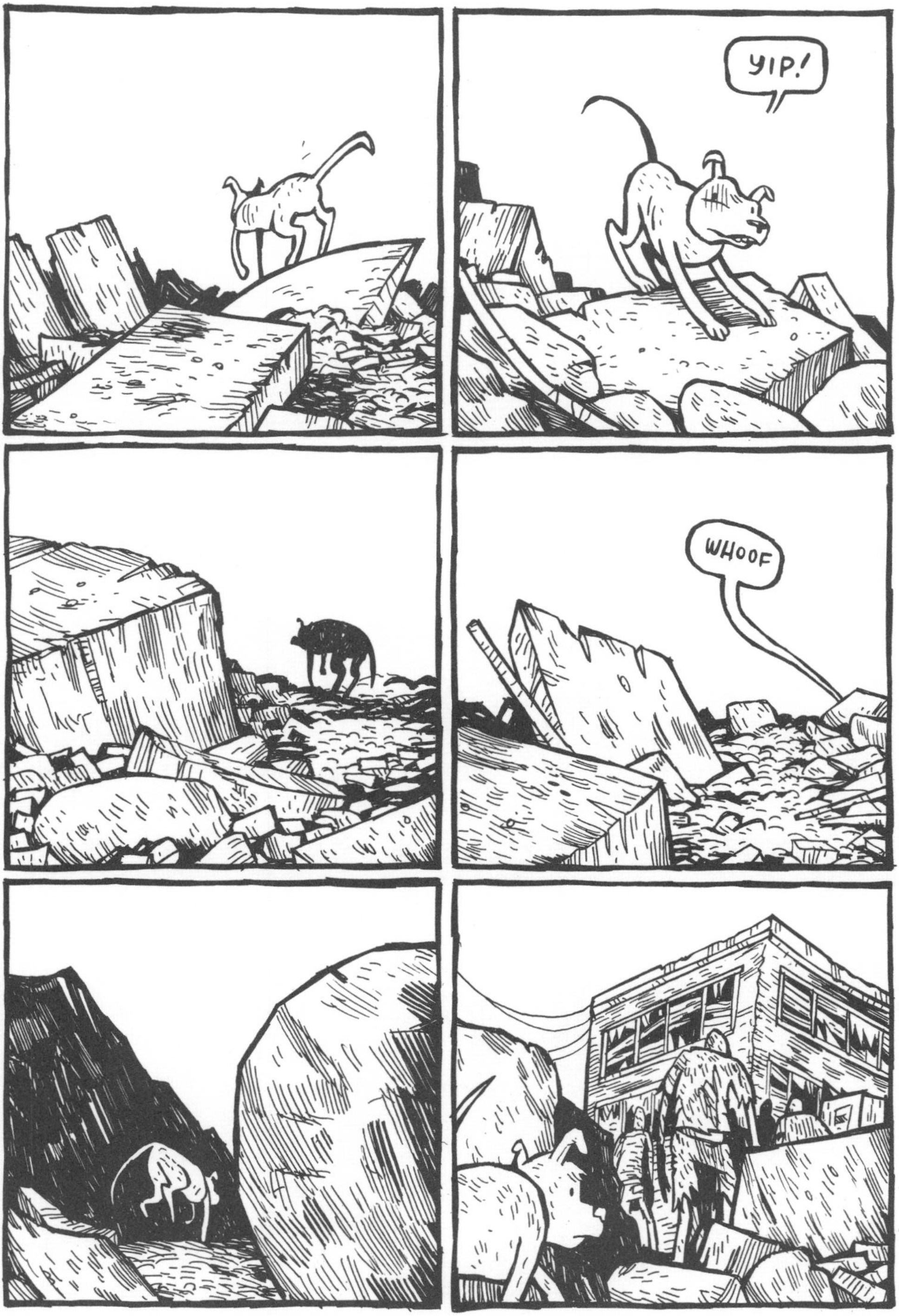
YIP!
WHOOF

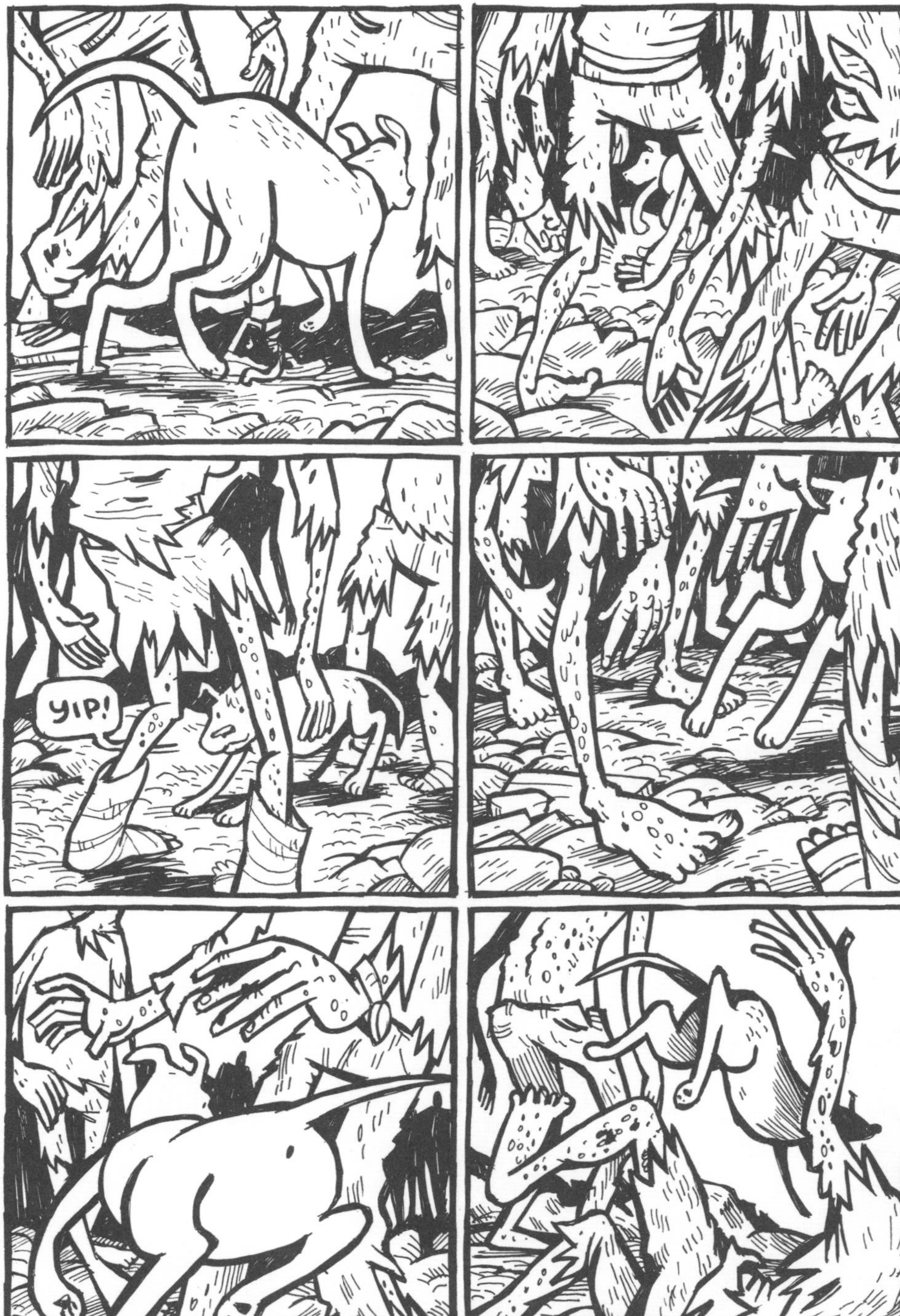
YIP!

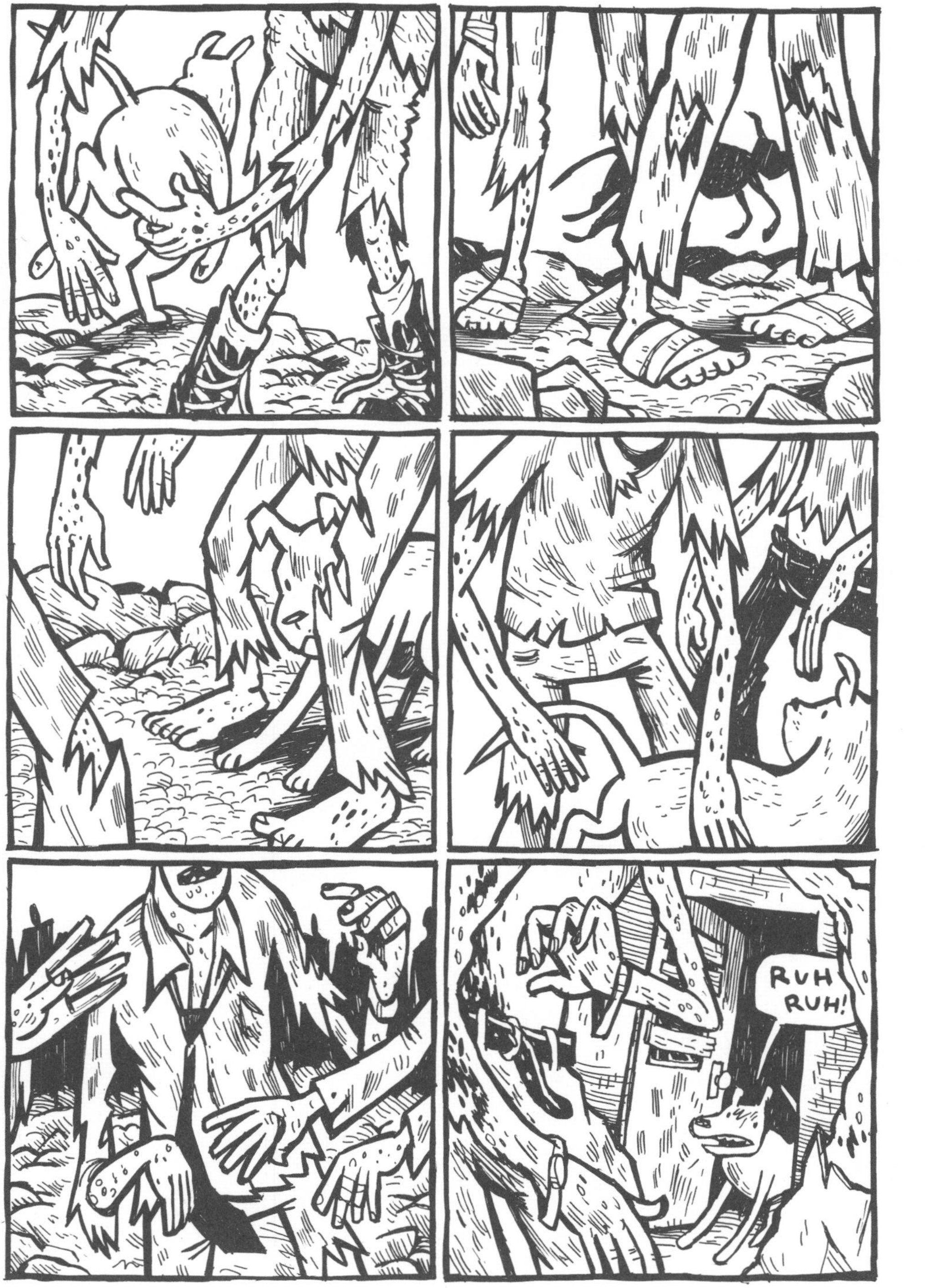
RUH RUH!

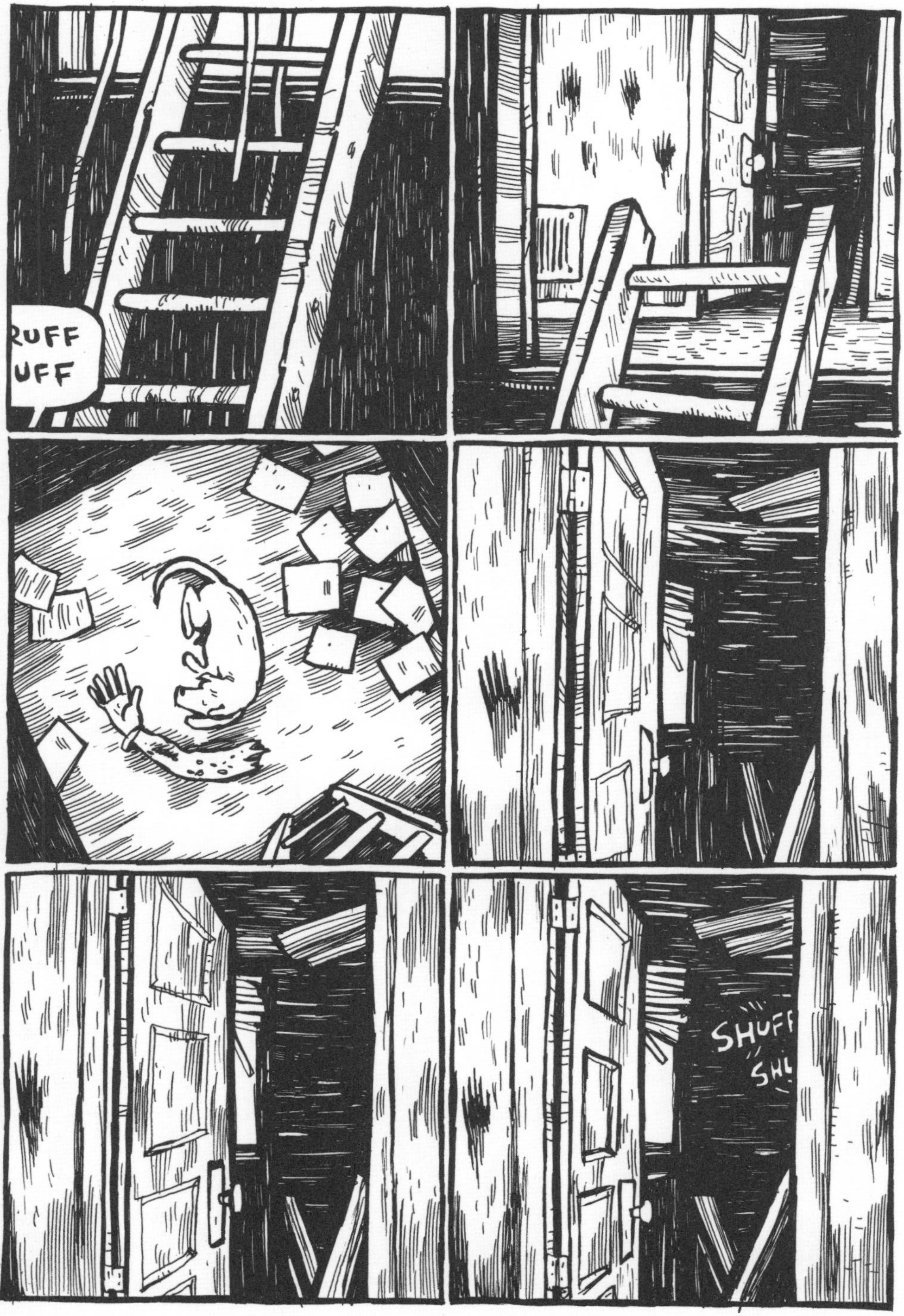
RUFF
UFF
SHUFF
SHU

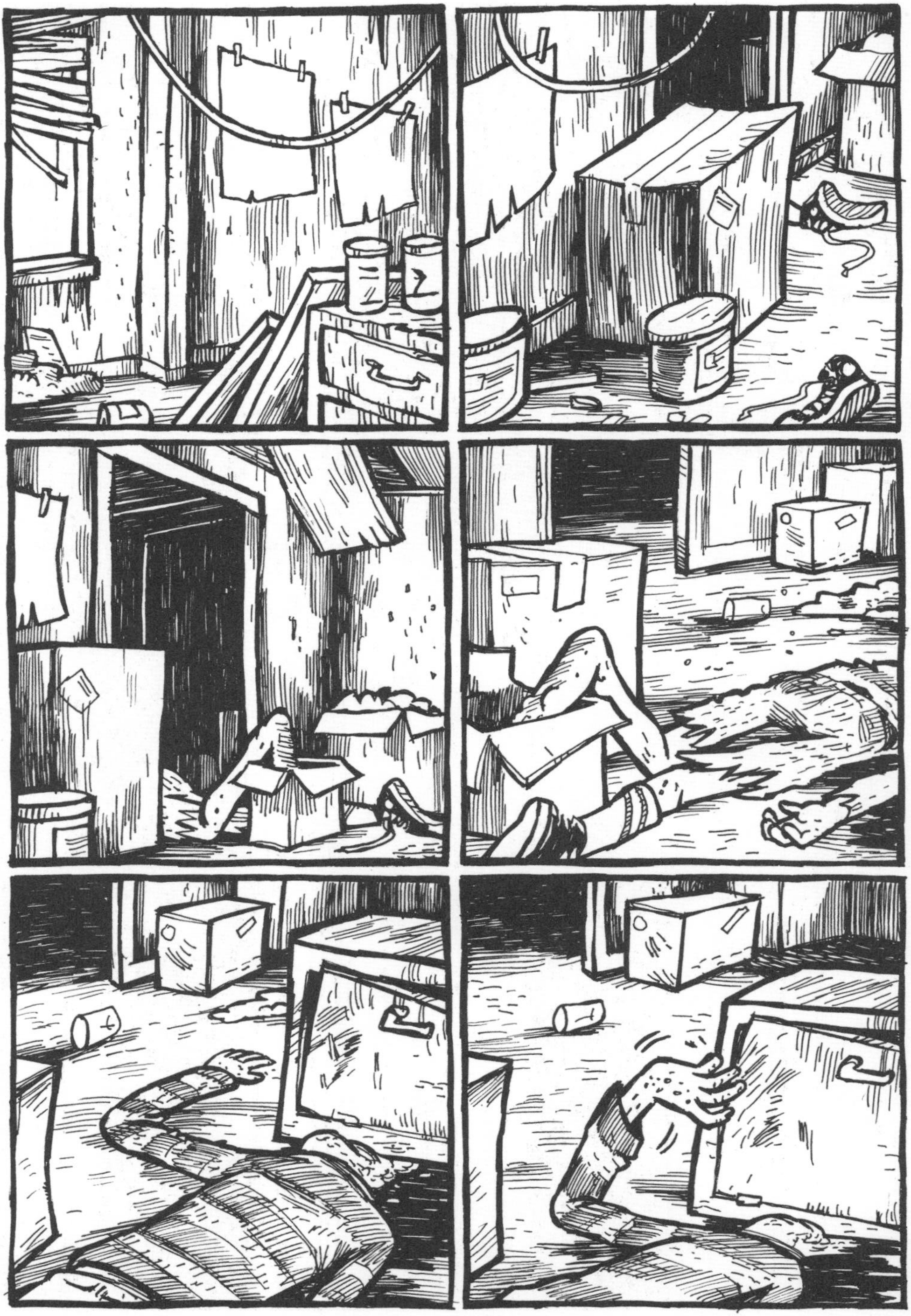

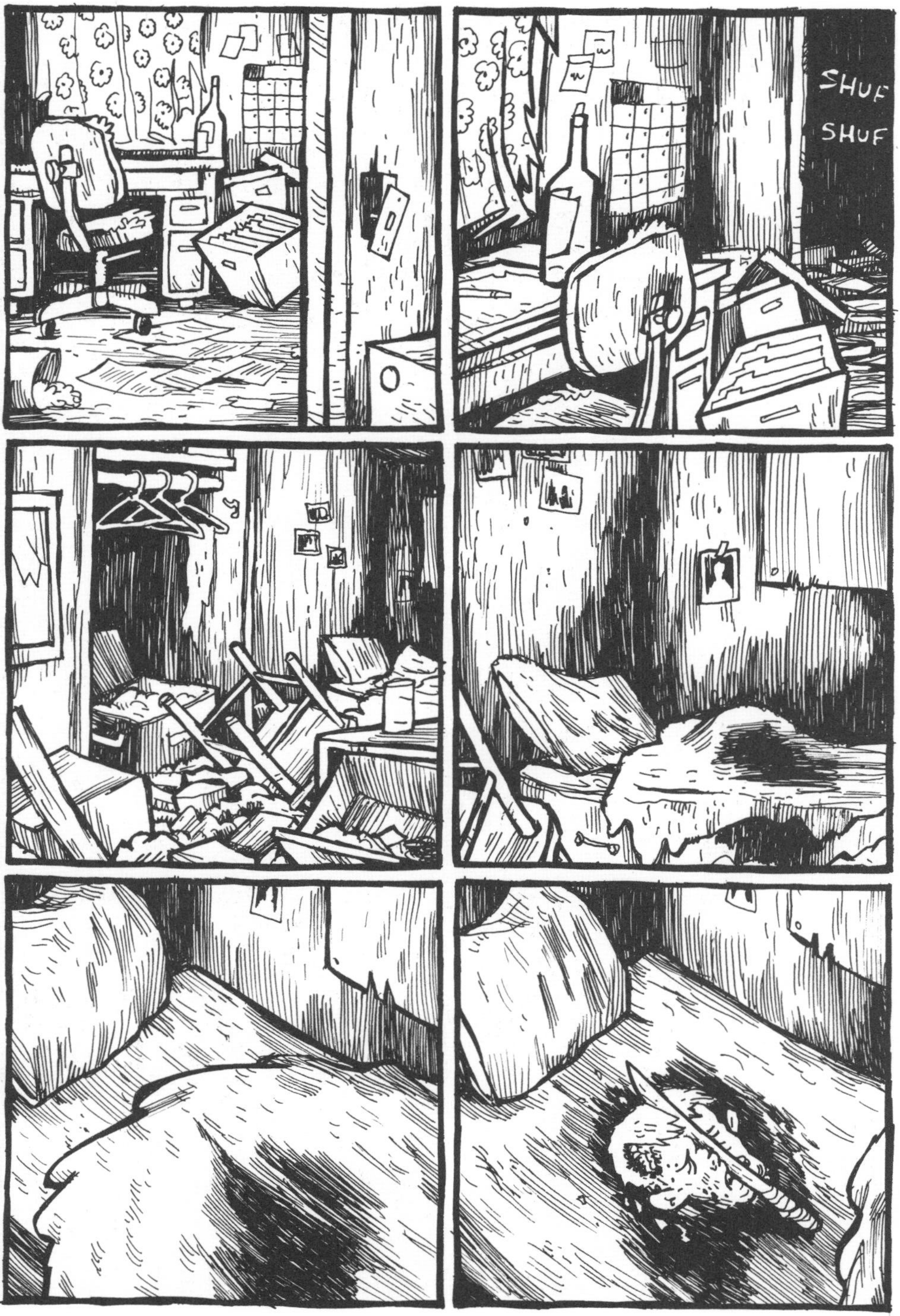
SHUF
SHUF

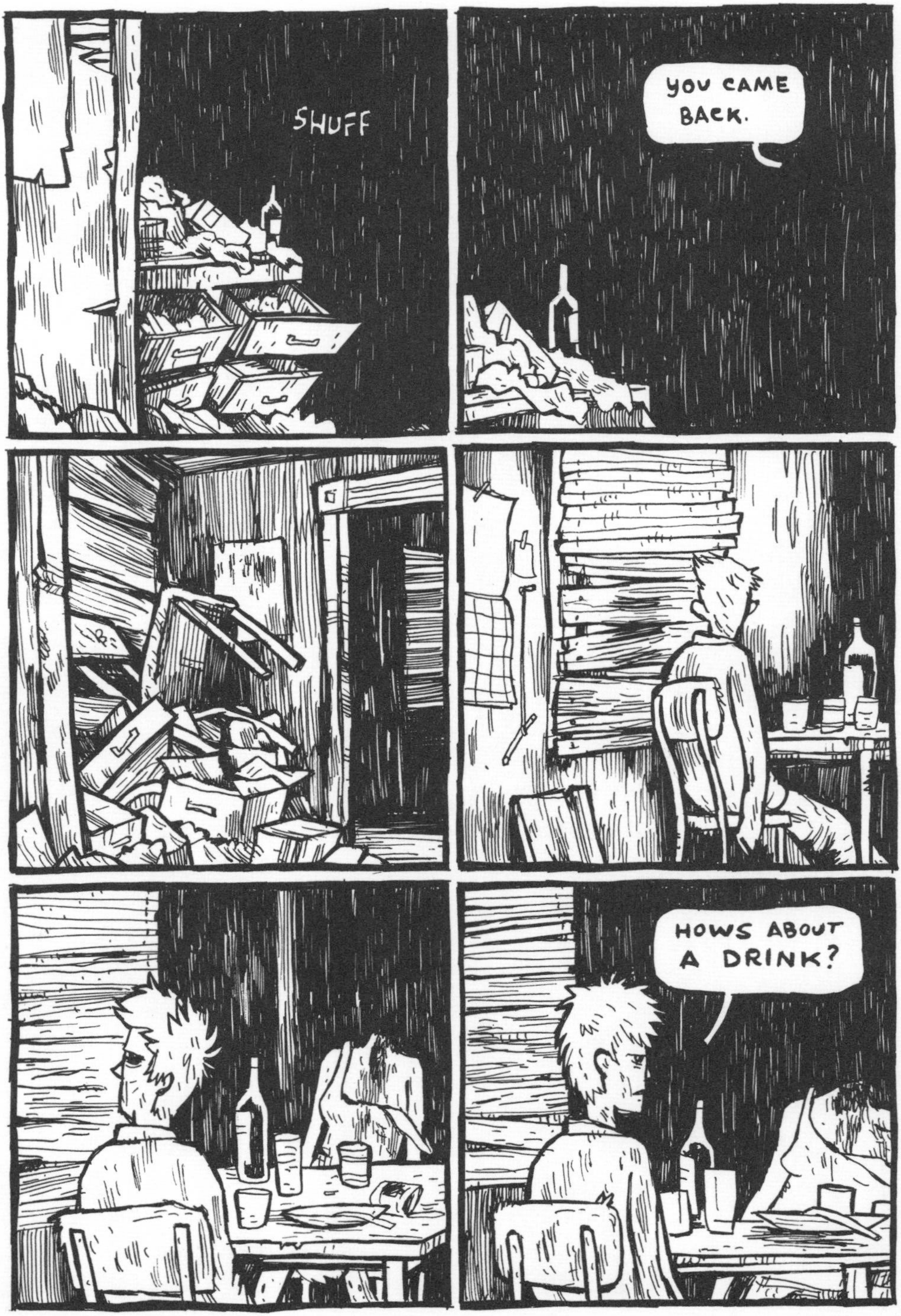
SHUFF
YOU CAME BACK.
HOWS ABOUT A DRINK?

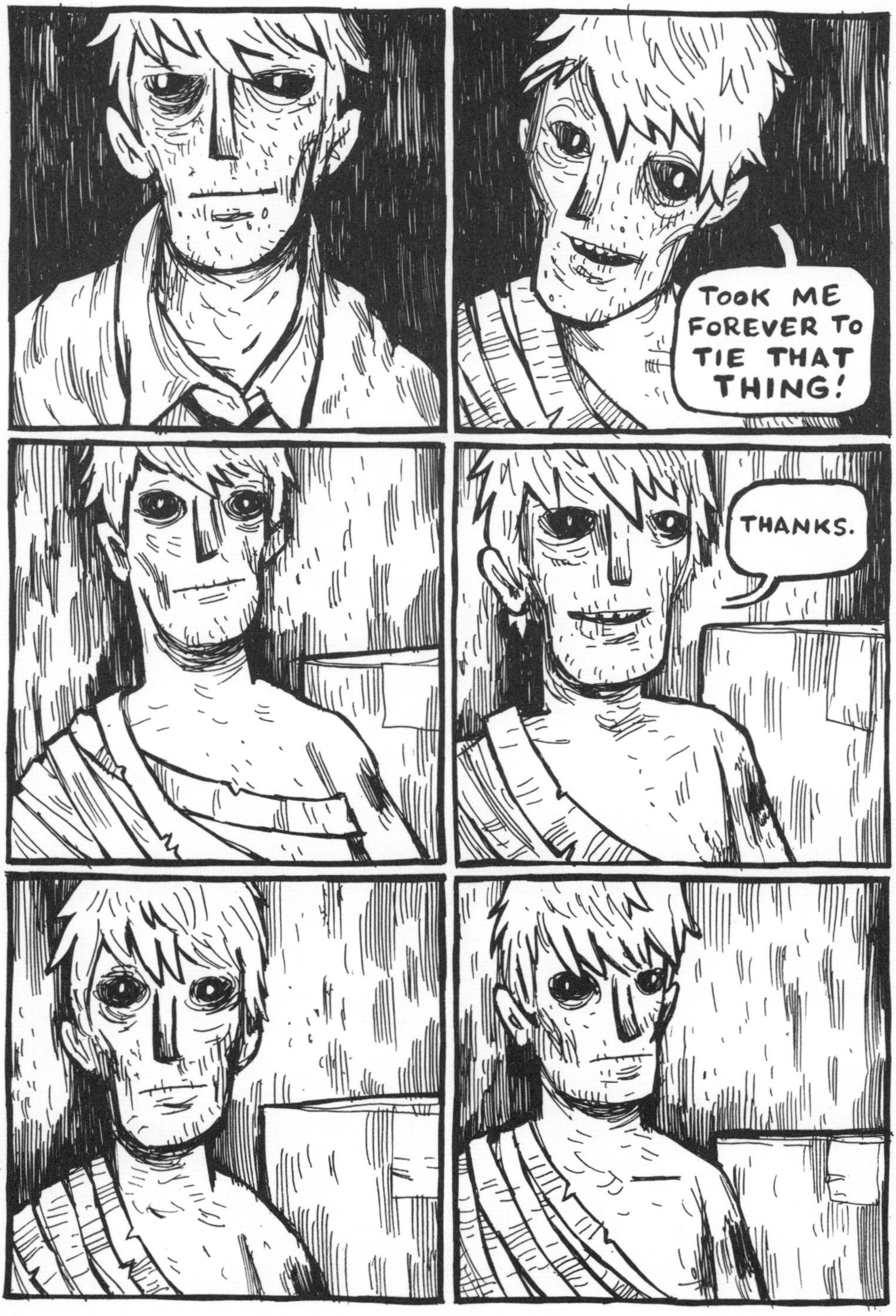
TOOK ME FOREVER TO TIE THAT THING!
THANKS.

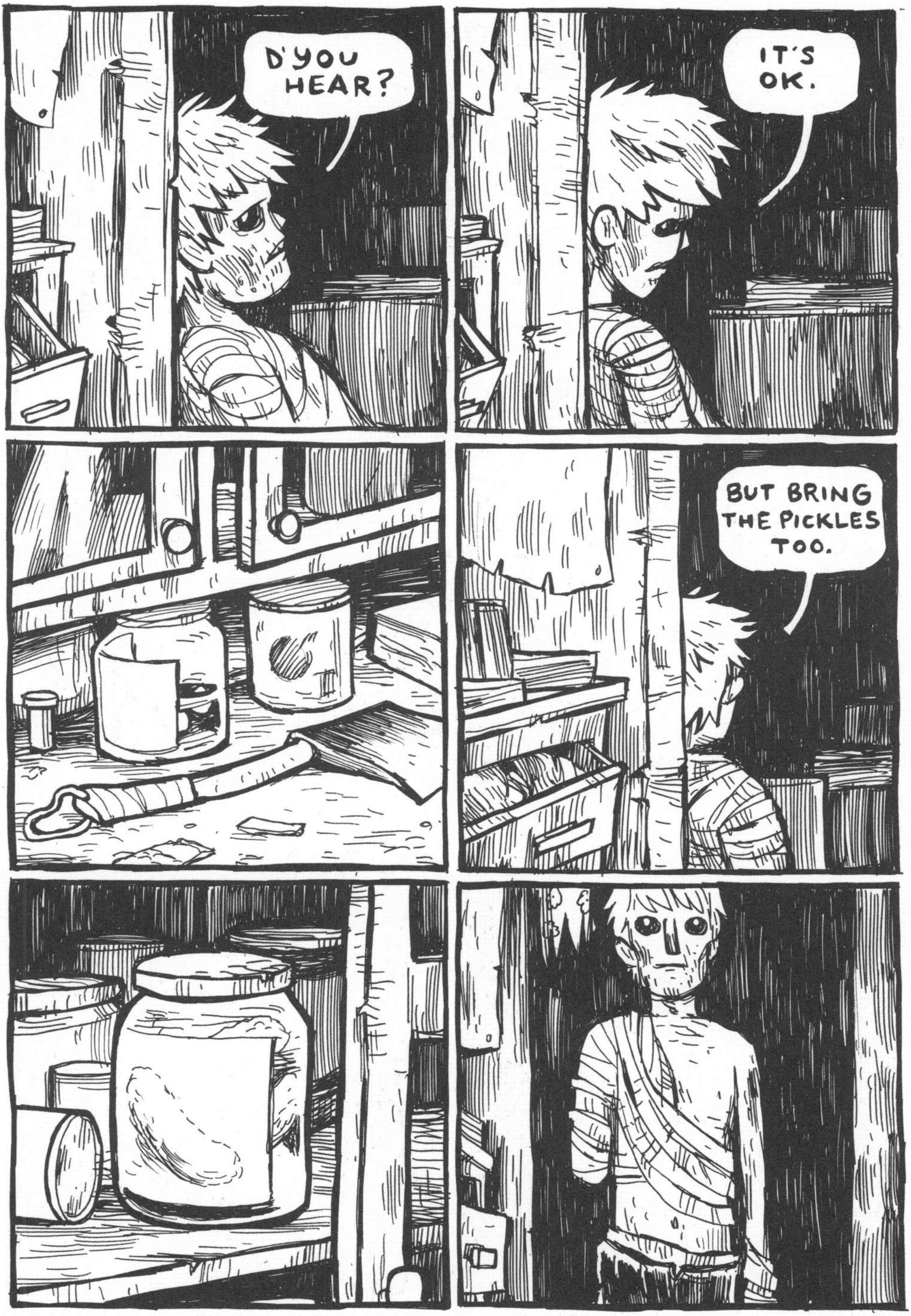
D'YOU HEAR?
IT'S OK.
BUT BRING THE PICKLES TOO.

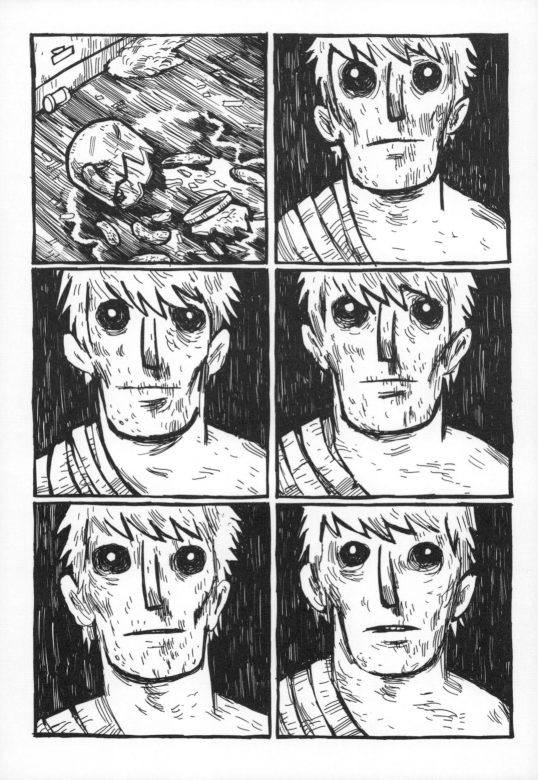

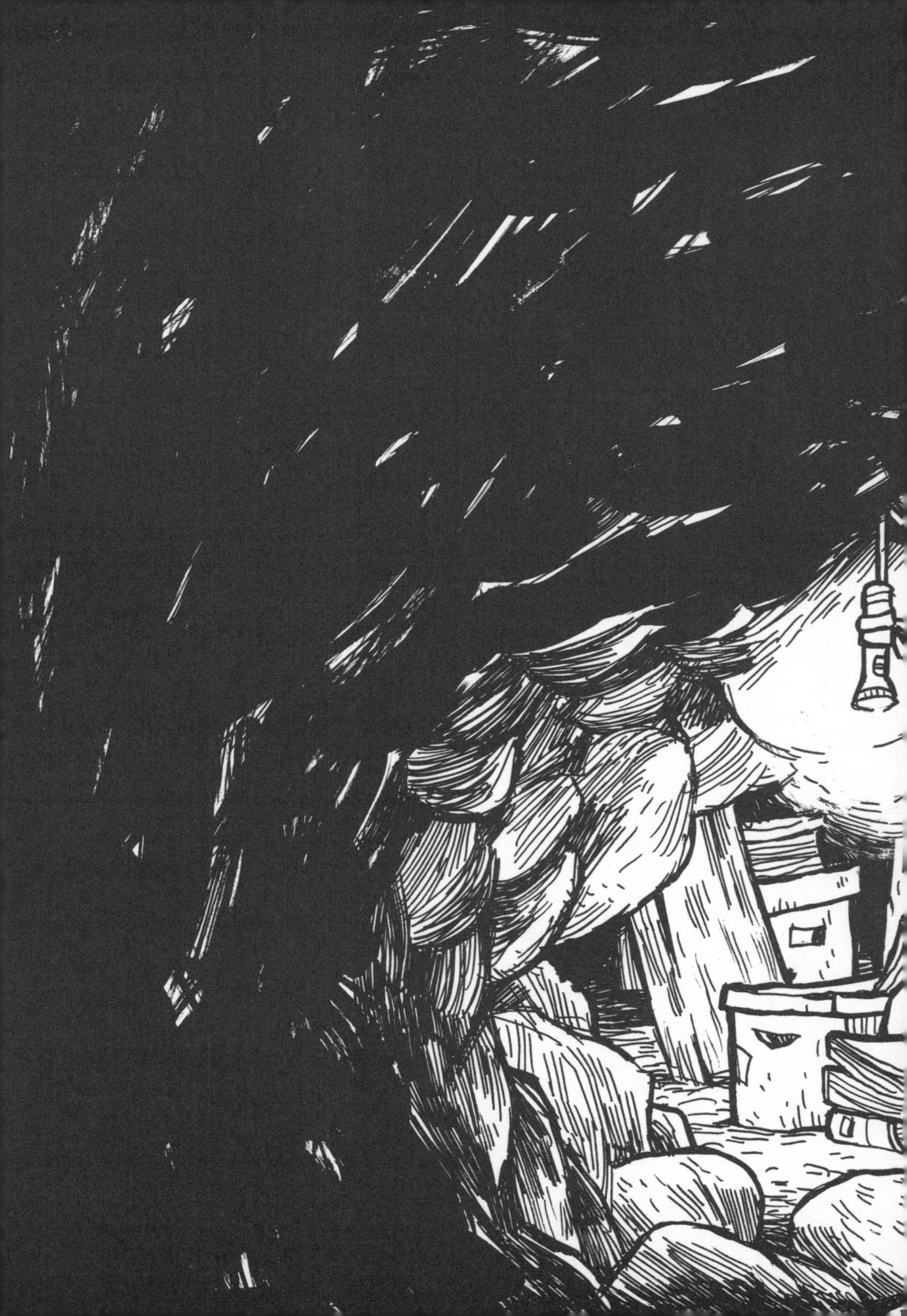

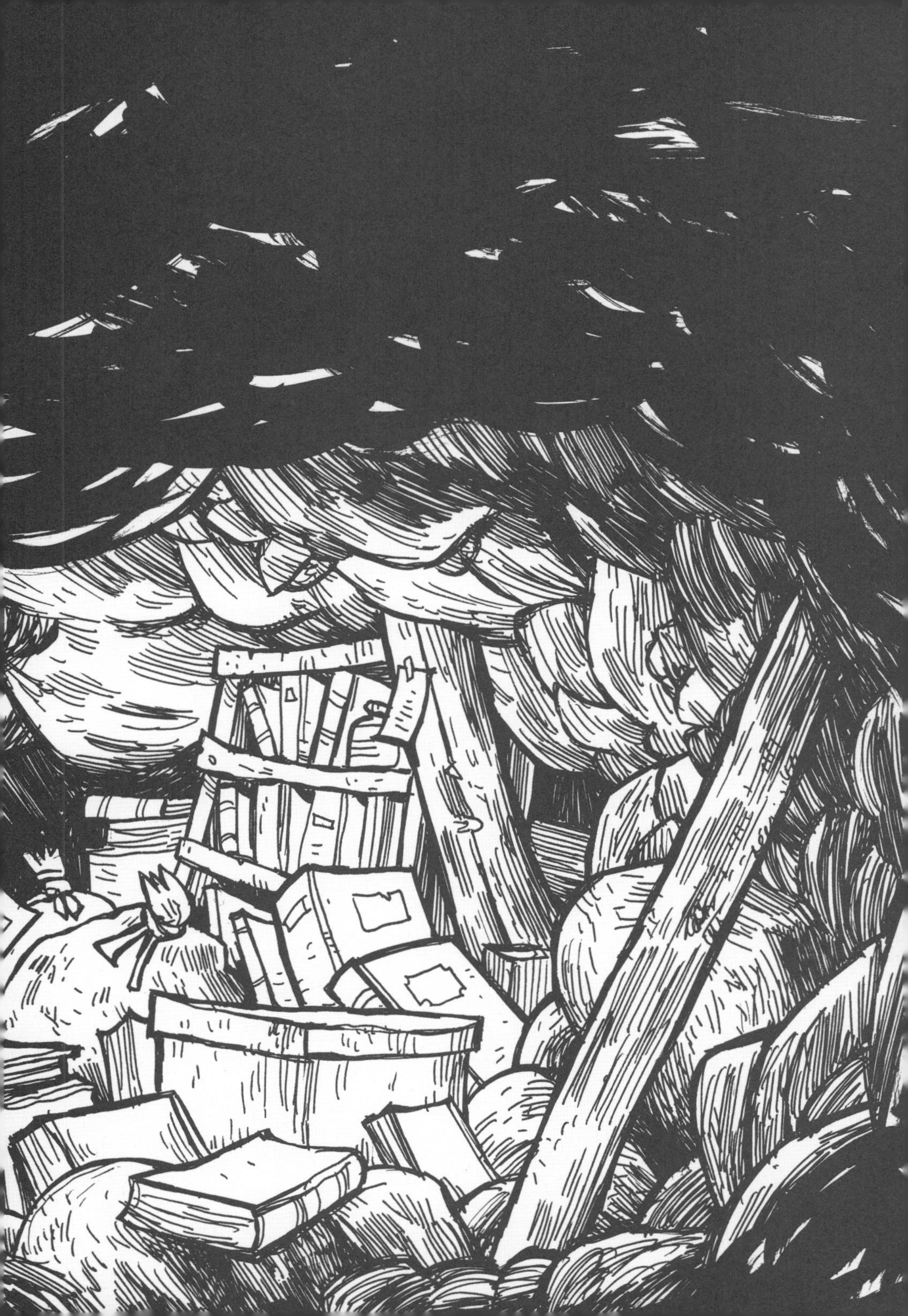

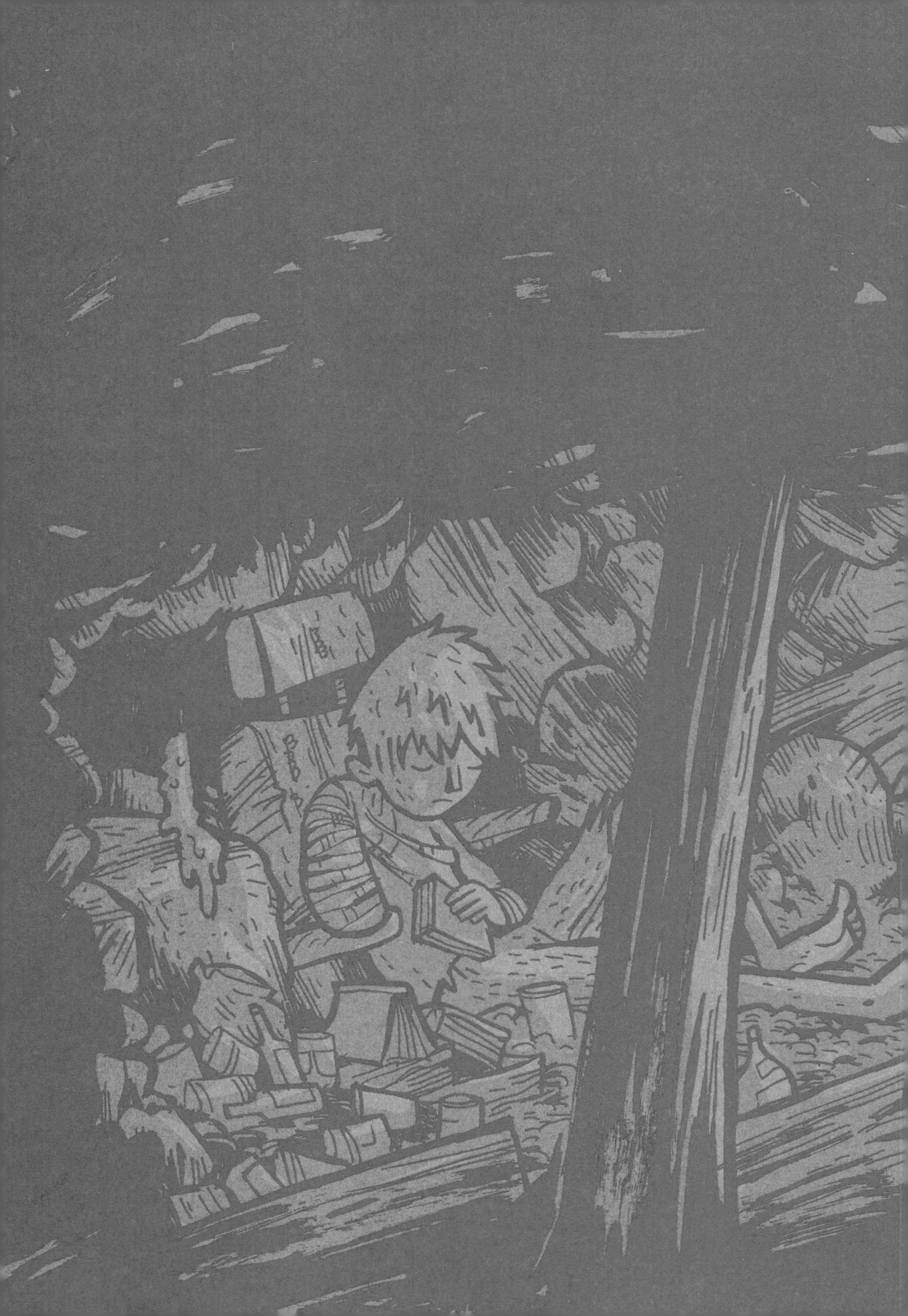